ACHIEVING
PHOTOGRAPHIC
STYLE

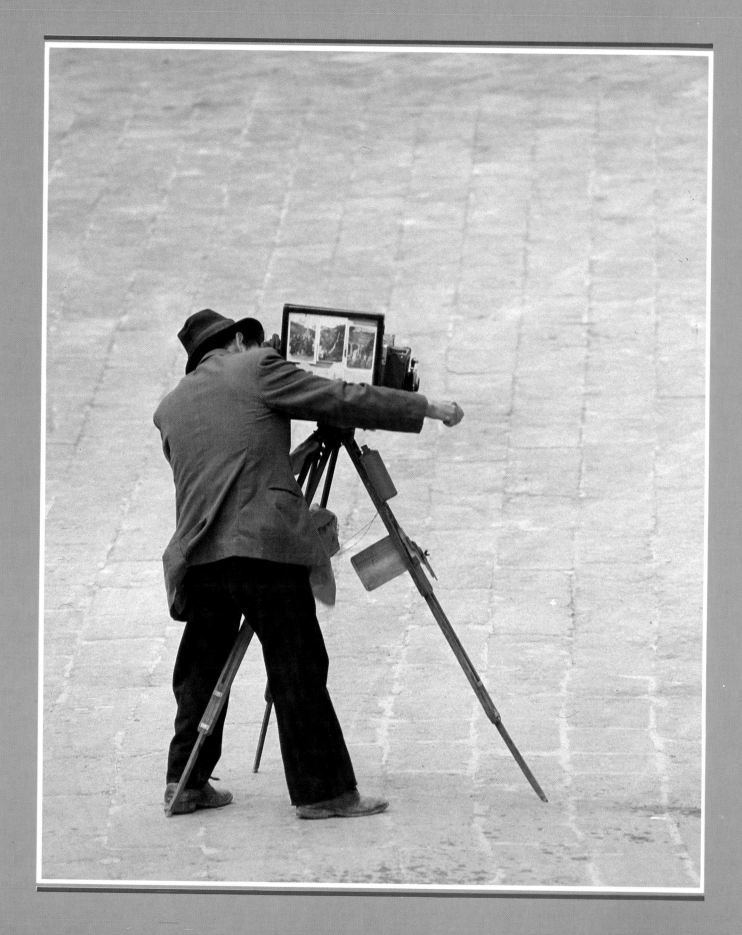

ACHIEVING PHOTOGRAPHIC STYLE

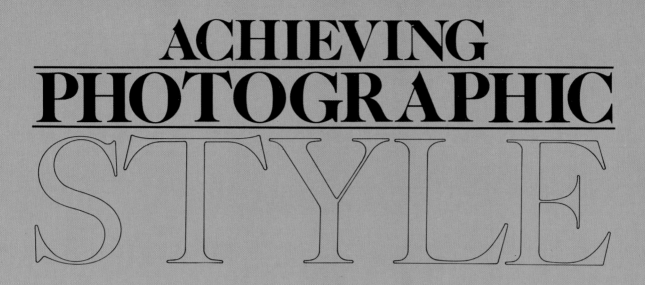

MICHAEL FREEMAN

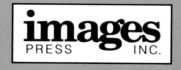

A QUARTO BOOK

This edition published in 1992 by
Images Press, Inc,
7 East 17th Street
New York, New York 10003
212-675-3707

ISBN 0-929667-15-8

This was designed and produced by
Quarto Publishing plc
The Old Brewery, 6 Blundell Street
London N7 9BH

Art director Nigel Osborne
Editorial director Christopher Fagg
Senior editor Liz Wilhide
Art editor Alex Arthur
Editorial assistants Deidre McGarry, Michelle Newton
Art assistants Elaine Cappi, Carol McCleeve
Illustrators Fraser Newman, Mike Pacey
Picture research Anne-Marie Ehrlich

Filmset by QV Typesetting Ltd, London
Origination by Rainbow Graphic Arts, Hong Kong
Printed in Hong Kong by Leefung-Asco Printers Limited

Quarto would like to extend thanks to Anne-Marie Ehrlich and
Shari Segel, The Photographer's Gallery and the Royal Photographic Society

Contents

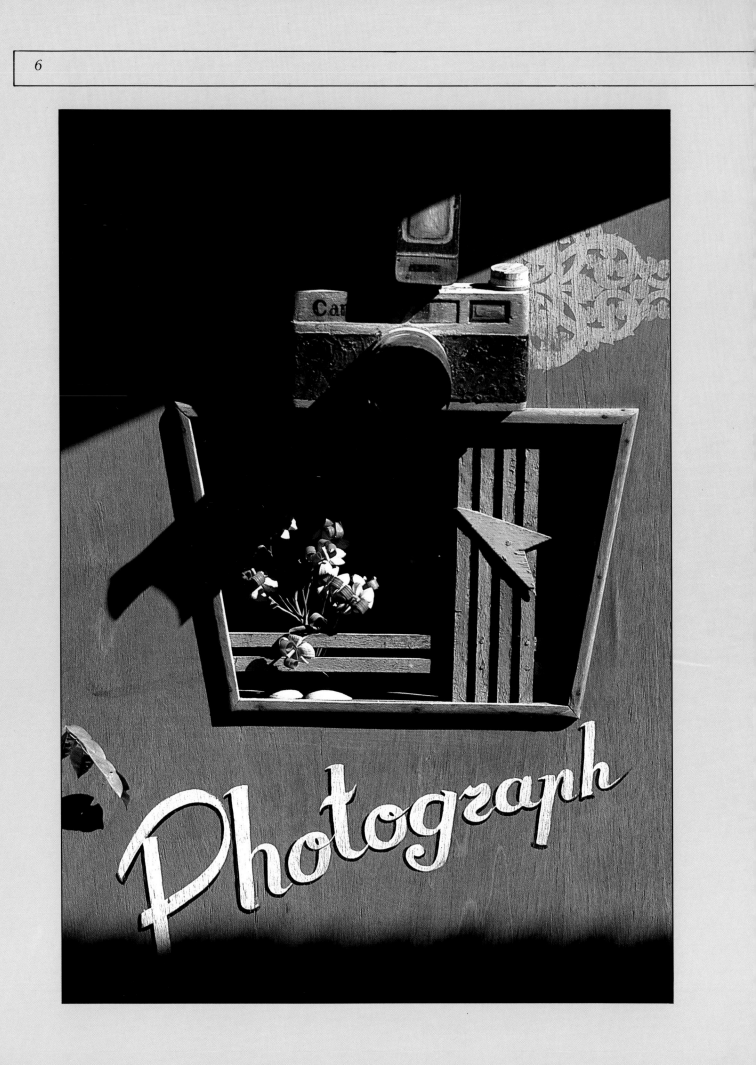

Foreword

It is hard to imagine a world without photography. 'The camera never lies', said someone (nobody is quite sure who) soon after its invention, and we all accept the evidence it offers our eyes. We know that men have been on the moon, that Jack Ruby shot Lee Harvey Oswald, that rain clouds are threatening northern Europe, because photographs have shown it to be so. Some people hardly see for themselves at all: tourists pouring from a sight-seeing bus start snapping the scenery before they have had time to look at it. Michael Freeman quotes American photographer Richard Avedon as saying that he knows the people he photographs better from their portraits than in person. And Freeman suggests, chillingly, that the world failed to register the full horror of the 1983 shooting-down of a Korean passenger plane, with the loss of all lives, because no photographs exist to prove it actually happened.

Yet we are aware, too, that photographs can be manipulated. When Stalin wished to deny the existence of a political rival, he simply had him removed from a group portrait. Advertisers convince us of the superiority of their product over others by using all kinds of technical tricks. Portraitists — in the past, if not so much today — took wrinkles off their clients' faces, and inches off their waists. Even so, there is no guraranteeing the response of those who see the results. Reactions to the work of one of the most admired artist-photographers of the twentieth century, Diane Arbus, whose favorite subjects were midgets, giants and transvestites, among others, are divided between admiration of her empathy with such people, and anger at her exploitation of them. In this book are two almost identical pictures from Vietnam, one taken by someone who confesses his fascination with the glory and excitement of war, the other by someone who is altogether horrified by it. Can you tell the difference?

The proposition here is that the difference between those pictures which make their intended point and those which don't is a question of 'style'. The work of such photographers as Julia Margaret Cameron, Bill Brandt, Frederick Evans and Yousuf Karsh, to name a few reproduced in this book, is always instantly recognizable.

Yet photography, whatever else is claimed for it, is initially a recording device, its starting point a slice of the real world seen by a camera lens. Even for Diane Arbus, 'The subject of the picture is always more important than the picture'. Many photographs are perforce taken 'on the wing'. People move and events occur unpredictably and, if a picture of them has 'style', it is partly because of the photographer's developed instincts, partly through his (or her) being wise after the event.

Photographers, amateur and professional, have been facing up to these contradictions for 150 years. At first they, and the critics, were sure the new medium was an art form, but when George Eastman invented his Kodak box camera ('You press the button, we do the rest', he boasted), photography seemed to surrender its right to be in galleries and art journals, and made its home in family snapshot albums. In time, it became a means of imparting news and information, of carrying out research, of expanding human vision.

At every stage of this progress, there have been accomplished practitioners to push out the boundaries of their craft and find a means, a style, to express themselves and the world around them. Yet few photographers today seem willing to look at the work of their predecessors, to benefit from their example and experience. Michael Freeman is an honorable exception, and his exploration of style in photographers as far removed in time and manner as Julia Margaret Cameron and Cartier-Bresson comes close to defining the partnership between aesthetics and process which is so special to photography (and which is, incidentally, the central theme of the National Museum of Photography, Film and Television). Of course, he cannot finally pin down its elusive nature. Nobody ever will. Photography is itself…unique, all-embracing, tantalizing. But I am confident that all who read his informed analysis, photographers or not, will learn to appreciate the medium — to see it, and to see through it — more clearly than they did before.

Colin Ford
National Museum of Photography, Film and Television

Introduction

*B*ooks on photography are generally either practical, which usually means that they explain how cameras work and how film works, or they confine their attentions to the aesthetics of the portfolios they contain. For such a popular and widely practised visual form, this represents something of an omission.

As photography is practised, the mechanics and aesthetics are often not the principal concern of the moment. While generalizations in this richly varied field may not be very reliable, it is unlikely that the major preoccupation of an experienced, sensitive photographer at the time of shooting is either the f-stop or the critical implication. What is often going on at the time is a complex pattern of decisions. These decisions may well involve the mundane mechanics of the process, and thought for the aesthetics, but there will be many others, fundamentally practical, as well.

What is explored in this book is the process of making photographs, a matter which is of much more importance to me, a professional photographer, than any subsequent discussions on artistic merit. If there is something to be learned from the way the most experienced photographers work, it surely lies in their decision-making at the time, not in subsequent rationalization.

Any book that looks beyond the equipment and selections of 'useful tips', as this one does, must touch on one over-worked topic: is photography art? I realize that this well-worn question is more likely to produce groans of exasperation than to stimulate interest, but in the context of the chapters that follow, it is unavoidable.

Most articulate photographers, and seemingly all photographic historians and critics, have passed comment on this at some time or another. Julia Margaret Cameron thought that photography was an art because, as painting, it sought beauty (highly questionable on both counts in view of subsequent developments). Paul Strand considered the question irrelevant, Moholy-Nagy thought it unimportant. Susan Sontag lays down stringent conditions; 'To be legitimate as an art, photography must cultivate the notion of the photographer as auteur and of all photographs taken by the same photographer as constituting a body of work.'

Personally, I share the sentiments of Harold Evans, former editor of both The Sunday Times and The Times, who, in the introduction to his book on photojournalism Pictures on a Page, kicks the whole issue unsympathetically to one side, saying, 'Is photography art? Nowhere in this book, the reader will be despondent to learn, will we land in this marmalade.' However, marmalade or not, at various points in this book, we will be looking at artistic expression in photography, but in terms of the how and why rather than the whether-or-not. That I feel that this is justifiable without devoting a chapter to the support or dismissal of photographic art is because the question itself arises from a confusion of terms.

Photography is a process, and can be applied in all kinds of ways to all kinds of subjects. It can be used scientifically, for instance, to uncover information that would otherwise be hidden, such as the tracks of sub-atomic particles. It can be used in a documentary way, to show what things look like. It can be used to beautify, as it often is in portraiture and advertising. It can also be used as art.

To qualify as art it needs little more than a declaration of intent by the artist-photographer, or a declaration of recognition by anyone who wants to try his or her luck as an art critic. Now, whether it is good or bad art is an entirely different question, and definitely not to be rolled into the same discussion. The most succinct piece of commonsense that I have seen written on the subject comes from Peter Rose Pulham who, in 1952 said, 'The question, whether or not photography is an art, has always seemed to me irritating, meaningless and beside the point. If photography is used merely as a technical process to record some visible fact, it is an adjunct to science. But if it is used to express, since all expression is emotional, selective and personal, it cannot avoid the use of art.'

I first came across this sound judgement in a book by Cecil Beaton and Gail Buckland called The Magic Image. *Adjacent to the quotation is their contribution to the question: 'We can but answer that if a dozen expert photographers are given the same subject and conditions, their pictures would be just as different as if a dozen painters had been set the same task.' This has a special relevance to the title of this book, for it is the perceived ability and imagination of 'expert photographers' that gives them what many people would call style.*

But is this always true? Certainly, when Time-Life, *in their* Photography *series, select a subject and assign a number of photographers to it, the results can be very different indeed. The catch, however, is that the subject must first be properly selected to reveal the differences and, in many situations the opposite may happen. The nature of the subject, the working conditions, or even the similar professional training and background of the photographers may result in a kind of convergence. Very similar photograpic solutions are frequently arrived at coincidentally; one immediate demonstration of this appears in Chapter Four, where two experienced photojournalists can be seen reacting on one occasion in the same way. The elusive quality of style, it seems to me, is more than a facile identification tag for individual photographers. It involves a visual coordination of the subject matter and the two-dimensional form of the image — a coordination that does some justice to its subject by showing it in such a way that it enhances or challenges our understanding of it.*

Style may be personally distinctive, as in the work of, say, Robert Frank or Richard Avedon, but it is much more likely to be a visual sensitivity that is shared by a number of other expert photographers. This, I hope, will be one of the lessons of this book — that what helps to produce good photography is sensitivity to and awareness of the subject, rather than the hunt for a trick, technique or visual fad to distinguish one photographer's work from that of everyone else. 'In photography', said Susan Sontag, 'the subject matter always pushes through.' And that is as it should be.

Michael Freeman ● London

CHAPTER 1

A Technological Art

'...focus-and-shoot automation that enables anyone to get great pictures on their very first try.'
Camera advertisement 1983

'My assistants know all that stuff, why should I?'
Art Kane

One of the popular assumptions in art is that, traditionally, the artist has been able to exert some kind of control over the process. According to this quite reasonable view, the result is the product of imagination and the skill to translate it. In the medium of photography, however, such a straightforward connection does not always hold, and a photograph can have power *without* the full intention of the photographer. There are occasions, many of them, when the machinery of photography takes over, or at least deserves much of the credit for a strong image.

None of this is meant to suggest that fine photography is without reason, or that it cannot be practised with full control. It usually is. Nevertheless, the simple fact that it *can* be seen to be successful and appealing as a result of a technical accident must change the standards by which we appraise pictures. Well-known examples are not hard to find.

One of the strongest images of the Second World War was taken by Robert Capa at the start of the D-Day invasion of France in June 1944 (*see* right). The picture is blurred, and only the crucial elements can be made out with any certainty — an American soldier sprawls in the surf to take cover; behind him in the distance are the angular shapes of tank traps. The photograph is rightly famous as an image of war. It conveys the urgency of battle just as effectively as a clearly focused and carefully composed shot and, some would argue, much better.

But consider what went into the making of this image. In extreme danger, there was no time to compose and make all the careful adjustments that photographs are commonly supposed to need. Capa snapped it, rapidly. Under fire himself, he prudently lay flat, working

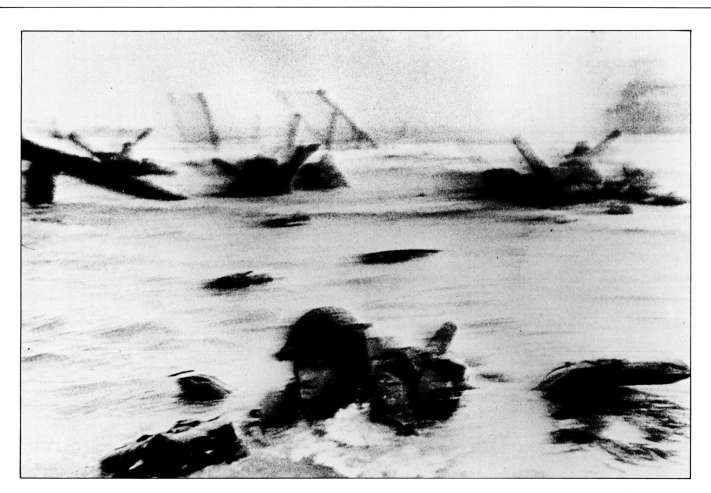

from an awkward position, and did not even manage to hold the camera quite steady. Technically, the picture is a mess, but its very imperfections are what make it stand out; it is obvious that here is a picture taken in the heat of battle. Capa was an experienced and skilled photographer; he knew the value of such immediacy in photographs and is quoted as saying: 'If your pictures aren't good enough, you aren't close enough. Grain and blur capture the coarse reality of battle action.' Nevertheless, it seems unlikely that on such a critical assignment Capa deliberately arranged for the shot to be blurred. He did his best in the difficult conditions, but on this occasion the technicalities prevailed — to the benefit of the photograph. Capa, of course, recognized a good picture when he saw one, and knew what he had when the film was developed.

Such rough edges in photography are by no means either solely due to extreme situations or evocative of them. In Robert Frank's well-known picture of an elevator girl in Miami, similar 'imperfections' have a different effect. Frank's extremely casual technique — the blur, imprecise composition and skewed framing — give a spur-of-the-moment, unplanned edge to the shot, an extremely logical way of treating what was, at the time, an ignored subject — the barrenness of everyday American life. In this case, although the exact effects of such a rough-and-ready camera technique could not be predicted, the principle was deliberate.

What photographs like these two examples illustrate so clearly is that the craft involved in making them does not necessarily matter in the same way as it does in traditional fine art. This is not the

Above The Normandy Invasion, *Robert Capa, June 6, 1944. One of the historic images of the Second World War, this photograph was taken by Capa just after he landed on a Normandy beach with the first wave of US infantry troops spearheading the liberation of Europe. By 'normal' photographic standards, the quality of the picture is poor: it is not only grainy, but also blurred and unfocused. While these characteristics may not have been intentional, and they were certainly the result of difficult, dangerous conditions, they convey, more than anything else, the urgency of the moment. Out of the 100 photographs taken by Capa of this event, only six survive. The rest were ruined during processing.*

beginning of a polemic on painting versus photography, and it will be one of the very few glances that this book takes in the direction of art history, but the comparison is very important for the appreciation of photography. Before the camera, all visual imagery demanded craft, time and effort. There was simply no way of turning an idea into a picture, or even of making a reasonable likeness, except by learning a repertoire of technical skills, acquiring proficiency in them, and then often spending an appreciable time in execution.

Photography has changed all this, and with a string of implications that go further than the immediately obvious. Just creating an image is a matter of optics and chemistry, and these are largely automated. As a result, anyone can make an image of some kind. Neither time nor special skills are absolutely essential if the aim is simply to fix a recognizable image, and now a regular and sophisticated industry caters to the non-technical public.

The nineteenth-century painter Paul Delaroche declared painting to be dead from the moment that photography was invented, and this now famous quotation has seen regular service ever since in the hands of photographic historians. Whatever Delaroche meant by his apparently histrionic statement, others have since used it to demonstrate the impact that photography had from the start. However, the realistic fixing of images is only an incidental part of painting. What photography *did* kill off was first of all portrait miniatures and, eventually, the kind of workmanlike illustration used by such magazines as *Harper's Weekly* and the *Illustrated London News* to present timely events to their readers, neither of which could be considered fine art. Nor did all artists share Delaroche's anxieties: Degas, Courbet and Gauguin were just a few of the nineteenth-century painters who used the new medium, some with appreciation and enthusiasm.

In the event, photography has certainly achieved mass popular appeal, but not at the expense of painting. The potential for using photography in newspapers, magazines, books and so on, is very much greater, and the question of competition hardly arises. There is now a continuous stream of photographic images in several different spheres of Western culture, as well as uncountable numbers of snapshots taken casually and confidently by millions of people who have no pretentions to art, but there has never been any question that these were roles for painting to fill.

Nor, to puncture a persistent myth, does modern photography owe a very important debt to painting, despite its initial influences in the nineteenth century. In the early years, there was a good deal of frank imitation, for a number of powerful reasons. The invention of photography did not meet any pressing demand — newspapers and magazines, for example, had no way of incorporating photographs until the invention of the half-tone process in the 1880s — and the new medium had no prior commitments in terms of role. It was quite natural that the first people to take it up were largely from the leisured and 'artistic' classes; Fox Talbot, for instance, was a landowner, and Julia Margaret Cameron the wife of a civil servant (and the friend of Tennyson, then Poet Laureate). Their milieu included painting and other fine arts, and photography began under this influence. Painting was also a handy referent for visual taste and conventions and most Victorian photographers naturally tended towards what was fashionable in the salons. Some went even further and deliberately aped the tableaux, themes, lighting, and even the textural qualities of painting.

The imitative genre photography of people like Oscar Rejlander,

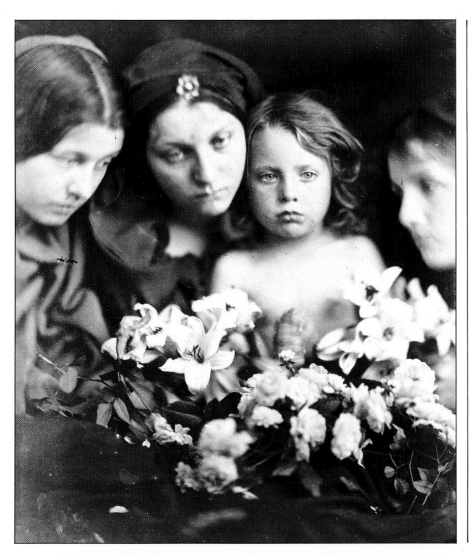

Left *Described in a recent exhibition as a 'Christian Pictorialist', Julia Margaret Cameron performed her 'mortal but yet divine! Art of photography' to create such religious tableaux as this example, made in about 1865 and entitled* The Return after Three Days. *Too cloying for most modern tastes, these pictures suited Victorian convictions perfectly. The two women and a girl, with roses and lilies, are generally taken to symbolize the three sorrowing Marys at the Sepulchre.*

Below *Oscar Rejlander, who studied painting in Rome before taking instruction in photography in 1853, discovered the techniques of combination printing while experimenting with depth-of-field. Having tended towards the sentimental and theatrical in his painting, he used combination printing to produce photographic tableaux. In this, his famous* Two Ways of Life (1857), *he photographed his models separately, combining the images to make this extraordinary Victorian allegory. Close inspection of the actual print shows where the separate elements have been joined, but at a normal viewing distance it is a technically successful image. The diagram shows the main elements combined in Rejlander's moral tableau: sirens, gamblers, religious penitents, workers and a happy family. Between the groups sits the veiled figure of Repentance.*

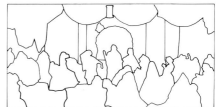

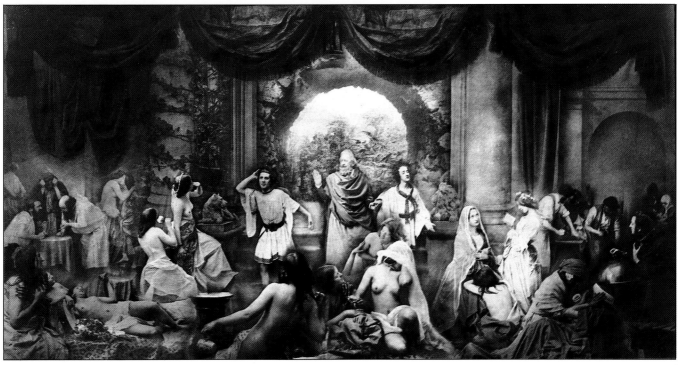

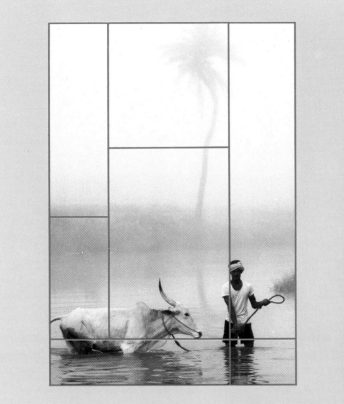

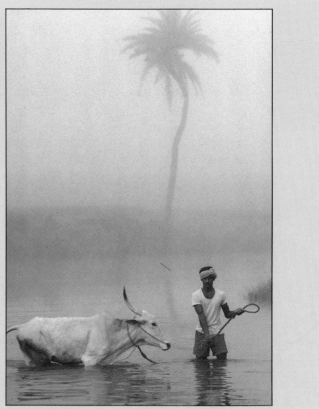

Above The grid overlaid on this photograph of an Indian farmer with a bullock has been divided according to the Fibonacci series, a mathematically derived sequence that dates from the Renaissance. (It is formed by adding two consecutive numbers to give a third, as 1, 2, 3, 5, 8, 13, and so on.) The relationship between the exactly calculated rectangle and the photograph are obvious, but actually false. The picture was taken quickly and instinctively, and although the photographer appreciated the dynamics of the design, the exercise on this page simply shows a coincidence. It is easy, and misleading, to read too much formality into photographic design.

Below The Golden Section is an enduring model of harmony in design. The diagram shows how a Golden Section rectangle is constructed. The value of the Golden Section is that it produces a number of integrally related areas.

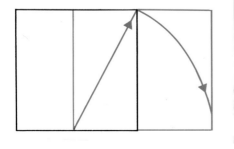

whose allegorical pictures were exhibited with paintings and sculpture, is obviously an important part of art history. It was also, however, a cul-de-sac, and one would be hard put to find traces of it in modern photography (advertising pastiches excepted). Rejlander's complex tableau *The Two Ways of Life* (page 13) is a marvellous curiosity, both for some of the Victorian moral preoccupations that it displays and for the technical skills involved in putting together one image from over 30 separate negatives. Although some considered the picture 'indelicate', Queen Victoria bought a copy to give to Prince Albert.

Such imitation was the high point of painting's direct effect on photography and, although there were subsequent occasions when photographic movements returned to painting for inspiration, such as the Linked Ring group in England in the 1890s and Photo-Secession in the United States, recent photography has largely pursued its own path, with little *specific* reference to other fine arts. What influence painting *has* had can be found in the fundamentals of design, and, even here, it is difficult to say to what extent photographers have, consciously or unconsciously, followed the examples of painters, and to what extent the aesthetic ground-rules are simply part of a shared sensibility.

Proportion, and methods of dividing a picture frame, have been preoccupations during certain periods of painting — during the Renaissance especially — and a number of very precise, mathematical systems have been followed by artists. Perhaps the best-known and most frequently adhered to is the ratio known as the Golden Section, known to the Greeks and widely used in later periods. What is considered to make it harmonious is that its divisions are all related to each other.

In painting, the whole process is sufficiently deliberate to allow such relationships as the Golden Section to be planned with geometrical accuracy, to the extent of working them out first on the canvas. The case with photography, however, is nearly always different; neither time nor the methods of viewing the image in the camera normally allow such planning. Yet, as the photograph at left illustrates, such tenets of classical composition are often followed. Care can be taken in still-life, architectural and most landscape photography, but in rapid shots such as this example, no calculations whatsoever can be made. Other systems of proportion exist, and other conventions in lighting, tone and color, but it can still be argued that such harmony can be achieved without recourse to calculations — simply because it feels right.

The difficulty in trying to pinpoint underlying influences on photography is that most photographers tend to compose intuitively, reacting quickly to their own visual experience. In terms of quantity, painting and fine art make up only a small part of most people's daily diet of images, and it is tempting to think that strategies such as the Golden Section are actually natural ones.

In fact, for a photographer to attempt to behave like a painter is usually impractical. In the way that the image is organized to appeal to the viewer's senses — its aesthetics — a painter has great choice, and is certainly not bound by any arrangement of objects in the real world. Composition, the balance of color and so on are *created* by the painter, and so the decisions concerning them come first. A photograph, however, is very much linked to the real world, and there are many situations where gross alterations to the image are hardly possible. Given this fundamental difference, the success of some of the most interesting and energetic photographs relies on the technical aspects of photography itself.

Below *Cuban-born American photographer José Azel took this wide-angle view of a crowd surging towards the Pope's helicopter as it took off from the village of Quezal Tenango in Guatemala, March, 1983. Most of the crowd, including the guard of honor, are bent over to shield their eyes from the flying dust — except for the central figure, arms dramatically outstretched. First featured in* The Observer *magazine, this photograph was subsequently chosen by* Life *as one of the pictures of 1983 in their end-of-year review, and also won the best news picture of 1983 award in the World Press Photographic Competition. A photograph ideally suited to the requirements of color magazines, this picture would lose much of its impact if reproduced in black-and-white.*

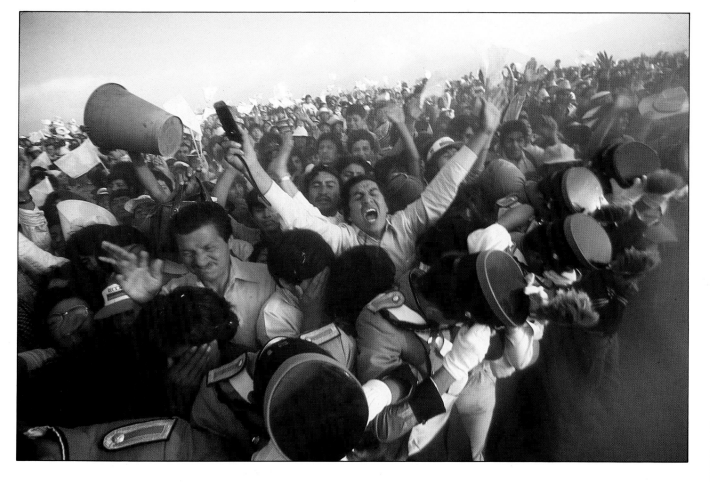

Strong emotion is the subject of José Azel's powerful photograph of the Pope's visit to a small town in Guatemala (page 15), and the religious ecstasy displayed by the central figure provides a focus. It is, however, a number of *photographic* aspects of this image that helps to convey the emotion. The lens used is an extreme wide-angle, and it has had the characteristic effect of increasing distortion towards the edges and corners of the picture, stretching the shapes, lines and general perspective outwards from the center. This, as often happens with such lenses, both exaggerates and creates a number of diagonals in the scene, and the result is to 'point' towards the center, where the focus of the photographer's attention was, on the upturned face. Even the green bucket and the elongated ovals of the guardsmens' hats direct the view inwards. These diagonal, directional elements in the photograph also induce a sense of movement and a dynamic into the situation, which help to bring across the vitality of the occasion. The distortion, in which such foreground elements as the soldier's epaulette at lower left seem extremely close, has the additional effect of drawing us into the crowd, and making us feel a part of the moment.

Since all this works so well, it is particularly interesting to see *how* the picture was taken. The viewpoint is unusually high, and given that there is a line of soldiers holding back the press of the crowd, it looks unlikely that the photographer was standing on anything just in front. The reflection in the man's spectacles at lower left reveals what we might have guessed — that the photographer held the camera at full stretch over his head, relying on his experience of similar circumstances rather than a direct view to compose. Through knowing what his equipment is capable of doing, this photographer has deliberately relinquished some control, allowing the technology to help suggest the image, and has been well rewarded for the slight risk.

Photography is almost top-heavy with technology. To fix an image simply and quickly in all its details calls for complex equipment and chemistry. Snapshots apart, control over the picture needs a good working knowledge of what the many different lenses, films, papers, filters and other materials can do. This is not simply a question of craftsmanship, but a full understanding of how photography sees the world. Although it is not always articulated, photography uses a different graphic vocabulary from other visual forms. The photographer is at liberty to ignore the technical constraints or to use them. It is worth looking at the main characteristics of photographic technology and to see how they can be made to carry the photographer's ideas further. A rough analogy is the way that some painters have used the methods of applying oils to enhance the image: heavy ridges of paint in some of Van Gogh's most famous paintings follow the lines of the image, and, in a more restrained way, Manet often emphasized depth by using the thickness of the paint to follow the contours of a subject.

Focus is one of the most purely photographic of features. The eye, of course, focuses like any other lens, but it does this so quickly that we are most of the time unaware that any part of our view is out of focus (except, that is, for people with deficient eyesight). A camera lens, however, is considerably less sophisticated than the human eye, and delivers an image that may be only partly sharp. Under the right circumstances, the photographer has a fairly broad choice of where to focus, and how much of the picture to keep sharp.

In Romano Cagnoni's photograph, *Terror of War, Biafra* (*see* right), it is the selective focus that makes the picture so disturbing. The staring, out-of-focus face is 'wrong' for most people because conventionally the closest subject to a camera is the focus of attention. It seems as if the boy has thrust himself towards us, demanding attention in spite of the photographer. The softness of focus distils his expression into a horrified stare, and fixes the viewer's eye. The 'wrongness' is, of course, skilfully deliberate.

Another visual effect that comes directly from camera technology is blurred motion. A subject moving too fast for the speed of the camera shutter is recorded with a very characteristic streaking; something similar happens if the camera is jerked. Often this is a technical problem that photographers would rather do without, but it can be very useful. It is not just an alternative method of making a picture indistinct, but through familiarity has acquired certain connotations, equating with speed, energy and urgency, as in Robert Capa's D-Day photograph. It is probably fair to say that while too-slow shutter speeds really were seen to spoil photographs in the early days, streaked images of racing cars, dancers and other active things are now perfectly acceptable — certainly to the many picture editors who select them. It has become such a popular device that it is fast approaching the status of cliché. Ernst Haas must take a share of the responsibility for making this technique over-popular. Images such as his bull-fighting series (page 18) were executed so elegantly that they have encouraged imitation ever since. Part of the success of these pictures lies in the fact that Haas managed to balance

Below *Most photographs with depth in the subject contain some areas that are out of focus, and these are traditionally assigned to what the photographer sees as the less important elements, such as a background. Here, (Terror of War, Biafra) however, is a good example of how focus can be used interestingly rather than conventionally. Cagnoni has focused beyond what would normally be the first point of interest in the scene, and the result, like the subject, is disturbing.*

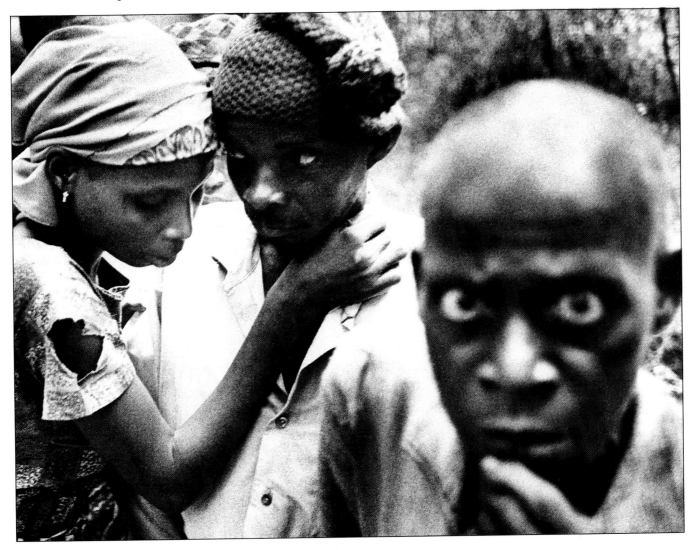

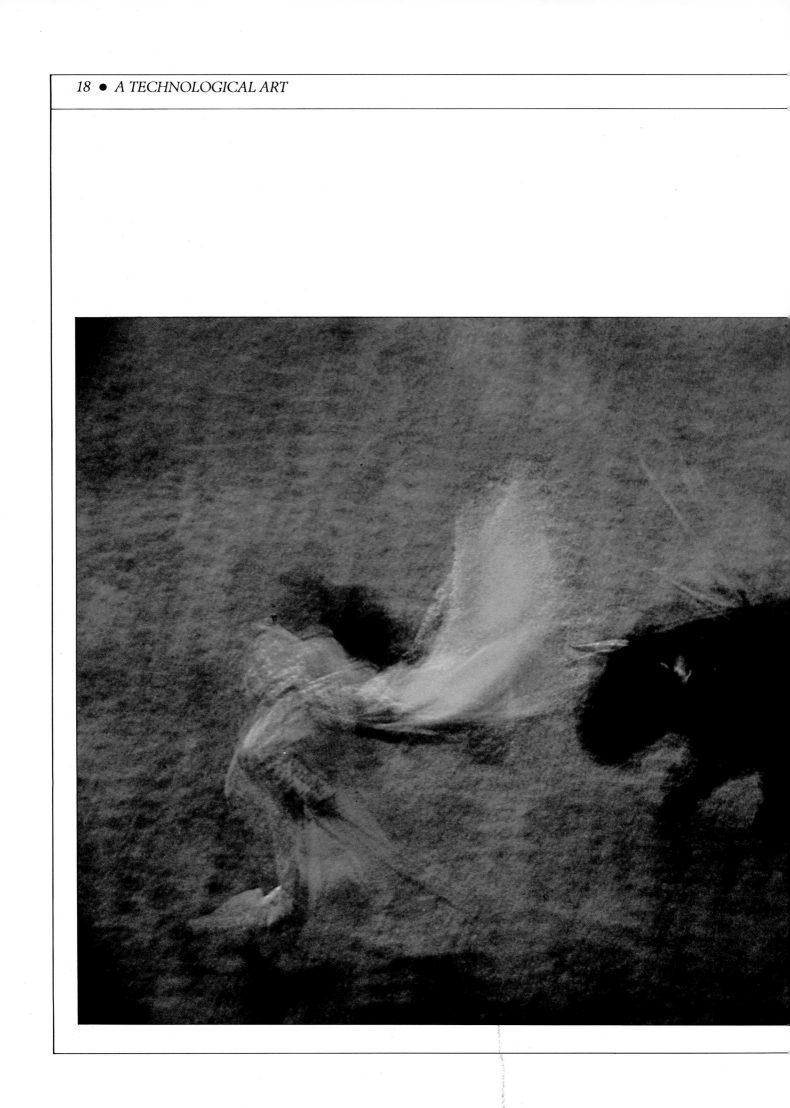

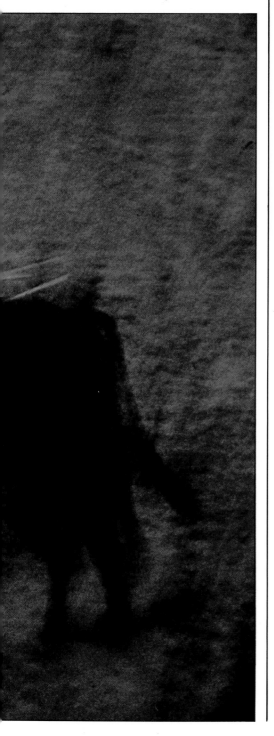

Below *Ernst Haas' fascination with and exploration of color led him to experiment with long exposures of subjects that would seem to call for short ones — bullfights, football games and rodeos. The movement, of both camera and subject, destroys detail and line at these shutter speeds (many at one-tenth of a second). What remains, however, is enhanced color.*

the flow of movement with a choice of subject that is sufficiently distinctive in its appearance to remain recognizable.

In a very different way, but one that is still essentially photographic, frozen action is another part of the camera's visual vocabulary. The macabre fascination of Brigitte Dahm's marvellously timed photograph of a bomb explosion in Northern Ireland (page 20) comes largely from the new evidence it gives us of what actually happens in such extreme events; such information is outside our own experience, and is derived from the high shutter speeds and sensitive film of modern photographic technology.

Two related visual properties of the camera are the compression and expansion of perspective. Both owe their existence to the fact that lenses of different focal lengths can be used. A standard lens, which has always been the mainstay of photography, is one that gives the same sense of perspective as our eyes. The definition is not quite as simple as this, because the final perspective effect depends on the size and distance of the photograph when it is viewed; nevertheless, without becoming mired in technicalities, a standard lens gives an image without any optical idiosyncrasies, which we would term 'normal'. A longer focal length, however, places a kind of stamp on the picture, and the longer it is, the more distinctive the effect. With a lens that is, say, 10 times the standard focal length (the actual figures in millimetres are irrelevant here, as they differ between sizes of camera), its graphic influence may be so strong that it dominates the photograph. While practically, at the time of shooting, much of the value of a long lens may seem to lie in its magnification — producing an enlarged image of something distant — the strongest visual effect is to compress the elements of the scene, as if they were stacked in a single, flattened plane. In both the photograph of the line of ceremonially dressed soldiers and the photograph of lily leaves on page 22, telephoto lenses have had this effect, partly abstracting each image and emphasizing respectively a pattern of colors and of shapes.

Long lenses are probably used most often for their ability to fill the picture frame when the subject is inaccessibly distant, but this is just a working technique and not nearly as interesting as the visual effect of compression. What makes it so distinctive is that such a perspective has come to seem almost normal with the advent of photography. Only since long lenses have been used for their magnifying properties in photography have the visual possibilities been fully explored — in juxtaposing the different planes of a scene and using the surprising way in which scale can be rendered for dramatic effect.

Photographic technology also makes it possible to *expand* perspective — the opposite of magnification. This is not quite so unusual as its long-focus opposite; we can easily create a sense of a wide-angle view just by looking quickly from side to side. Nevertheless, a wide-angle lens, with its short focal length, not only records an essentially panoramic view, but also exaggerates the perspective, making the foreground seem unusually large. This effect seems less odd when the photograph is large and is seen from close up, but reproduced in a small format, as in the pages of a book, the forcing of the perspective can be quite severe. In the photograph of sand dunes on page 23, an extreme wide-angle lens covers, in one sweep, everything from the fine textural detail of individual grains to the far distance. The angle of view from top to bottom is here in the region of 140 degrees, much more than the eye experiences, and an additional feature, noticeable in the sky, is a curved distortion from the lens itself.

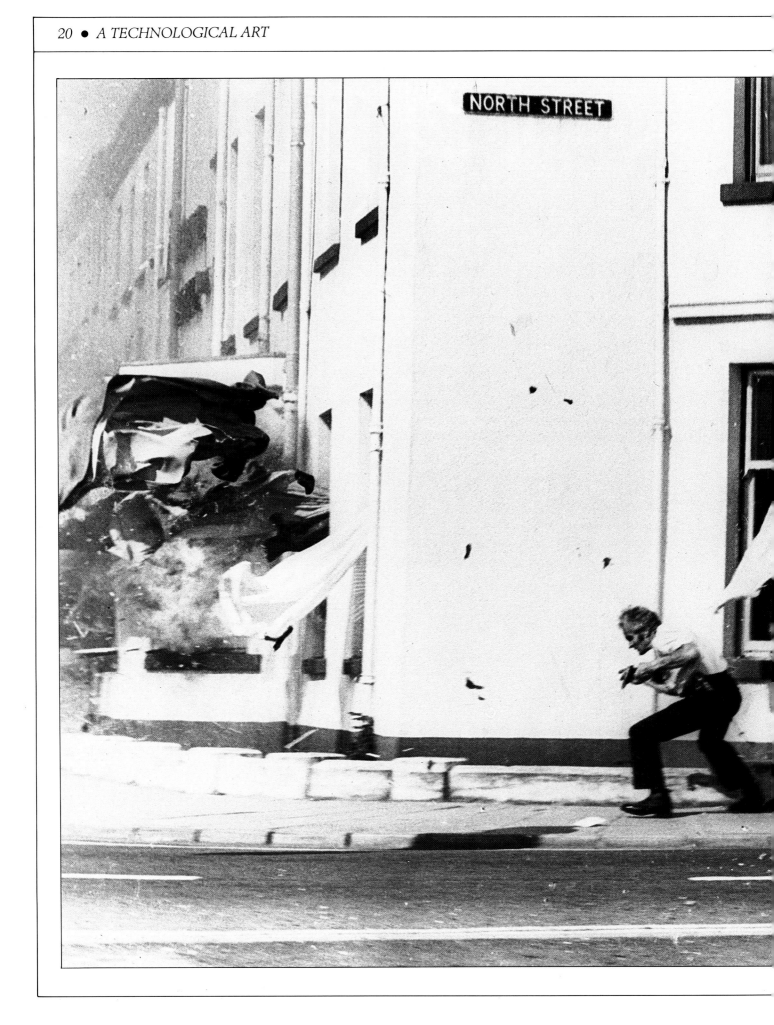

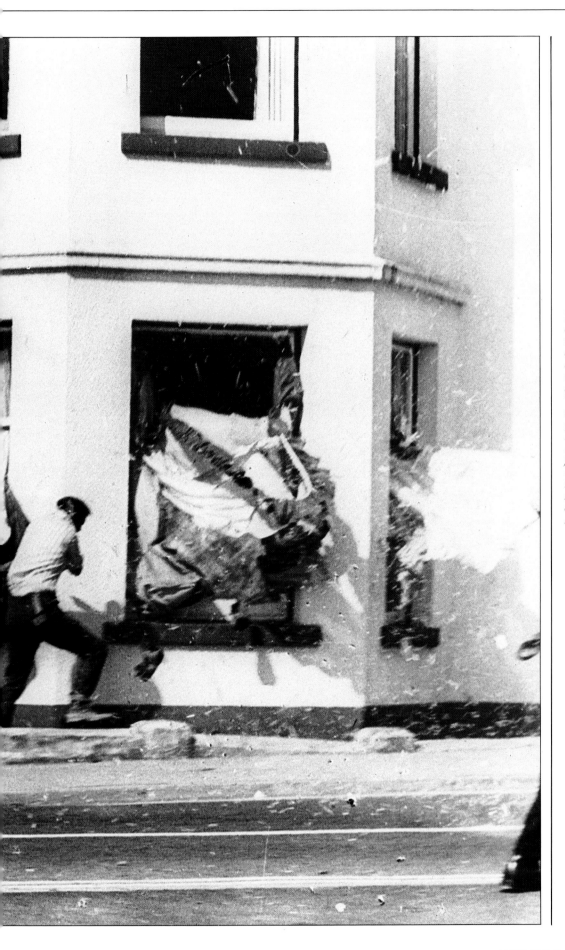

Left *In the presence of fast action, eyes and brain fail to register all the details; if the action is violent as well, shock and other nervous reactions make it even more difficult to appreciate what has happened. This near-invisibility of such events gives this type of photograph an extra fascination. Here we can actually see the bizarre details of flying fragments and the power of the blast . . . and wonder what happened to the two men. Brigitte Dahm photographed this explosion at the Marine Hotel, Ballycastle, Northern Ireland.*

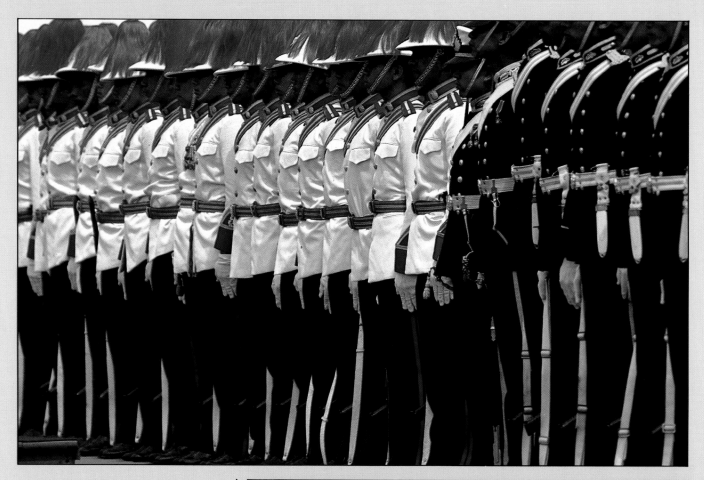

Above *True perspective is only influenced by the viewpoint; it changes when the camera is moved closer or further away. The apparent perspective, however, changes dramatically with focal length. Here, a 600mm lens magnifies a small portion of a scene, and appears to compress its proportions. The explanation lies in range — here we see a very much larger view than we would have seen with our own eyes.*

Right *In this photograph of giant Victoria Regia lily leaves, the compressing effect of a moderate, 250mm telephoto on a 6×6cm camera, combined with the selective framing of a small part of the scene, give a rhythmic effect to the lines. This kind of abstraction is one of the functions of long-focus lenses.*

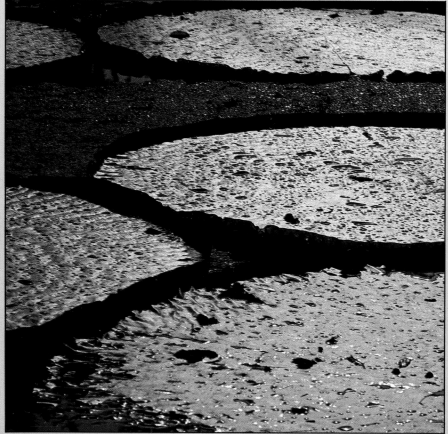

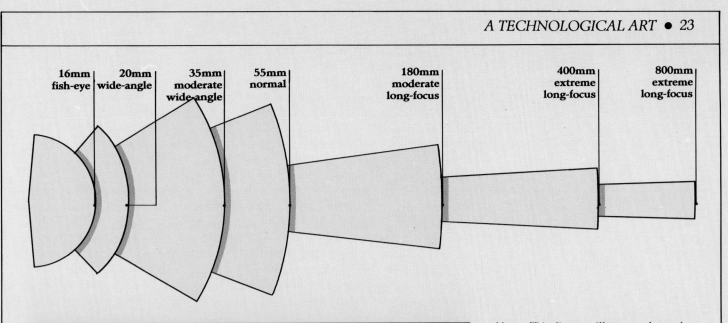

| 16mm fish-eye | 20mm wide-angle | 35mm moderate wide-angle | 55mm normal | 180mm moderate long-focus | 400mm extreme long-focus | 800mm extreme long-focus |

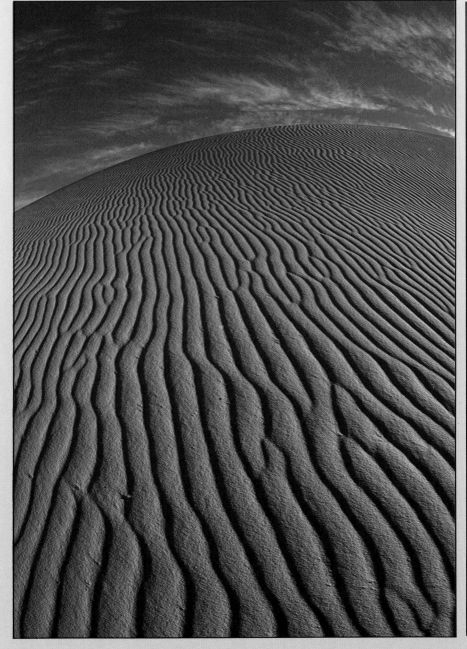

Above *This diagram illustrates the angles of view of lenses of different focal lengths. The lenses available for modern 35mm cameras vary in their angles of view from 200° to 1°: hence choice of lens can have an important effect on composition. Lenses in the middle of the range are generally considered 'normal' — in other words, they cover approxomately the same angle of view as the human eye, without perspective distortion.*

Left *Just as a telephoto lens alters the proportions of an image in one direction, so does a wide-angle lens in the other. Photographed with a fish-eye lens — so-called because of its curved, barrel distortion — these sand-dunes would never look like this in reality. The angle of view from top to bottom is nearly 140°, and the effect is further exaggerated by being reproduced on this page in a relatively small format.*

These are the main *technical* features that help to give photography its visual flavor and, as the examples show, they can be entirely incidental to the image, or used trivially, or they can be put to work to give an extra dimension to the photograph. Together, they are a part of the framework that defines the special nature of photography.

But at a deeper level, the technology of cameras affects the way in which photographers approach their subjects, practically. Taking pictures is an activity that, in general, has to fit in with the way things are. However it is finally used and manipulated, the camera is a device primarily for recording, in a way that a painter's or illustrator's tools are not. But very few photographers exert no influence on the way the image falls into place. Most have the natural desire to organize the elements of a scene so that the picture is in some way pleasing or effective. The result is that working photographers have had to develop certain strategies for overcoming, or at least for dealing with, the limitations imposed by real events. A large number of these are related to composition. In street photography and any other kind in which the subjects are not amenable to being rearranged, the chief means of influencing the design are the framing of the shot, the position of the photographer and the focal length of the lens. If objects cannot be physically moved in a photographic situation, images of them can often be excluded by framing the picture in a certain way or choosing a viewpoint from which they are hidden by something nearer the camera; a wide-angle lens will make nearer objects appear larger and more distant ones smaller; a long-focus lens will make objects at difficult distances appear closer to the same scale. The kind of ballet that many street photographers and photojournalists can often be seen performing is at least partly a design technique in itself.

Other strategies are aimed at dealing with inadequate technology, such as when the level of light is insufficient to allow a shutter speed fast enough to freeze a particular action, or when the depth of a scene is so great that not all of it can be rendered sharply. These are problems, of course, only if blurred movement or selective focus is not actively sought. As in Haas' bull-fighting picture the technological limitations often inspire creative solutions, turning such problems into virtues. In the photograph of a pig being roasted on an open fire, for instance (page 26), the techniques used to overcome the dim lighting and extremely high contrast were to use a very fast lens with a shallow depth of field, to shoot directly towards the flames to give a silhouette of the men and as bright an image as possible, and to use a slow shutter speed. The result, with flare, some softness of focus and swirling traces of the fire, is arguably more effective for its impressionistic character.

Limitations such as these are a fairly logical consequence of the way cameras form images, and the solutions are essentially ones that come naturally to photographers. There is, however, another quite arbitrary limitation that photography suffered from until quite recently — one that has been solved so successfully that, paradoxically, it is now seen more as a special, *positive* quality than as a problem. Though it may seem a little odd to think of it in this way now, the fact that early photography could only be performed in black-and-white was a real hindrance. Most Victorian photographers would have dearly loved to be able to work in color, hence the considerable efforts made to bring some variety of hue to prints and glass slides. With an admirable perversity, generations of photographers have since found ways of working creatively within monochrome images, so that for many this medium is actually *preferable* to full color.

Now that black-and-white photography has a creative cachet in galleries, it is not easy to appreciate the Victorian point of view, yet black-and-white is a result of nothing more interesting than the primitive state of film technology in photography's early days. After all, what photographer would have deliberately chosen to restrict his palette? In the event, there was not a great deal that could be done until the invention of Autochrome in 1907 and other color processes, but this was not for lack of trying. Hand-coloring and chemical toning were hardly major creative aspects of photography, even when performed skilfully and subtly as they often were, but they were a measure of the dissatisfaction that many photographers felt at not being able to cover the one outstanding gap in realism.

In the hands of an expert, toning could be impressively successful in compensating for color. Unfortunately, subtleties are largely lost in printed reproduction and this, being most people's experience of toned prints, has probably done most to give toning a bad name. Certainly, the aim of photographers such as Fox Talbot was not to produce a flat, uniform monochrome; he made deliberate use of impurities in the chemicals and papers to create variety in tone and color. Further alterations to the chemicals and to the time that the print was allowed to soak in the baths extended the range of possible hues, to permutations of brown, red, blue, ocher, purple and yellow. Sometimes the hues would vary slightly within one print. The result could be a remarkable sense of depth and a quality that was not exactly a substitute for color but which could take the edge off its absence. It is hardly coincidence that the classic age of the toned and crafted print drew to an end as photographers were coming to better terms with monochrome.

This can be seen as a special strategy for working within a limited medium, and it has been so spectacularly successful that two important bastions of black-and-white photography are still fairly healthy. One is gallery photography, the other is photojournalism. As a kind of reaction against the improved technology of new color films, which has had the effect of making things almost too easy, a large proportion of exhibiting photographers are happy to stay within what is now a rather specialized medium. In photojournalism, black-and-white has survived for the more prosaic reason that color reproduction has, up to now, been too slow and expensive for most newspapers. Possibly even more important, color reproduction was for several decades not even possible, let alone economically feasible, and the legacy of photojournalism's formative period is that gritty, unromantic black-and-white is now thoroughly associated with hard news. Only slowly are news photographers beginning to learn and use color and, even so, compromises must remain. It is a feature of news images that they are frequently syndicated to different publications, so that for simple visual efficiency, a photograph taken in color must work in black-and-white. *Time,* for example, will normally run a feature in color in one of its regional editions, but in black-and-white elsewhere. For events of real journalistic significance, black-and-white can even have the edge in realism due to its associations — something that a Victorian photographer would have found difficult to comprehend. All this because a couple of generations of photographers were successful at working within technological limits.

Such strategies for dealing with technical restrictions are really a practical matter. Most of the time, most photographers perform them without worrying too much about deeper intent. In this chapter, the examples have been chosen for what they show of practical, sensible

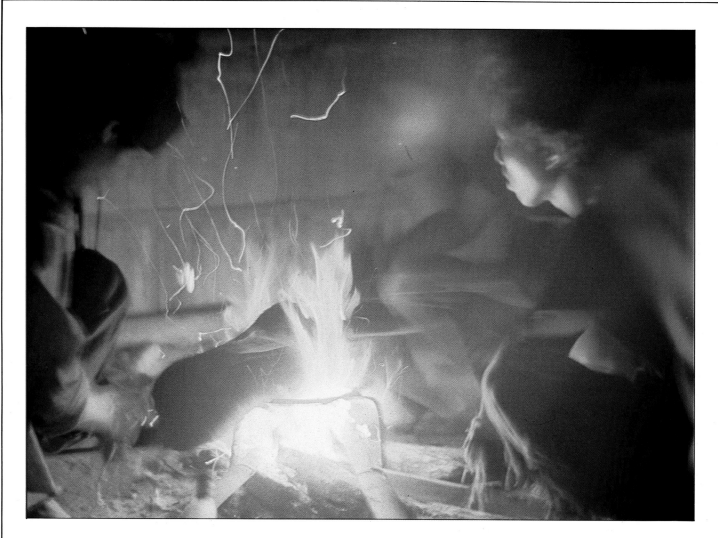

Above *The only illumination in this tribal house in Thailand was the fire on which the pig was being roasted. Since flash would not have captured the right mood, other techniques were employed to record an image under the low light conditions. These were to use fast film, a fast lens at full aperture, and a slow shutter speed (one-eighth of a second). The combination of very shallow focus, flare from the wide-open lens, and moving flames and sparks, give an impressionistic effect that, while not exactly deliberate, makes a strong image. Photographs taken under these and similar conditions are not completely predictable, and so often contain an element of surprise for the photographer when processed.*

solutions — essentially, the craftsman's approach. However, what is obvious, even here, is that these skills are open to abuse. Because photography *is* mainly tied to the real world, it is widely assumed to *show* reality. As some of the later chapters explore, photography starts with a long line of credit in believability and this can be exploited, sometimes innocently, sometimes unscrupulously. Photography began ingenuously enough, but over the decades photographers have become more adept at solving the problems of the trade, and in so doing have acquired the ability to manipulate their audiences.

In the course of looking for ways to outwit clumsy natural arrangements and technical limitations, photographers occasionally come across surprises. Ernst Haas' picture of the bull-fight on page 18 is essentially an exploitation of a type of photographic accident — the photographer finding a creative use for what must have originally, in the nineteenth century, been simply an odd streaking effect. The multicolored view of a tropical storm over Rangoon on page 30 is another example of effects not visible to the eye; here the green light on the buildings is a result of the special way in which photographic dyes react to fluorescent lighting, while the violet sky is due, not to the actual color of the lightning, but to the long exposure, for which the film is not designed. In addition, the actual appearance of the lightning flashes, which are cumulative, was completely unpredictable.

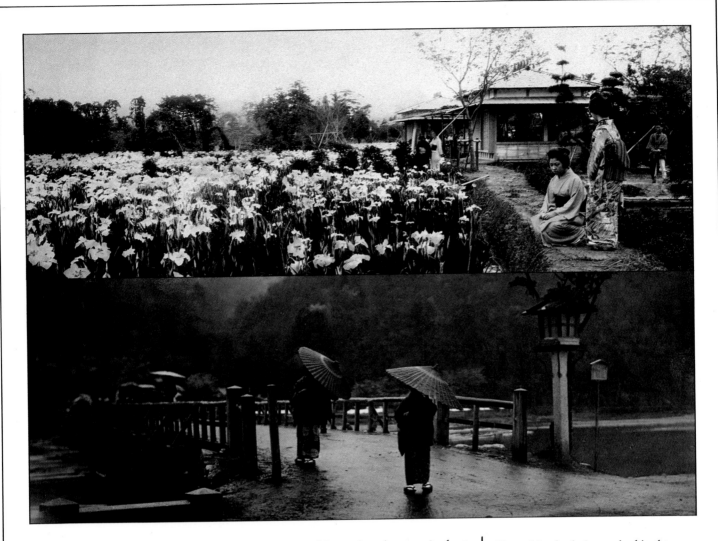

A different kind of surprise picture is rooted in technology — in fact, in the experimental area. Every so often, developments in imaging processes throw up entirely new ways of seeing the world. Thermography, which is a process of visibly recording heat, uses special infrared sensing apparatus cooled to extremely low temperatures, and the image is displayed on a video screen, in the form shown on page 31. In this unusual image of a camera, each color represents a particular temperature range, and the result is a kind of contour map of heat. A camera, of course, produces no heat itself, unlike the human body for which thermographic equipment is mainly designed; in this example, a hair dryer was used to heat the camera selectively.

Similarly, polarization, in which light is manipulated by means of special filters so that it shows different properties according to the way it vibrates, produces a particular kind of visual information. Overlaid on a normal image, it can produce vivid and luminous colors, as in the close-up arrangement of artificial fibers on page 31. The deep rich violet background is actually strong backlighting that has been almost extinguished by the crossing of two polarizing screens, while the multiple colors of the strands are evidence of internal stress patterns made visible by the process.

If the beauty of these pictures comes from the technology of new sensing and processing systems, the pictures must also be seen as being substantially automated. The argument that they just represent more sophisticated developments of existing camera technology, and that

Above *Hand-coloring evolved in the nineteenth century as a means of adding the 'naturalness' of color to photographs, denied this element because of the early deficiencies of the technology. It became a minor art-form. These hand-tinted platinum prints, showing typical scenes from Japanese life, were made in the 1890s and probably sold to European tourists. The photographs were taken with a type of panoramic camera and painted with water colors.*

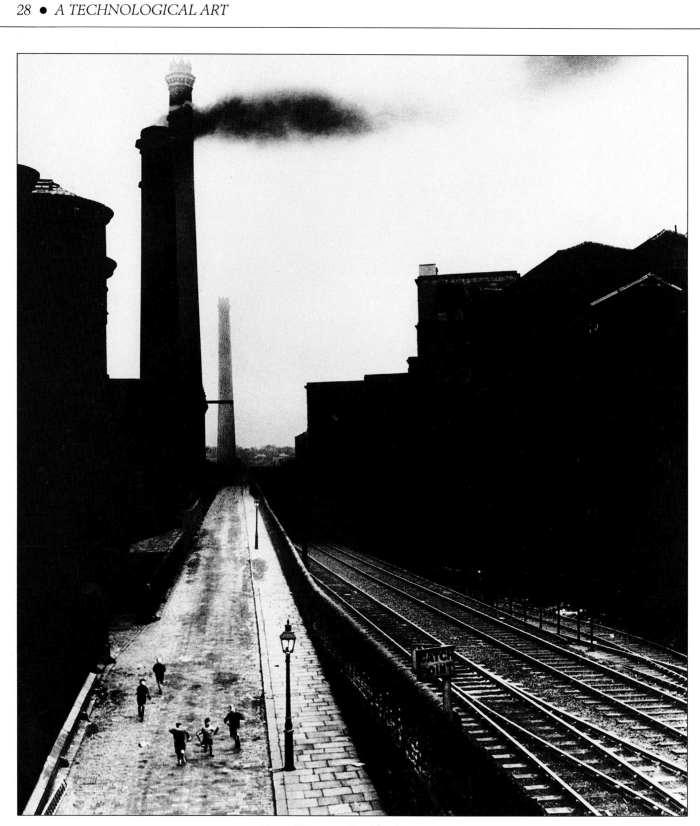

Above *This view of Halifax in the 1930s (Shadow of Light) is in many ways typical of Bill Brandt's monochrome skills. Through strong and distinct use of tones and shapes, most of Brandt's photographs work within the monochrome format, and never appear as if they would have benefited from being in color. High contrast gives dense, sooty blacks, which suit, in a brooding sort of way, Brandt's feelings about his subject matter — here the industrial landscape of the north of England. His wife said, of such dark northern buildings, that they 'looked to him as if they might have been built of coal.'*

photographers are directing them and using them in the same old way, will not do. 'Straight' photography, as Edward Weston called it, accords with the way we see the world. These exotic images, on the other hand, are in a different league. They are essentially unexpected gifts from imaging systems that are usually directed towards scientific ends.

From here it is only a small step to considering fully automatic photography. Although familiarity has dulled some of their edge, the most outstanding are the deep-space photographs from the American planetary probes. Some, like the photograph of Io on page 31, have an intrinsic beauty that places them among the best of exotic landscape photography, while even the most workmanlike are surprising documents, given what we know about how they were taken. Even photographs of rocks and sand in a Martian desert, taken in 1976 by a Viking lander, which have little to recommend them aesthetically, have durable curiosity value thanks to their extraordinary location. Precisely because photography records something of the real world, the pure aesthetics of a picture are difficult to isolate. The picture of Io provokes amazement as much because of what it is as what it shows. What is intriguing about this picture is that it is the work of a true robot. The human creative element has been restricted to the role of art director — making the selection and tidying up the image — yet it is undoubtedly a remarkable photograph. Clearly, although this is an extreme example, photography cannot always be treated as the outcome of deliberate intention and craftsmanship.

Photographers as a whole have something of an ambiguous relationship with their technology, a relationship that oscillates between admiration and disdain. Camera technology is seductive because it allows opportunities for avoiding some of the more difficult creative issues. Cameras, like hi-fi equipment, can function as adult toys, a role for which they are increasingly being designed and produced in the mass market.

Recognizing the trivial appeal of gadgets, flashing information displays and high-tech design, many photographers react to this technology in a rather odd way — in public, at least, it has become customary to play down the technical side of taking photographs. The motive is usually to defend what a photographer assumes to be his or her artistic integrity, as if to say that only a special inner vision is at work, not a mass-produced camera as well. This kind of denial is understandable in the face of an audience of millions of other people who also use cameras, but it is not reasonable to deny the role of technology. Nor should it be allowed to cloud the real issue, which is that technological influences on photography are complex and variable, and are part of the context in which any photograph is seen.

Clearly, in appreciating photographs, a new set of standards is needed. A photograph is not a painting or a sketch, nor does it necessarily hang on a gallery wall. The standards for judging it must allow for its different uses — photojournalism, for example, has a different aesthetic from that of, say, fine art photography. It must also allow for images that owe more to accident than design and for others that are created with little obvious craft. Photography's ability to be reproduced means that images are rarely precious objects in the sense that an old oil painting is. These new standards must, above all, recognize the different visual language that photography uses, and make allowances for the context of the image.

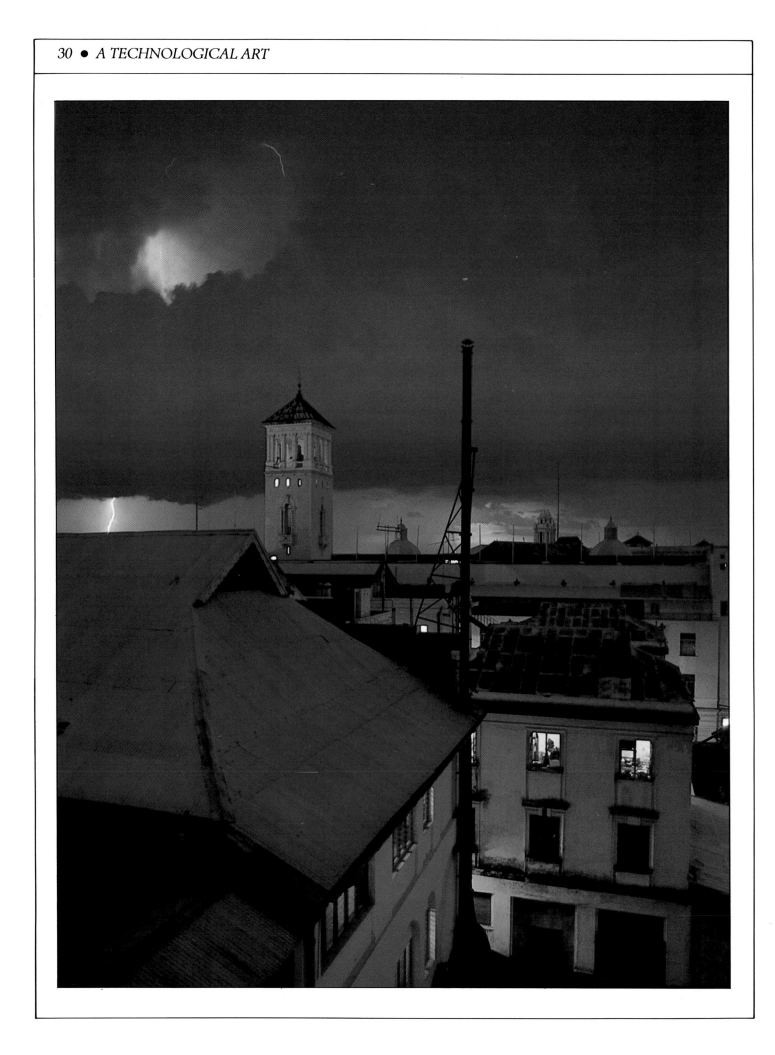

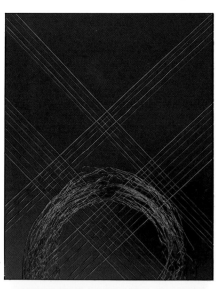

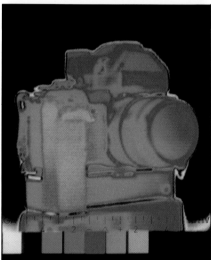

Photographs play a large part in everyone's visual experience, and most of the people who see them regularly also know at least something about using a camera. As popular a subject as it is, however, photography still seems to come in for some particularly dense and over-reflective criticism, as if it were some mysterious and exotic art-form. Can a critic who describes a recent picture by William Eggleston (the subject is a 'straight' photograph of a patch of wasteland) by suggesting that the photographer's 'vision is sometimes apocalyptic, involved with the Four Last Things — death, judgement, heaven and hell', really be talking about photography? It seems a pity to be so convoluted about such an interesting, vital medium. The solution lies in understanding *how* photographs are made, from the tactical decisions taken on the spot to the more philosophical issues involved in approaching a particular type of subject.

The following chapters explore these practicalities, beginning with pictorial elements—composition rather than content—and moving on to the major preoccupations of the medium.

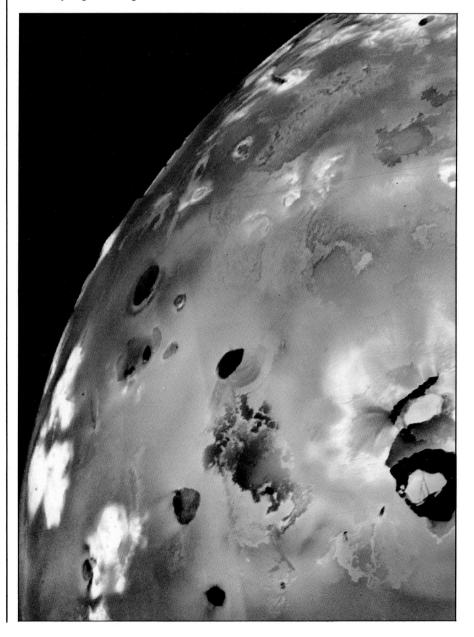

Left *Here, in a late evening view across the rooftops of Rangoon, the combination of colors comes from reciprocity failure (the exposure was 30 seconds), green fluorescent and orange tungsten light (both unfiltered on daylight-balanced film), a residual sunset and lightning.*

Top *Internal stress patterns in artificial fibers are transformed into polarizing filters, one between the light and the subject, the other between the subject and the camera.*

Above *This thermographic portrait of a camera was recorded by a super-cooled heat detector and then displayed on a video monitor. The temperature profile, exaggerated by playing a hair-dryer on the camera, is color-coded by the equipment.*

Right *Two years after launch, the deep-space probe Voyager I sent back images of astounding resolution from Jupiter and its moons. Received digitally, these have since been processed by one of the US Geological Sturvey's computers to produce color photographs such as this, of the moon, a mosaic in which high-resolution images furnish spatial detail and low-resolution images provide color information.*

CHAPTER 2

The Lively Surface

'The so called "rules" of photographic composition are, in my opinion, invalid, irrelevant and immaterial.'
Ansel Adams

...teaches you how to frame your compositions. Position your subjects. Use different viewpoints. And much more.'
Advertisement for Kodak book, *Take Better Pictures*

Above right *A classic and well-known photograph by Cartier-Bresson, this view of a family picnic on the banks of the Marne (1938) demonstrates this photographer's consistent ability to make cohesive compositions quickly from candid situations. Most of Cartier-Bresson's best-known photographs contain moments of action, as here, even if they are small ones such as pouring a bottle of wine. Cartier-Bresson uses activity as an element in the photograph's design.*
Below right *One of the great difficulties in analyzing the design and composition of photographs is that, however tempting, it is never reasonable to ignore the content. Nevertheless, photographs are seen on different levels by people. This enigmatic situation, photographed in Mexico in 1934 by Henri Cartier-Bresson, is uncharacteristically formal in design, yet also portrays powerful emotions.*

Organizing the image is a skill that ultimately plays a major part in the success of most photographs. Design, however, is something that many photographers are strangely reluctant to discuss in any detail. Part of the reason is that the decisions taken are often hard to pin down; also, however, there is the fear that a bald description of how a picture is composed will somehow rob it of magic. How much justification there is for this attitude varies considerably among photographs and photographers; with some, the techniques are actually rather simple and probably best left undiscussed, but others enjoy more complexity and subtlety than might be obvious at first glance. Composition and similar visual attributes of a picture are certainly important enough to merit a close examination, but they also need to be treated cautiously, for the role they play in photography is not the same as in painting and illustration. So much happens intuitively, and nearly always quickly, that there is a real danger of assigning too much importance to what are essentially design skills.

Whatever their subject matter, all pictures are designed in some sense, whether the composition is arranged with great care in a studio, selected from a number of alternative shots of the same subject or achieved quickly and instinctively as is liable to happen in location photography. The relationship between the content of a photograph and its composition is a dynamic one which, ultimately, involves questions of appropriateness and meaning. For this reason, the analysis of form, line, color and so on can be a slippery road, sometimes ending up in a wonderfully theoretical description that bears absolutely no relation to the way in which the picture was made.

A number of years ago, one photography magazine ran a regular

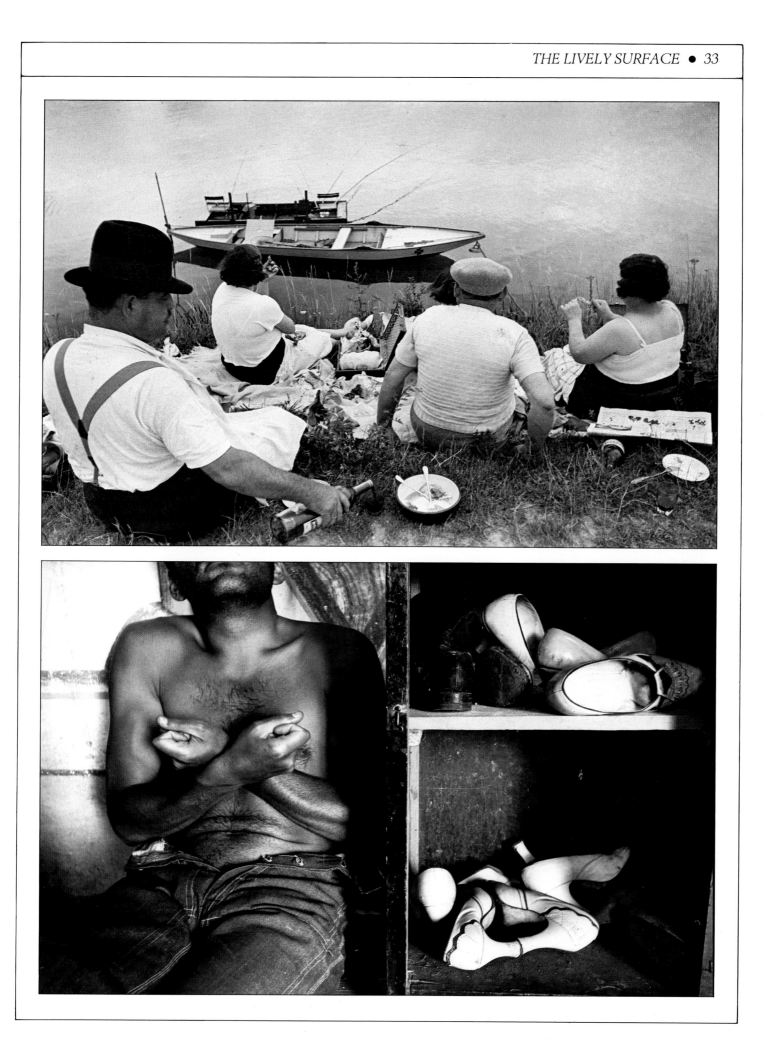

column in which photographs were analyzed with the help of small sketches — and with additional sketches to show how the picture would have been better if composed differently. What was unintentionally entertaining about this popular feature was that occasionally the editors would become so carried away that they even proposed major changes to the landscapes being photographed. Most of these descriptions were, as might be expected, fascinating and quite irrelevant. There is something almost irresistible, when the opportunity allows, about considering the alternatives and nuances of different framings and points of view, and this is the kind of treatment that photographs tend to receive in critical appraisal. There is no real harm in this but, to be of any value, such a judgement *must* take into account the conditions under which the picture was taken. A quickly observed moment such as Henri Cartier-Bresson's *Banks of the Marne* (page 33) requires intuitive composition — born of experience, practice, decisiveness, and a certain maturity of seeing. At the moment of shooting there is often just no time for the kind of analysis to which it may later be subjected.

Even devoting the whole of this chapter to the design elements of photographs carries some risk. However balanced and reasonable we are, the tendency is bound to be towards emphasizing the surface patterns of a picture. This can be particularly unrealistic in photography, where events and situations carry equal weight. Look at one recent example from an encyclopedia of photography, typical in its way. The photograph being described, shown here on page 33, was taken by Cartier-Bresson in Mexico in the 1930s. Here is what was said: 'This picture by Henri Cartier-Bresson shows his strong feeling for geometric constructions, plus his ability to observe odd similarities between dissimilar objects (such as the hands and the shoes).'

All that is certainly true, and by delving further into the design of the picture we could probably find other correspondences and visual nuances. But the photograph is *not* an exercise in composition; the composition helps to create the enigma that is essential to this photograph, and is not an end in itself. Why are the man's hands clenched tight to his body? What are the emotions caught in this picture? The way the photograph is composed cannot be discussed in isolation from these issues.

Although what now follows is a look at the structure of photographs, this treatment of Cartier-Bresson's picture should be remembered as a cautionary tale. The basic design elements that exist in photography are approximately the same as in other graphic arts, and the visual sensations created by points, lines and shapes are undoubtedly real. While these elements are often dominated by what the photograph is actually showing, the tension between content and design can be creatively exploited.

Separating composition from content is rather like taking the sound out of music. A useful exercise, however, is to examine pictures that have actually been motivated by an *interest* in composition. This is not to say that their content is unimportant, but that some aspect of design has triggered the photographic process. What distinguishes most of the pictures shown here is that the photographers have been attracted to the design possibilities at the start, rather than simply making the best of a situation in which the intention is to photograph a particular subject.

The most basic design element is the single point, but in photography (aside from studio set-ups) it occurs distinctly on fewer occasions than

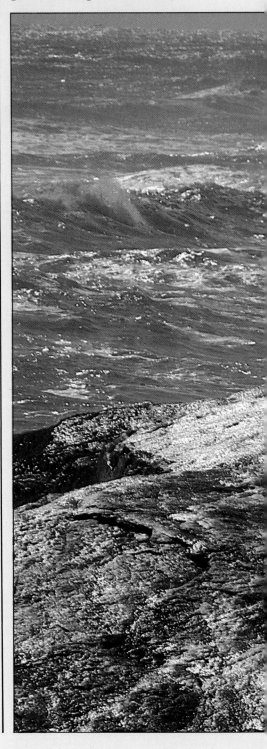

Below *Two women stand on a promontory overlooking the sea at Cape Comorin, India. Backlighting and a heavy sea wetting the rocks gives a consistency of tone and texture to the setting that, in effect, isolates the figures as a single point in the design. This point is off-centered for logical reasons: the women are looking in one direction, and their position in the frame places them in relationship to the sea rather than to the land. Placing them to the right gives visual weight to the sea at left.*

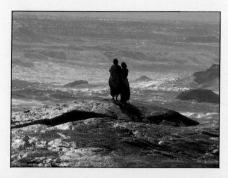
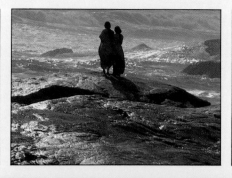

Left *and* **far left** *These alternative compositions illustrate how important framing can be in determining the visual dynamics of a picture. With the figures in the center, the composition is static and flat; with the figures moved to the top of the frame the overall effect is one of truncation.*

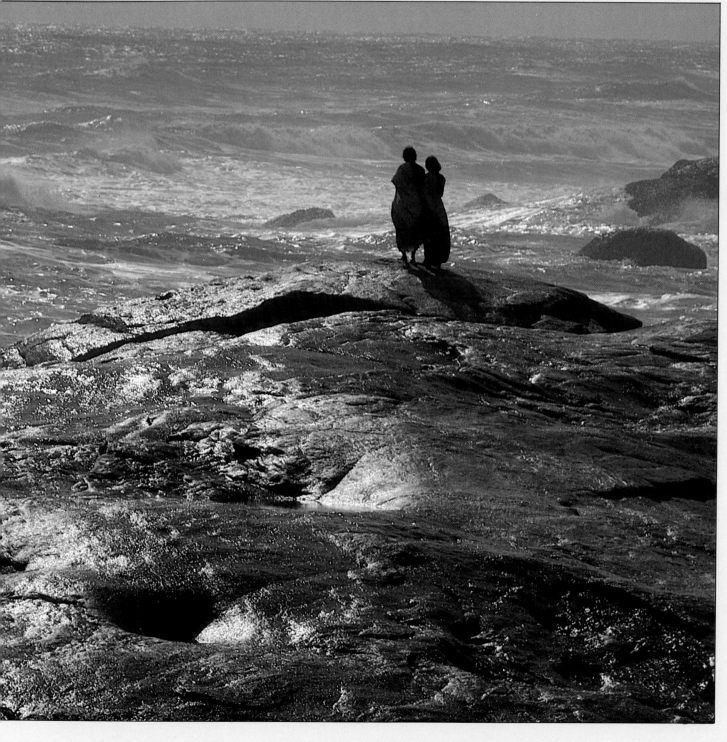

one might expect, largely because a main prerequisite is an even, uncluttered setting or background for a single object. Figures in open spaces, such as in the photograph on page 35, are among the most typical of single-point images. This graphic treatment is only one of a number of possibilities; a closer approach or a longer focal length would, for example, make much less of the setting. Given, however, that the subject is to be treated as a point, the principal decision becomes where to place it in the frame. In the dynamics of design, the point implies location, and has a forceful relationship with the space around it, and with the frame edges in particular. The symmetry of a central position is not necessarily very interesting, and, in this example, the stance of the two women looking out to sea suggested a logical place for them at the right of the picture.

More often, points in photographs are implied; if there are several, other relationships are established. Two or more together encourage the eye to travel between them. In the photograph of a Greek Evzone's ceremonial dress being critically inspected by an NCO (page 52), the position of the camera is responsible for the head seeming to peer in from one edge of the frame. The result is to take the viewer's attention across the picture.

Right *At a very quick glance this close view of a human midriff by Ralph Gibson, might seem to be a single-point design. In fact, as a longer look confirms, the design is more subtle, for the shapes in the top left and lower right corners pull the attention across the frame. Gibson was trying to convey motion in this photograph, and printed it so that 'by having a highlight on the left and a shadow on the right there would be a certain stroboscopic effect that carries the eye back and forth'.*

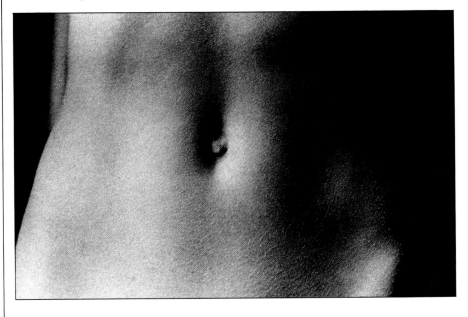

When several points make up a regular, or at least recognizable, pattern, they begin to imply the second most fundamental design element — the line. Whereas the point tends to be static, lines generally have energy and direction and, as a result, often acquire further associations. Horizontal lines, such as the series of escarpments in the photograph below right, suggest stability and flatness, while horizontal and vertical lines together, as in the picture of a desert road (*see* above right), tend to produce a sensation of balance and regularity. It is usually more interesting if the lines owe at least something to the optics of photography rather than simply the subject as in, say, the window pattern of a building. In the case of the photograph of escarpments at right, an aerial view would reveal them as a pattern of indentations, but a low, long camera view has a tendency to flatten many elements into horizontal lines. Diagonal or curved lines, which in photography are often created by an off-axis camera position, introduce other qualities — those of dynamism, particular direction, and even speed. The long, downward

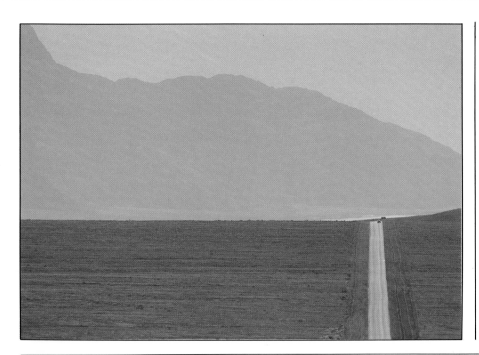

Left *Viewpoint is totally responsible for the precise juxtaposition of vertical and horizontal lines in this photograph of a Death Valley road. In principle, a combination of flat and the upright can be expected to induce a sense of order.*
Below *The perspective in low-angled views tends to favor horizontals. The horizon itself is usually level, while even the various directions of the pale-edged escarpments in this view of Utah's Canyonlands are converted to nearly horizontal lines.*

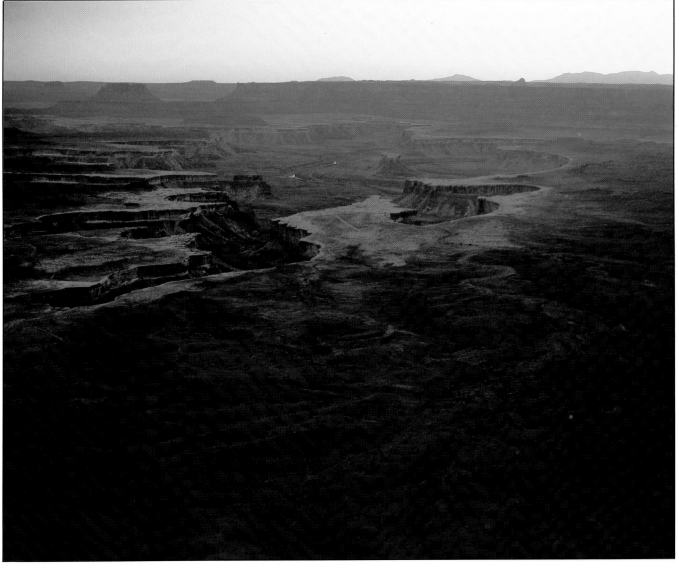

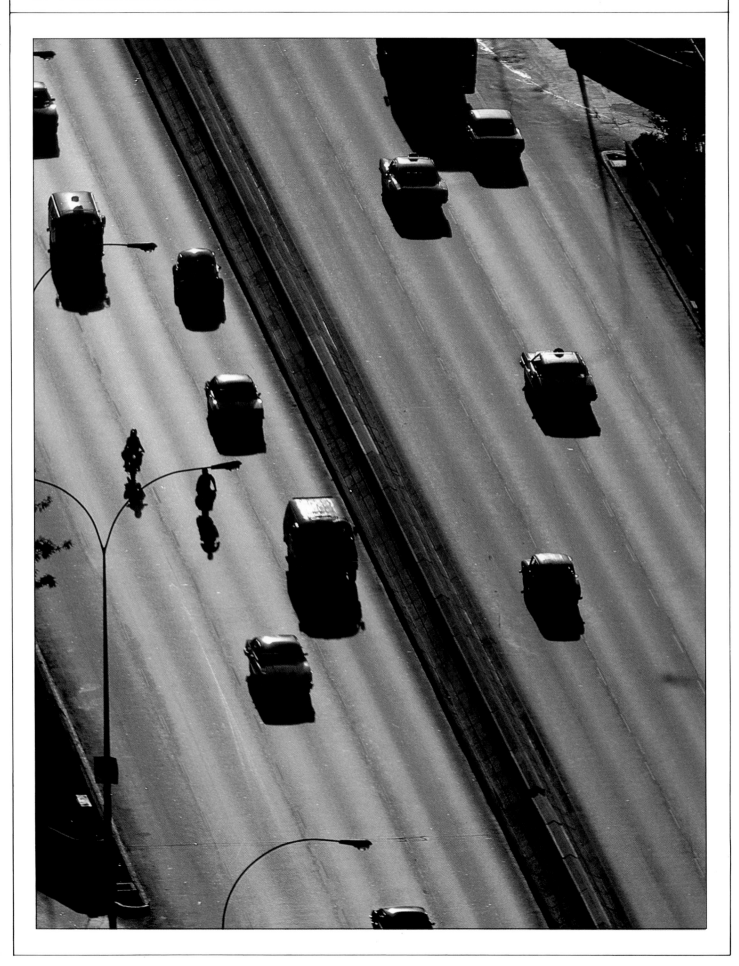

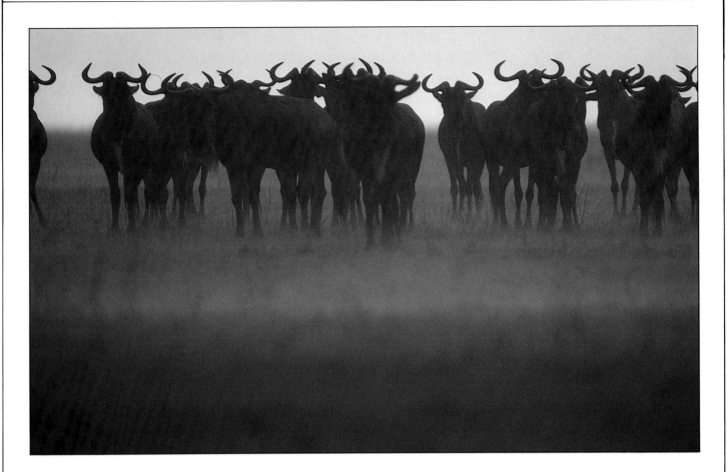

shot of an expressway (see left) is a fairly uncomplicated demonstration of this, aided, perhaps a little unfairly for this example, by the content of the picture. Varieties and combinations of lines can introduce yet another dynamic sensation into an image — that of rhythm. Both the line of standing wildebeest (see above) and the backlit pattern of giant waterlilies on page 22 rely as images on repetitive patterns, in one a linear sequence of similar shapes, in the other zigzagging lines.

As points can imply lines, so both lines and points can make up the basic planar figures that can dominate pictures as shapes. The three most basic of these figures are the triangle, circle and rectangle, of which the triangle, in photography at least, is the most commonly used, both unconsciously and deliberately. Why this should be so must be due partly to its geometric simplicity — it needs only three points to suggest it, and these need not be in any precise position — and partly to the fact that most of the normal effects of perspective suggest triangular convergence. A substantial number of photographs, particularly those taken with standard or wide-angle focal lengths, are taken by aiming the camera slightly downwards towards a receding view, and this frequently creates triangular compositions with the base in the foreground and the apex in the distance.

One of the most valuable properties of basic shapes in a picture is cohesiveness, something that is, on the whole, more useful to photographers as a way of imposing order on untidy scenes than it is a design restriction. As the three photographs on pages 40-1 show, shapes can be more or less distinctive: the unequivocally circular view of the dome of the Library of Congress utterly dominates the frame, while in the aerial picture the triangular arrangement of surf pointing to a small island at the apex is simply fortuitous. In the dense woodland scene, the choice of

Far left *Diagonals tend to convey movement, and never more simply than in this downward view onto an expressway. Several lines and the flow of vehicles repeat the direction, while the strong backlighting from the afternoon sun removed color and form, making an abstract design composed of shapes and lines.*

Above *In another picture where color and details are suppressed, in this case largely by heavy rain, a line of wildebeest stop in their migration route to watch the photographer's vehicle with apprehension. The outlined horns and heads set up a horizontal rhythm across the frame that becomes the dominant element.*

Right *The very simplicity of triangular composition — any combination of three points or implied lines will generally do — makes it easily found. It tends to give coherence and a sense of stability and is a natural strategy for many photographers.*

Far right *The visual unification of the circle is unmistakable in this upward view of the dome of Washington's Library of Congress. The dynamics of this design are formal and rigid, but make an irresistible image. A wide-angle lens and a low tripod, with a grid screen to check the alignment, ensured a formal composition to suit the subject.*

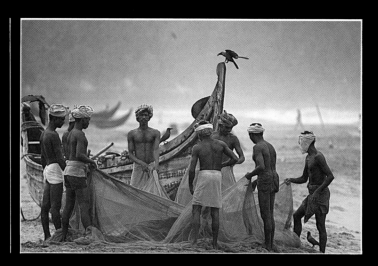

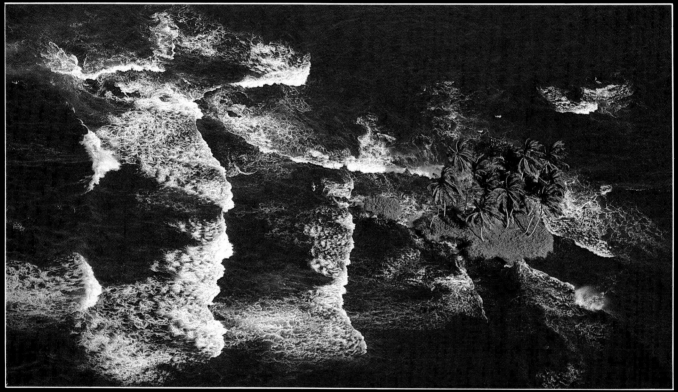

Above *Photographic images being inextricable from the real world, the shapes and lines that make up designs are often only suggested, not obvious and dominant. In this aerial view of a tropical coastline in South America, the convergence of the lines of surf on the small island make a triangle.*

Right *In contrast to the very obvious circular design of the photograph of the Library of Congress, the construction of this photograph of a dense, leafy oak forest works gently to unify the image. Unification was needed, or the complex vegetation would have appeared to dissolve into an unstructured mass of green, and was provided by a careful choice of viewpoint, by a curving branch, and by using a fish-eye lens that added its own, optical curvature. The result is a hint of a spiral that draws the elements together.*

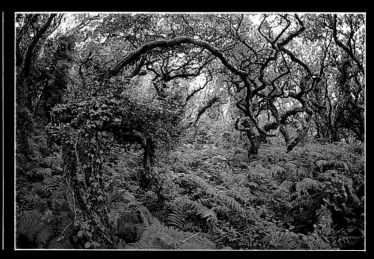

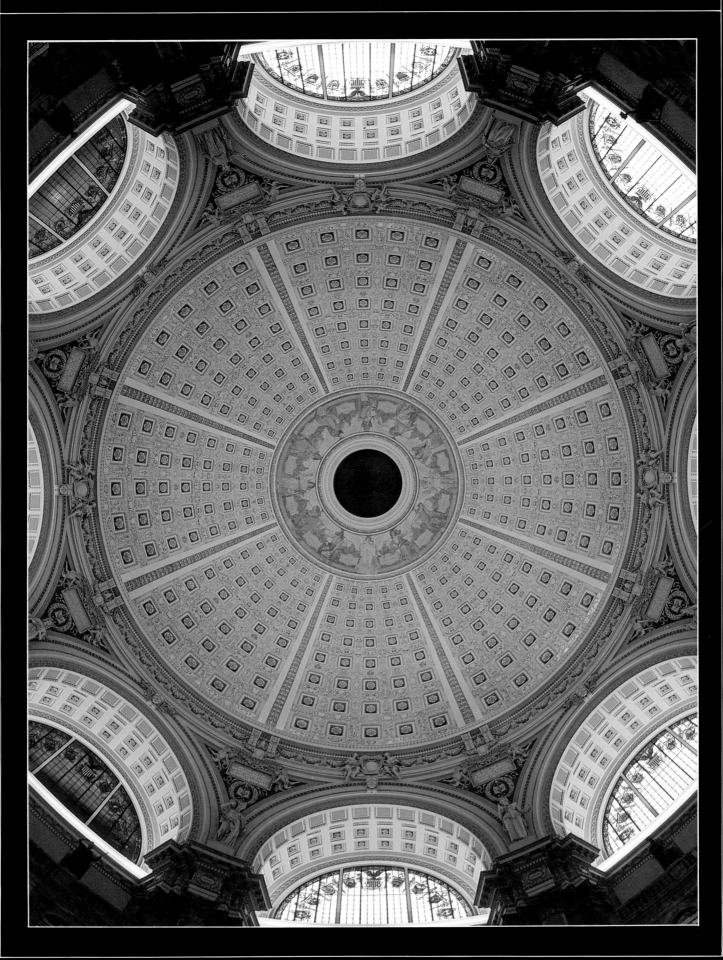

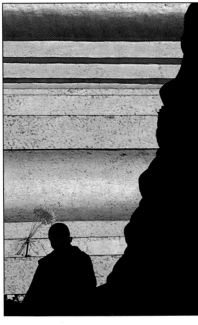

Right *Many photographs can be considered as having two components, the figure and the background. Figure-ground relationships offer an area for graphic experiment, at least when the two elements are distinct in tone or color, as in this photograph of a silhouetted monk sitting against the side of a stupa, with the golden background of the main pagoda beyond. When the areas of figure and ground are nearly equal, a slight visual conflict is often set up.*

Center *Contrast, particularly when contained with pattern, can be an important element in photographic design. In this view down into the Colorado River canyon, the angle of the sun in the late afternoon catches the top edges of the walls but leaves the depths in shade.*

Far right *A midday shaft of sunlight strikes a group of sculptures in Chartres cathedral, and the surrounding glow where the direct light is reflected from the stone helps to make the illumination as much the subject of the photograph as the artefacts themselves.*

viewpoint, close to a curving branch, and the curvilinear distortion of a wide-angle lens, together bring a circular, almost spiral, structure to the image, but one that is suggestive rather than definite.

Another way of looking at the design of a picture is in terms of the spatial relationships between the different elements — how their arrangement influences the sensations of weight and balance. Figure-ground relationships, seen in the silhouetted photograph of a monk (*see* above), are one of the dominant varieties and can, when the contrast is very distinct, be quite striking. Any relative combination is possible, given sufficient freedom to move around the subject and use different focal lengths — from extremes of proportion, as in the photograph of the two women and the sea on page 35, to virtual equality, as in the picture of the monk. In painting and illustration, such a close proportion between the two areas can give rise to a phenomenon known as alternation, in which the viewer is never quite sure which part advances from the picture and which recedes; in photography, the reality of most subject matter removes obvious confusion, but the image can still have a sense of spatial ambiguity.

The element of contrast and comparison is, in fact, never far from any examination of spatial relationships and simply the range and quality of the differences between tonal values, for example, or textures, can be of sufficient interest to justify a photograph. A shaft of sunlight illuminating a sculptural frieze in a cathedral (*see* far right) creates a full and unusual distribution of tones, while a low sun in clear air details the texture of canyon walls (*see* right), emerging from smooth black shadows.

In the graphic arts, color plays an intensely subjective role, and although it is possible to construct a framework for the crude relationships between different colors, the most interesting combinations are generally very subtle. While a painter has the opportunity of experimenting on the canvas, and has absolute choice in the palette, colors in photography are largely found, albeit subject to manipulation. In fact, when compared with the tonal controls used in the photographs of Brett Weston, son of Edward Weston and noted for his studies of landscape and nature, the extra dimension of color actually limits the ways in which the image can be altered. Using a strong colored filter simply adds

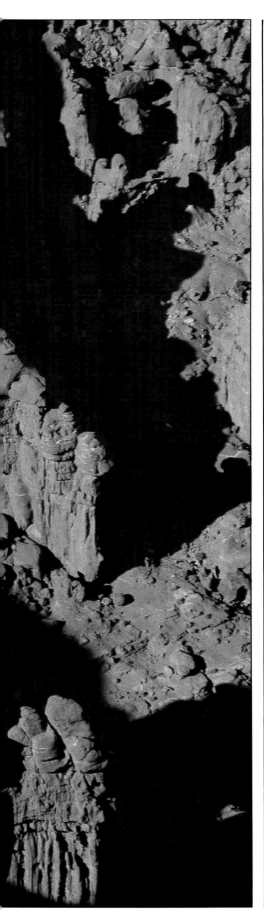

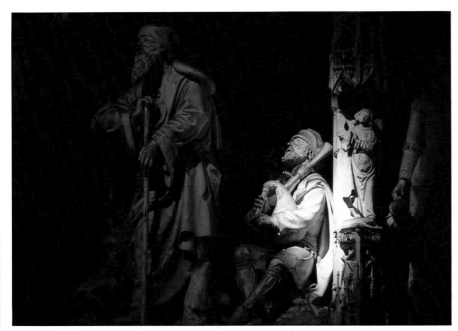

an overall color cast, and the effect is much more likely to be crude than interesting.

In all events, the greatest influence on the use of color in photography has been its late arrival. Most of the basic pictorial conventions had already been worked out by the time that color became usable for most subjects. This, and the relative difficulty in influencing color relationships in a photograph, meant that it has attracted little serious experiment until recently.

The area of *possible* experiment is mainly limited to choice of subject and choice of lighting. Popular taste in color tends to favor the spectacular and unusual, with most people seeing luxuriant, dramatically colored photographs as an ideal, expert version of what they themselves sometimes attempt. Pete Turner's picture of a barn and road sign in Sweden (page 45) is an example of professional photography that/taps the sensual appeal of rich, saturated color. It is typical of a large body of work, principally American, and is used heavily in the commercial areas of advertising and annual reports. The popular appeal of this photograph rests on the visceral sensations of color: the strong hues are the real focus of interest, and this strikes the viewer immediately and easily, without the need for any analysis.

Joel Meyerowitz' image on page 44 shows the same selective skills, evidence of anticipation and very careful timing, but the intentions are more restrained.

Throughout the history of photography, the structure of the image has fascinated certain people and has become, at times, a preoccupation. The critical label for such an approach is Formalism, a word that is perhaps a little too grand and academic for what is really a straightforward treatment. For photographers such as Edward Weston and his son Brett, Aaron Siskind, Harry Callahan and others, an important direction for at least a part of their careers was experiment with the structure of the image, whether they were photographing flaking paint, cracked window panes, weathered wood or other mundane subjects. To paraphrase the French philosopher Victor Cousin, this is photography

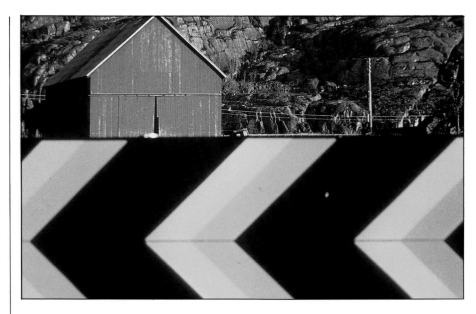

Right *Intense and brightly contrasting colors are a hallmark of much of Peter Turner's work. In this photograph of a chevron-patterned roadsign against a red Swedish barn, virtually all other elements, including the content, are subordinated to the juxtaposition of hues. Even the camera height has been selected so that the middle ground between barn and sign is hidden (presumably it would have had distracting, uncolorful detail).*

Far right *No less celebratory of color and color relationships, but strikingly different in approach, is this Miami poolside scene photographed by Joel Meyerowitz in 1978. Here the restrained use of color helps to suggest a mood and reinforce the content of the subject. The complementary shades of orange and turquoise suit the art deco architecture and underline the atmosphere of stillness and nostalgia. Meyerowitz achieves this type of effect by taking great care in color printing, working from large-format negatives.*

for photography's sake, contrasting, for example, with photojournalism, in which acquiring a picture of some kind of a specified subject is the first consideration. In the Formalist school of photography, the importance of the subject matter is that it has allowed the photographer to explore visual relationships. True, Edward Weston talked about his famous pictures of nautilus shells as having spiritual significance and being 'a sublimation of all my work and life', but he was at the time a little carried away by the effusive reactions of his friends. His earlier notes, made when he was actually taking the pictures, show that he was mainly concerned with a fairly down-to-earth visual exploration of shapes and textures. He writes about looking for suitable backgrounds: 'I wore myself out trying every conceivable texture and tone for grounds: glass, tin, cardboard, wool, velvet, even my rubber rain coat!' and similar practical design matters. In that his daybooks show something of his working method, his immediate notes are probably more instructive than later reflections.

One of the interesting things about photographs taken in the Formalist tradition has been their popular success. The photograph by Brett Weston on page 46 is fairly typical — refined, but not concerned with any difficult issues of content. It raises no moral or social questions, unlike the majority of the photojournalistic pictures in this book, neither is it provocative. Formalist pictures as a whole rely very much on elegance of design and, judged as fine art which they evidently can be, are a fairly safe area of exploration. Being unobtrusive, pleasant to look at and not overly concerned with the non-visual properties of subject matter, they have a broad, and probably timeless, appeal. Even the methods of presentation — notably the print quality — have been developed to the status of a sophisticated craft. All in all, these are photographs to be hung on a wall, stimulating to the eye when they are good, and inoffensive in every other way.

For some, the appealing nature of such photography, which ensures high prices in galleries and a consistent following among amateur photographers, is something of a limitation. There is not so much opportunity to stimulate, and there are at least some grounds for thinking of Formalism as a cul-de-sac for development. For Weston's generation, design in photography was still an area with many possibilities for exploration; there were also fewer photographers pressing ahead with

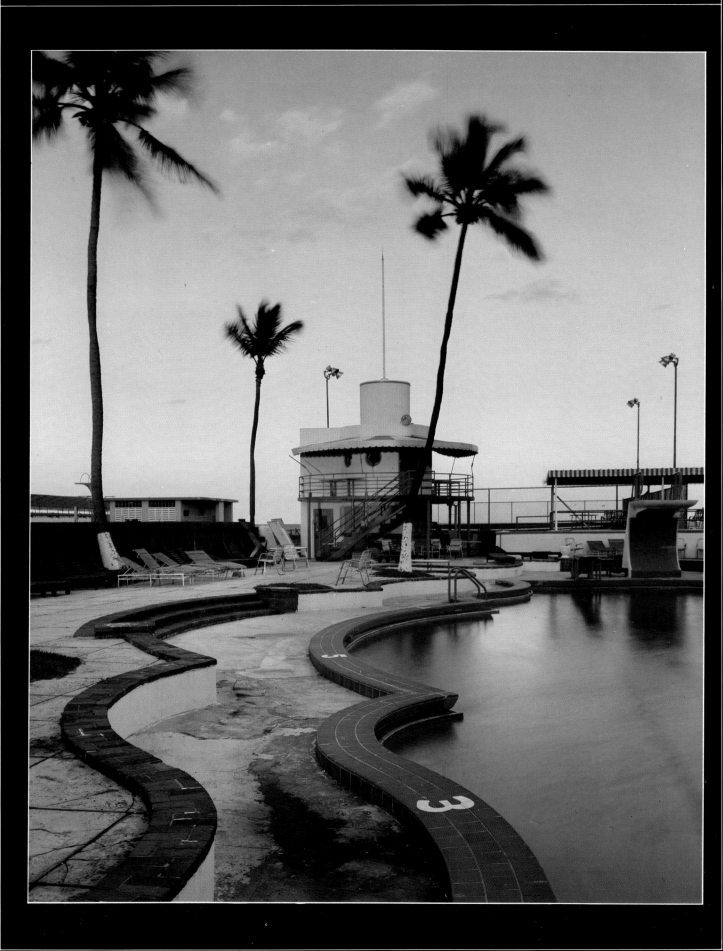

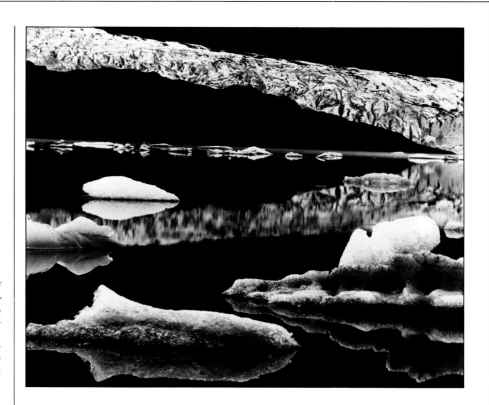

Right *Brett Weston's explorations of the formal components of design use their subject matter more as a vehicle for the photographer than as things requiring comment or explanation. Hence, in a manner typical of most Formalists, the nature of the objects is usually of secondary importance, be they found objects, details or elements of a landscape.*

new ideas and in different directions than there are now. Not surprisingly, therefore, since this classic period of investigation little real development has taken place in the Formalist area until quite recent times.

The most acclaimed work of this type has taken place in America in the past few years, by photographers such as Joel Meyerowitz, William Eggleston, and Stephen Shore. It inevitably has a label — New Color — and although this is not a perfect description, it does give an idea of the main drift of experiment. Briefly, the argument for this photographic movement is that while the monochrome design elements have had a full share of attention over the years, color has eluded serious investigation and has been used mainly for sensation and beautification. This new school explores the subtleties of color relationships without seeking out or forcing glamour and excess. That, at any rate, is the case for it, although it is only fair to say that there are probably many people who find the results incomprehensibly plain. Interestingly, photography's early preoccupation with black-and-white left behind some odd attitudes towards the role of color. Having for so long been compelled to work without this extra dimension, which was not widely available for high-speed, small-format use until after the Second World War, many photographers in the 1950s and 1960s seemed to view it as a new ingredient that somehow needed a well-defined function, rather than as a natural, unremarkable element of any scene. Even Helmut Gernsheim, an important photographic historian, wrote: 'In monochrome the massing of light and shade and the reproduction of texture are of the utmost importance: in colour photography, the imaginative use of colour rather than truth to nature.'

Nevertheless, for our purposes here, it is interesting to see what success such a recent surge of Formalism has had — whether close attention to the design elements alone can in fact create really interesting new photography. Joel Meyerowitz has had more critical success than anyone else in this movement, although, when discussing his Cape Cod pictures, he admits the photographs are just as much about light: 'Color suggests that light itself is a subject. In that sense, the work here on the Cape is about light.' Still, this is probably splitting hairs, as one is inextricably linked with the other. Meyerowitz, certainly, exercises about as much control over both as is possible, given his subject matter.

With such naturally lit subjects, anticipation, careful observation and, above all, patience, are essential; in addition, Meyerowitz uses a large-format camera for detail and control in the image, and color negative film in order to be able to produce the exact, delicate colors in a print.

William Eggleston is perhaps even closer to the core of New Color, and his work probably touches the limits of understatement. The complete lack of *any* sense of beautification or slickness in his photograph of a patch of waste ground (*see* left) is an odd sort of achievement, but at least marks one kind of boundary in the organizaton of images. Understandably, Eggleston's work is by no means universally popular and, having few commercial applications, is not widely published. That he has a particularly important role in the eyes of those critics who identify themselves with the New Color photography is almost certainly because, of all the output of this school, his is the furthest removed from the popular, vivid use of color and design. For one biographer of the New Color photography, Sally Eauclaire, Eggleston's approach is a necessary antidote to the 'school of slick, sensationalized "creative"

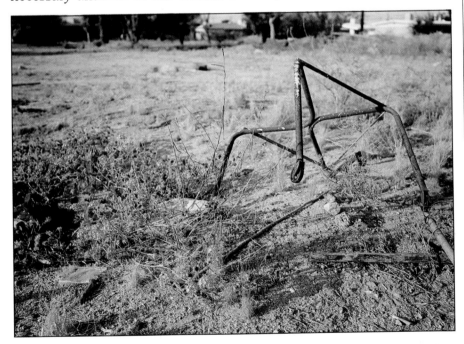

Left *Elliott Erwitt used the term 'anti photograph' to refer to his pictures of street dogs — subjects not normally deemed worthy of a photographer's attention. Probably the most extreme example of work that deliberately concentrates on the thoroughly mundane is the photography of William Eggleston. A scene such as this — a patch of wasteland in Memphis — is in real life so uninteresting to most people as to be virtually invisible. Eggleston controversially challenges the normal priorities of attention.*

photography that has saturated the public's (and artists') consciousness of the medium for the past quarter century'.

The important common denominator in the work of photographers such as Eggleston, Meyerowitz, and Mitch Epstein is restraint, but restraint is a somewhat limited direction for creative development. Having put up a case for a more subtle use of color in the structure of pictures, as it has, the New Color photography now suffers from not having content as an anchor. This is the difficulty with other types of Formalism — in a medium that directs attention to the reality of its subject matter, pictures that are concerned principally with design can come to look like exercises.

Whatever the intention of the photographer, however, the basic design elements of a picture can be controlled only up to a point; appreciating the dynamic effect of diagonal lines is relevant only if they can be made to fall into place in the picture. Armed with an appreciation of how the structure of the image can be made to work, the photographer faced with a subject may at best be able to bring only a small part into play. A studio, naturally, offers more control, and so a better opportunity to structure the image, but on location and in situations where the photographer is the observer rather than the director, events and chance often overwhelm design. In the end, the *practical* design limitations in photography can never be ignored.

The picture frame is one such control. It is, as we have seen, an integral part of the image, working with and against other parts of the picture. Under the right circumstances it can be put to work as much as any other design element and can, in theory at least, be chosen to suit the image. In practice, however, most photography is performed within a fixed frame of certain dimensions, and this tends to dominate the design possibly more than it should. The range of film formats is fairly restricted for reasons of standardization, the most common by far being the 2:3 proportions of 35mm film (there are some panoramic cameras that stretch these proportions, but they are specialized equipment). A long way behind in use and popularity are the more evenly proportioned formats of rollfilm and large-camera sheet film — 6:9, 4:5, 6:7 and the less dynamic 1:1 square format.

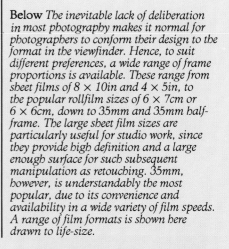

Below *The inevitable lack of deliberation in most photography makes it normal for photographers to conform their design to the format in the viewfinder. Hence, to suit different preferences, a wide range of frame proportions is available. These range from sheet films of 8 × 10in and 4 × 5in, to the popular rollfilm sizes of 6 × 7cm or 6 × 6cm, down to 35mm and 35mm half-frame. The large sheet film sizes are particularly useful for studio work, since they provide high definition and a large enough surface for such subsequent manipulation as retouching. 35mm, however, is understandably the most popular, due to its convenience and availability in a wide variety of film speeds. A range of film formats is shown here drawn to life-size.*

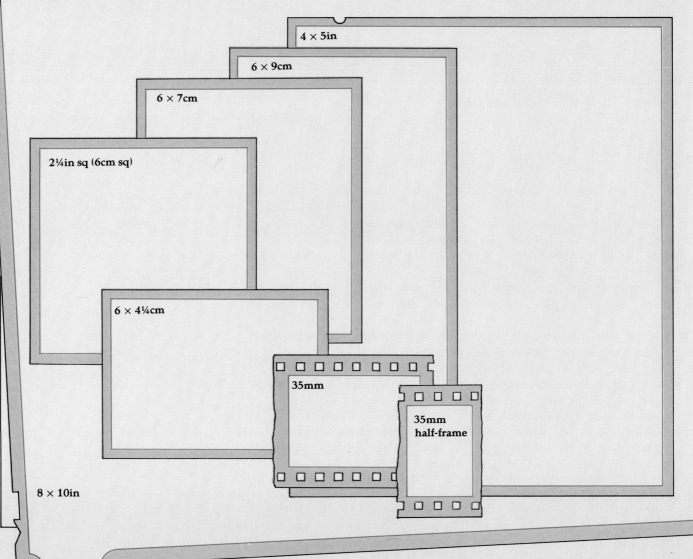

4 × 5in

6 × 9cm

6 × 7cm

2¼in sq (6cm sq)

6 × 4¼cm

35mm

35mm half-frame

8 × 10in

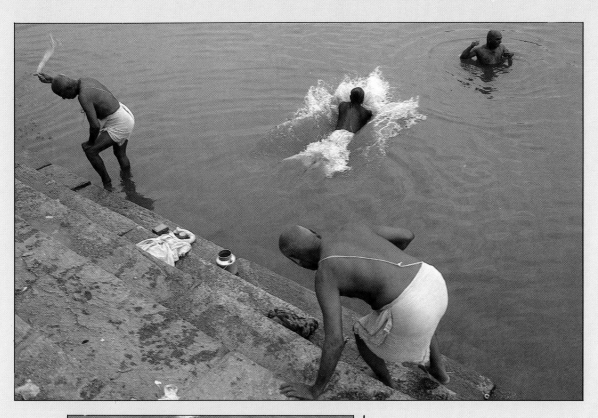

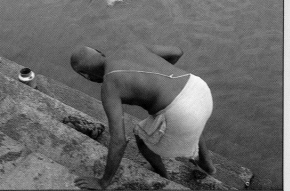

The limits to which a photograph can be
cropped — by someone else, such as a
designer, or art director — are often set by
the coherence of the composition. In this
example (**above**), the photographer has
intentionally framed the shot in such a way
that the action extends to the very edges
and corners of the picture. The examples of
cropping (**left** and **below**) do not make
any improvement to the image at all. The
crop to the proportion of a 35mm frame
(**left**) and the square crop (**below left**) lose
too much information; the upright crop
(**below**) is the most descriptive but destroys
the composition.

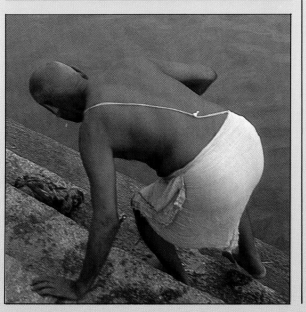

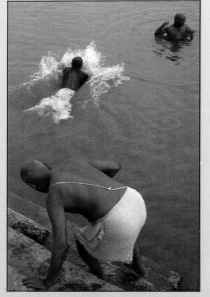

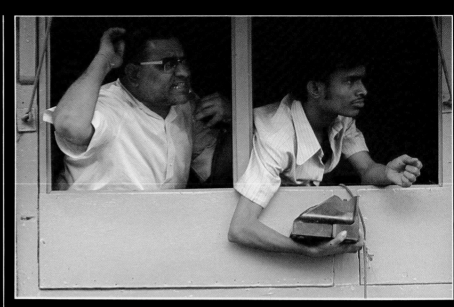

In contrast with the photograph on the previous page, the compartmentalized structure of this image of a commodity exchange in Calcutta (**far right**) makes it easy to crop in at least two ways. Cropping has two distinct functions. One is to fit the photograph into a designated space, different in proportion to the original picture — a designer's problem. The second is to make the photograph do a different job or tell a different story — an editor's problem. The version showing two men is an acceptable way of making the picture fit a horizontal space, with some loss of the sense of group activity. The man at left holding the base of a telephone but not the receiver may also appear slightly odd. The one-man version (**below right**) ignores what interested the photographer, but is a little more enigmatic. Several people can suggest collective bargaining; one alone is a puzzle.

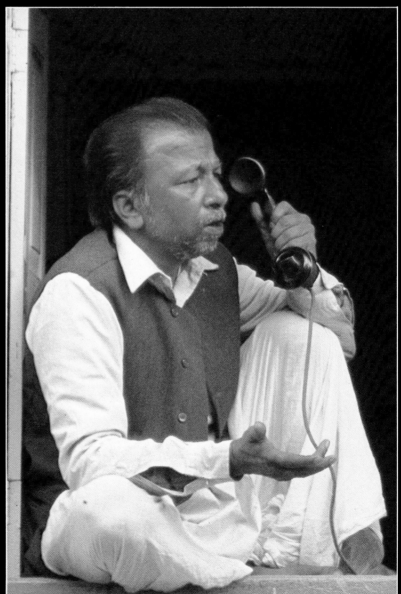

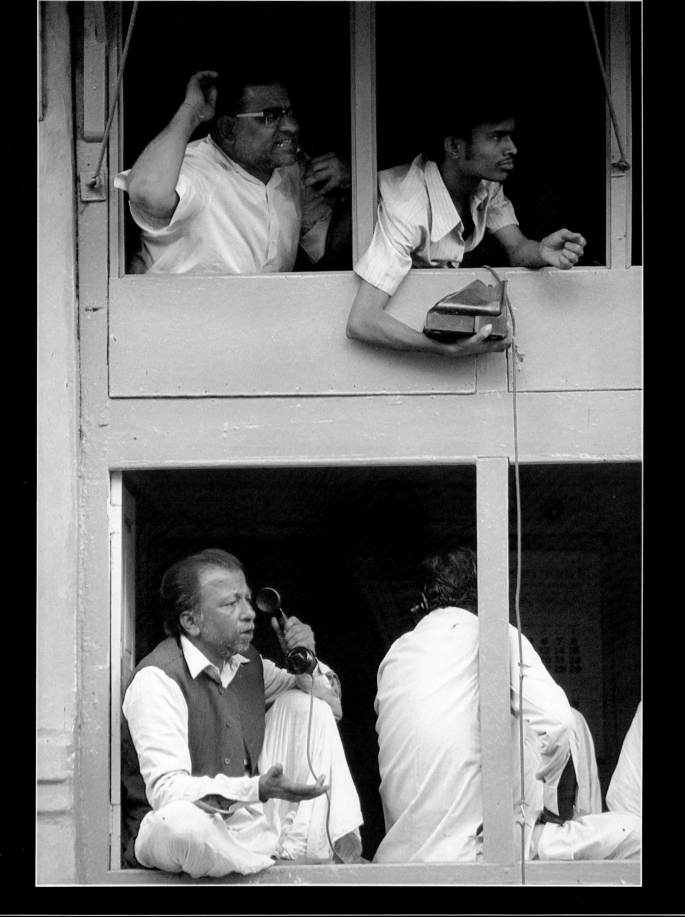

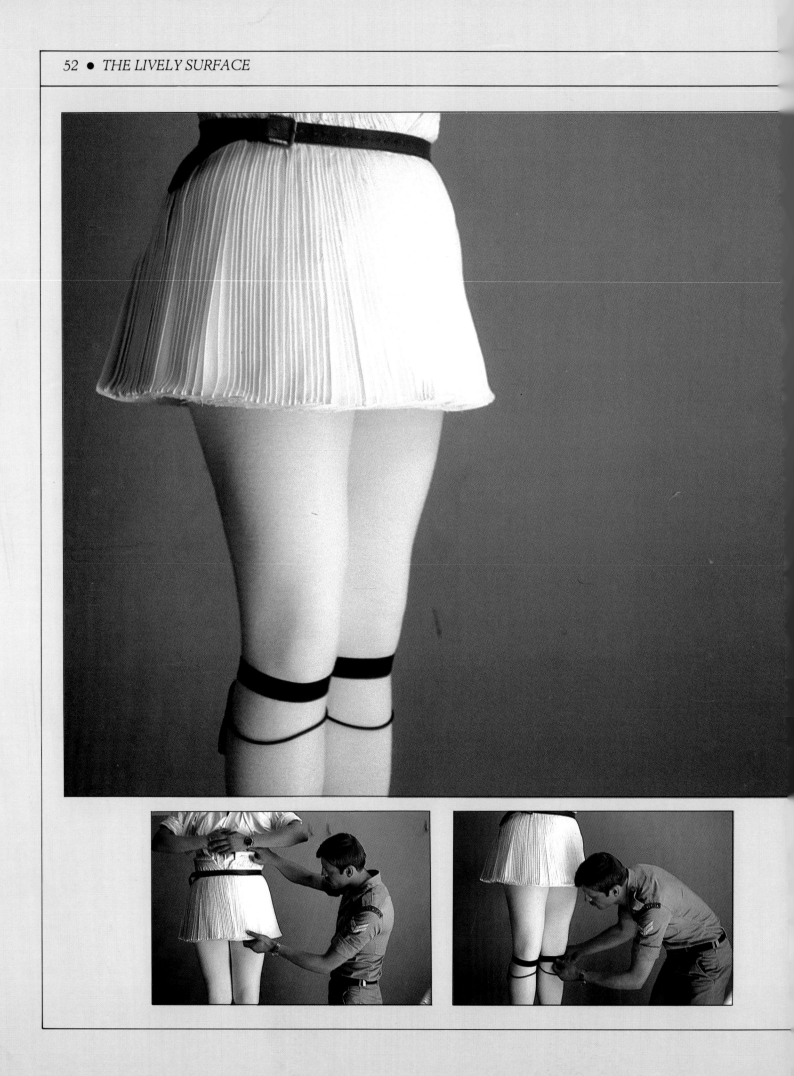

There is no pressing reason why the shooting format — that is, the proportions offered by the viewfinder — need be adhered to. If the photographer is later to make an enlarged print, or if the picture is to be reproduced on a printed page, there are infinite opportunities then for cropping the image. Indeed, when black-and-white was the standard medium, delicate cropping with the enlarger easel was a normal and essential part of the process. However, in order to do this successfully, the photographer has to anticipate the final cropping and allow sufficient space for it when shooting. Such foresight really only suits certain kinds of situation and types of photography — those in which there is time to plan the image before shooting. Landscape, architectural and most studio work is clearly ideal for this treatment, while large-format cameras are in all cases so slow to use that they encourage a deliberate way of working.

Nevertheless, photographers generally compose by eye rather than by calculation, and often make adjustments simply by moving the camera and seeing what effect this has on the image. It is so much more natural to sense the play of elements within the viewfinder that most photographs are in practice balanced to the film frame. This is particularly so with 35mm film, despite the fact that 2:3 proportions are often a little too stretched for comfort for many subjects. With a horizontal image, the problems are not too apparent, as the eye tends naturally to scan from side to side, but vertically these proportions are usually difficult. The result is that in practice a great deal of photographic composition includes a degree of accommodation, with some distinctive devices for filling a longer-than-ideal frame. The photograph of the Evzone (*see* left) uses one method — that of separating the subjects so that they are close to the edges of the picture.

Another practicality of photographic design is the near inevitability of depth in the picture. In most situations, a photograph reveals a three-dimensional world — in two dimensions, certainly, but in such a familiar way that distance and perspective are rarely questioned by the viewer. The clues to three-dimensionality are usually inescapable, and flat planes and abstraction have to be fought for if the photographer is bent on destroying a sense of depth. Far from employing graphic devices to *create* perspective, as a painter might do, the perspective exists in the subject already. Getting rid of it, as one popular way of exercising control over the image, needs a special repertoire of techniques. These need to be directed against the specific clues to perspective that occur in photographs: convergence towards vanishing points, aerial haze, receding blues and advancing reds, comparisons of size between recognizable objects. A telephoto lens has the useful effect of compressing the image into planes and reducing convergence, and is employed regularly to confuse the sense of depth, as in Romano Cagnoni's photograph of lines of Ibo recruits (page 54). A composition that divides the image into a few distinct, contrasting planes, as in the photograph of the monk and temple on page 42, also diminishes perspective (often with the help of a telephoto lens). Reversing the expected distribution of colors in depth, so that a nearer object is from the cooler part of the spectrum and the background warmer, also helps to make the perspective more ambiguous, as does the simple condition of clear, unhazy air, the effect of which can be enhanced by using a polarizing filter, seen in the photograph of canyon spurs on page 42. On the whole, however, normal photographic conditions produce perspective unasked for.

A more immediate practical issue is the point of view. The photographer may well be able to imagine an ideal camera position, but

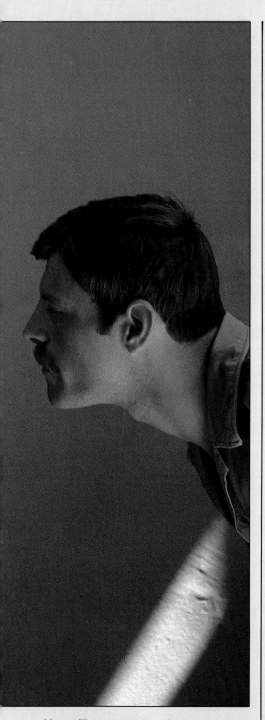

Above *The composition of this photograph of a Greek soldier's dress being inspected was designed to create both humor and a sense of balance. To the majority of viewers, who would naturally associate this kind of dress with a woman's short skirt, the seriousness of the inspection and the atmosphere of barrack-room masculinity seem unusual, and the photograph plays on this. The sequence of shots (left and far left) leading up to the final picture captures most, but not all, of the interest in the situation. What gives the final picture its edge is that the corporal's head appears to have just pushed its way into the frame.*

Right *Romano Cagnoni was impressed by the mass effect of the shaven heads of these Ibo recruits and, using a 500mm mirror lens and a vantage point on the terrace of a house that looked out onto a Biafran parade ground, he planned the shot to display compressed proportions. He waited four hours for this, the most effective composition.*

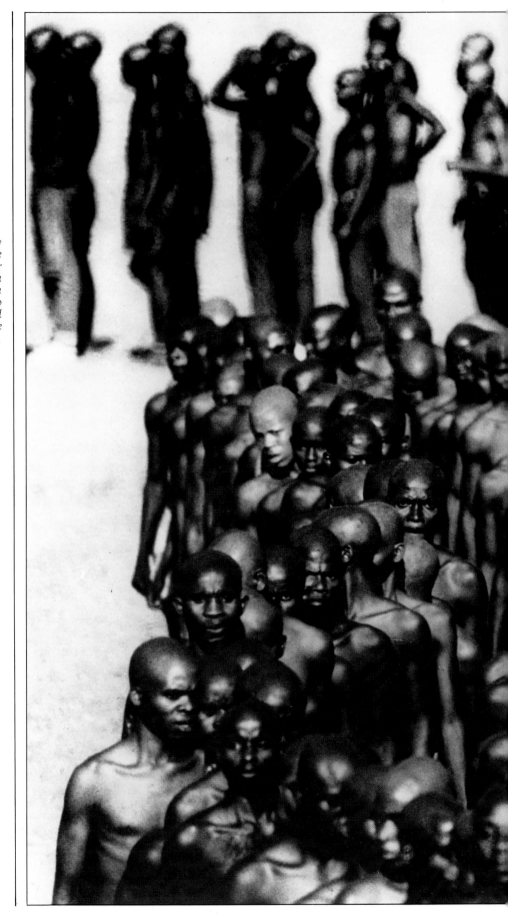

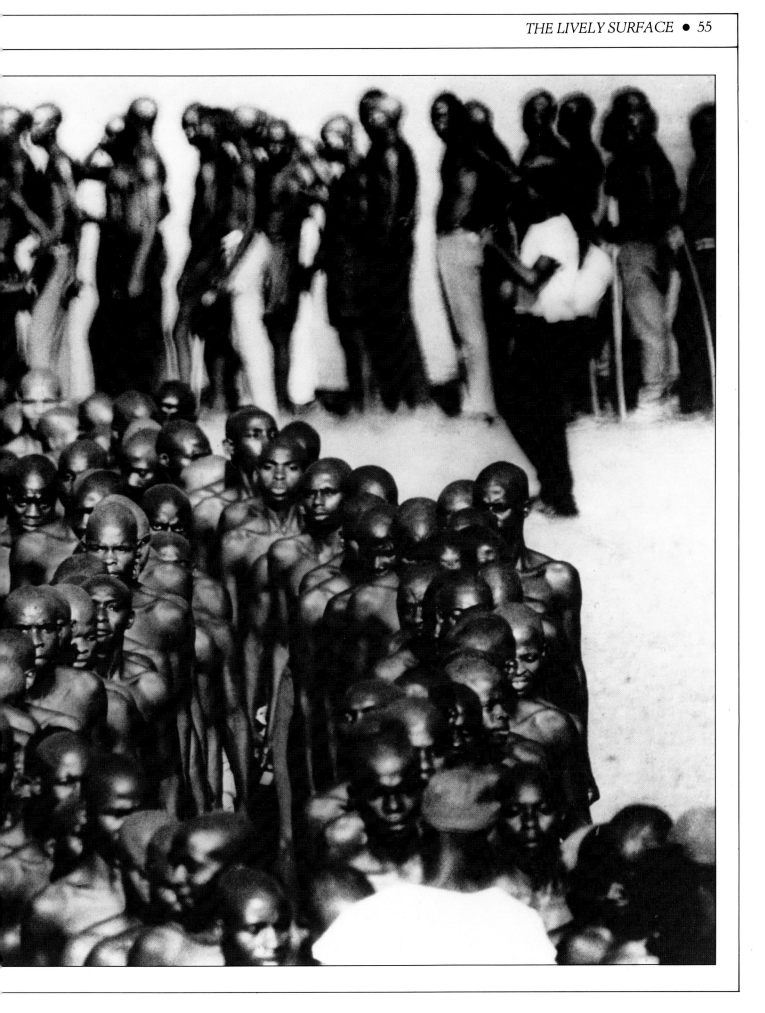

getting there may just not be possible. This is the kind of workaday problem that can bring photographic design right down to earth and swamp whatever skills the photographer might otherwise be able to bring into play. Some successful images, in fact, owe as much to the good fortune of finding a good viewpoint as to anything else. In the more mobile situation of an event involving people, the rules of the game change yet again and the viewpoint may be restricted by time rather than by place. Especially with street photography, the natural style of pictures tends to be participatory, which means that camera positions are generally accessible; however, shifting positions, expressions and gestures keep the photographer constantly on the move, avoiding obstructions in the foreground and readjusting the balance of elements, while waiting for a moment that seems to make the picture gel.

Below *James Nachtwey's involving photograph of an incident in the Lebanon (Withdrawal from Yamit, 1982) gains its power from drawing the viewer directly into the scene. The wide-angle lens introduces diminishing proportions, which take the eye inwards, while the movement of the soldier in the right foreground, half-cropped from the picture, takes the action out of the frame. The fact that the soldier in the foreground is looking at the viewer also aids involvement; direct eye contact is always hard to resist.*

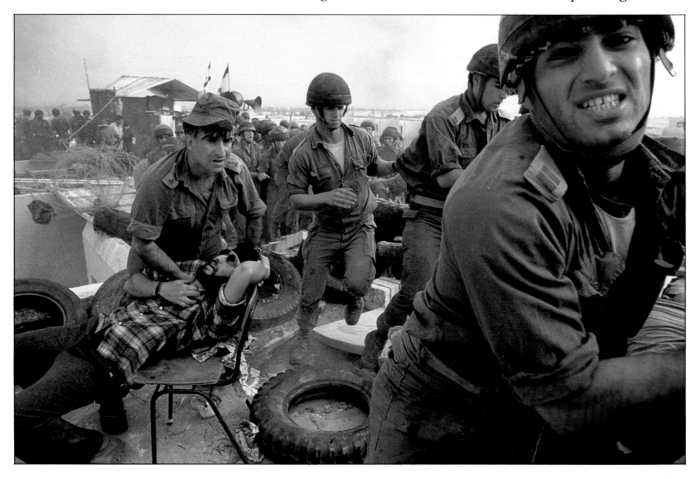

Another direct effect of photography's strong links with the real world is that the presence of the camera is easily felt. This is particularly noticeable in candid photography, where the viewer is, by proxy, the photographer. In looking at Nachtwey's photograph (*see* above) the sense of involvement is almost tangible and this illusion is often exploited deliberately by good street photographers. This technique projects the viewer into the scene, and suggests that the picture continues beyond the frame, as indeed the real scene did. Two strategies enhance this extra dimension: the use of a moderately wide-angle lens, which has the effect of partially wrapping the scene around the viewer, and the abrupt cropping of the figures on both sides, which emphasizes what has been cropped out of the picture. Eye contact further reinforces the camera's presence.

Most people looking at this photograph naturally fix their attention for at least a moment on the face, not so much because the lines of the image converge on it but because there is direct eye contact. This is perhaps the strongest example of a special phenomenon in photography — the psychological 'weighting' of certain subjects. A human figure, for instance, attracts more attention than its size and position in a picture might merit; a face attracts even more, while a pair of eyes looking directly at the viewer is nearly irresistible. Similarly, lettering, numerals and pictures are 'weighted' subjects, drawing an excess of attention. Whereas a painter can vary technique to alter their emphasis, a photographer generally has to balance them with composition. For example, in the photograph of a sailor (*see* below), the letters and the numbers distract attention from the man's face.

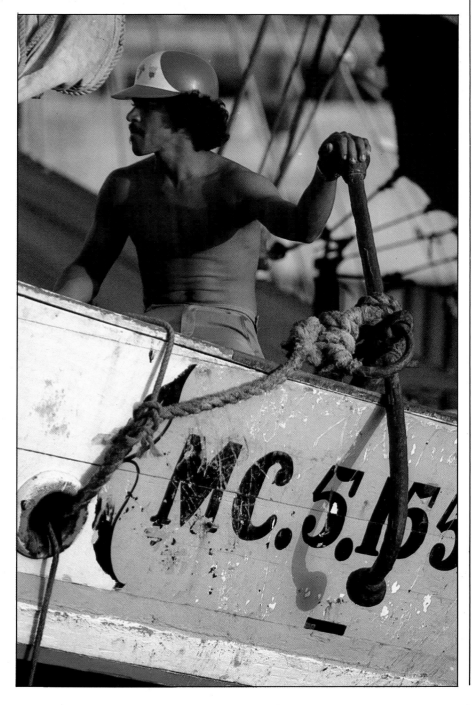

Left *Symbols, in particular letters and numbers, carry extra visual weight in a picture, and tend to pull attention away from other areas. As a demonstration, cover over the ship's letters in this photograph — the attention shifts strongly towards the man's face.*

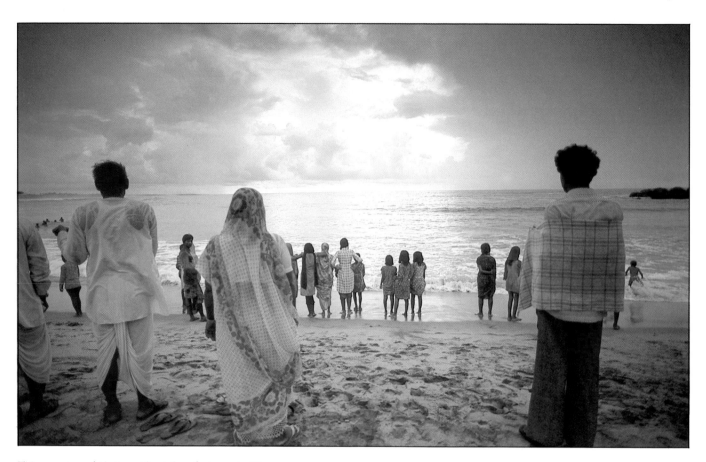

*This sequence of photographs, taken during a break in the south Indian monsoon, illustrates some of the practical design decisions in photographing on location. For the first attempt (**above**), the photographer used a wide-angle lens to make a feature of the crowd of people waiting patiently at the water's edge for the rain to end.*

In practice, the taking of a photograph can be a complex orchestration of all these different elements and influences. This is, in fact, a good opportunity to look at the inner workings of the photographic process by taking one picture and examining, step by step, the sequence of decisions that went into making it. Naturally, one image is in no way typical of others, but jumping from the general to the highly specific should at least give some insight into the ideas, techniques and time involved. This kind of analysis is inevitably retrospective, and may make the picture-taking process seem more structured and uni-directional than it really is; the fluidity of most of the situations in which photographs are taken creates a very complex set of influences, which are then handled, or ignored, extremely quickly by the photographer. It is perfectly normal for a photographer to explore several directions at once.

One of the reasons for choosing the picture of bathers in India that appears above for this exercise is that the motivation for taking it was not strictly defined, and as such is absolutely typical of much photography. There was no specific brief to shoot a particular subject, unlike in news reporting and advertising; although such directed needs stimulate problem-solving approaches, these tend to be very ordered in a specialized kind of way. In this case, the motivation was simply to present the photographer's personal view of southwest India during the late monsoon, over a period of time. This photograph was therefore a part of a much larger set of images, and the product of a daily routine of exploration, eventually to appear in a travelling exhibition.

Over the preceding days a number of images of certain types had already been taken, and the photographer was looking for images that were visually different. The monsoon was, in fact, unseasonably

*Further attempts at making a composition with a dominant foreground (**below**) were unsatisfactory, and the photographer abandoned the idea when the sun came out more strongly and a few people ventured into the water (**below center**). The final result (**bottom**) exploits the diagonal line made by the bathers, leading straight towards the sun; the two raised legs were a last-minute bonus, which reinforced this geometry.*

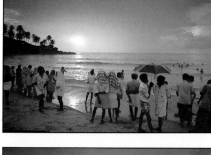

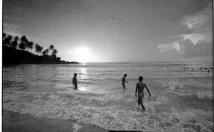

extended that year, dominating practically every aspect of life in the area, and so became a natural theme for the photography in progress. In fact, although the weather conditions were interesting visually, they offered little variety — day after day of muted tones and veiled landscapes. As a result, when the rain stopped one afternoon, the photographer set out to make use of the changing light, without any particular subject in mind. He noticed that a small crowd of local people was beginning to gather close to the beach, simply to watch the weak sunlight that might mark the end of months of rain.

Sensing that here was a potentially interesting subject, which had some relevance to the monsoon, the photographer decided to wait out the remaining half hour of light on the beach. At first, people remained standing facing the sea, and, as the first attempts show, the photographer tried to make something out of this uniformity by using a wide-angle lens to look over the shoulders of one rank to those nearer the water's edge. Dissatisfied with this, and disappointed that the image was not coming together as he had hoped, the photographer was relieved when a new opportunity presented itself — one or two people began to shed their clothes and wade into the surf.

Stepping forward to the water, the photographer abandoned the idea of a dominant foreground to concentrate on the bathing. By now, the sun was breaking through more definitely, and so began to play a more important role in the composition. Together with the strong dark shape of the headland, this suggested an off-centered position at the left of the frame and to balance it, the photographer started looking for a bather at the lower right.

Now working quickly before the light faded, he noticed one bather

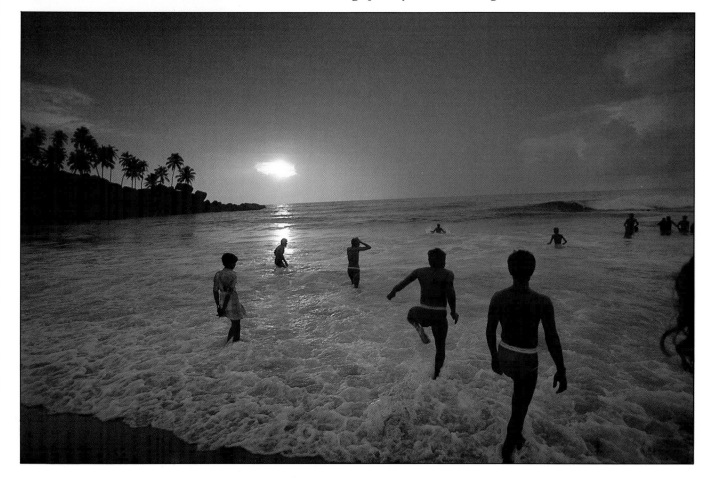

entering the water from his right, saw the possibility of a diagonal line leading straight towards the sun, and moved forward a few feet. At this point, another bather also entered from the right, reinforcing the diagonal line visible through the wide-angle lens. When both of these bathers coincidentally raised their left legs, the photographer knew that he had the best possible version of this shot. What was irresistible about the image at the time was the geometric organization of the different elements, while the small coincidence of the two raised legs was a welcome bonus.

Dissecting the anatomy of a picture in this manner gives some of the flavor of the practice of photography, and is a useful sampler. As a means of analyzing photographs regularly, however, it is rather cumbersome, and most photographs can be enjoyed with only a general awareness of the *kinds* of decision open to photographers.

A tendency among some critics, which appears slightly ridiculous to the photographers whose work is under discussion, is to drag in all kinds of convoluted and often psychological influences. Given that the real events in front of the camera severely limit the photographer's imaginative contribution, many photographs are really not suitable subjects for deep probing. Except for a relatively small proportion of planned, constructed shots — mainly in the studio — most working methods are rapid and reactive.

Moreover, what appears as a final product on a printed page or a gallery wall has been rigorously selected, an important, if hidden, part of the creative process. Very rarely does any photographer know in advance that he will have a success on his hands, and one good image is often at the end of a line of experiment that is composed of a number of attempts that did not work out. This is normal, but the context in which a photograph is seen by the public can create around it a misleading air of certainty.

So far, we have seen how some photographers have experimented with the basic design elements and how others *react* to the design constraints. The same methods can also be used more forcefully, to emphasize something that has an unusual interest for the photographer, and even to exaggerate a point that he wants to make. All these techniques can be thought of as ways of drawing attention to a specific feature of the scene — a way of ordering or directing the viewer's response to the picture.

A subtle method of playing with the viewer's attention is used by Joel Sternfeld in his photograph of the effects of a flash flood in California (*see* right). While the natural temptation might have been to dramatize the wrecked car and to give it a dominant place in the image (this would certainly have been necessary in any news photograph), Sternfeld instead has designed the picture so that the disaster becomes apparent only slowly. The objective, distanced treatment, and the seemingly conventional composition, ensure that the eye is first caught by the central, parked car, in what appears to be a fairly ordinary view of the type that a real estate manager might use. Careful control of the color balance also helps to subdue the events that have occurred in the lower right of the photograph. The final effect, quite cleverly, is one of delayed surprise, with some humor. Such detached views have almost become Sternfeld's trademark.

The role of design in photography is by no means clear-cut, and is complicated by the different degrees to which situations permit graphic

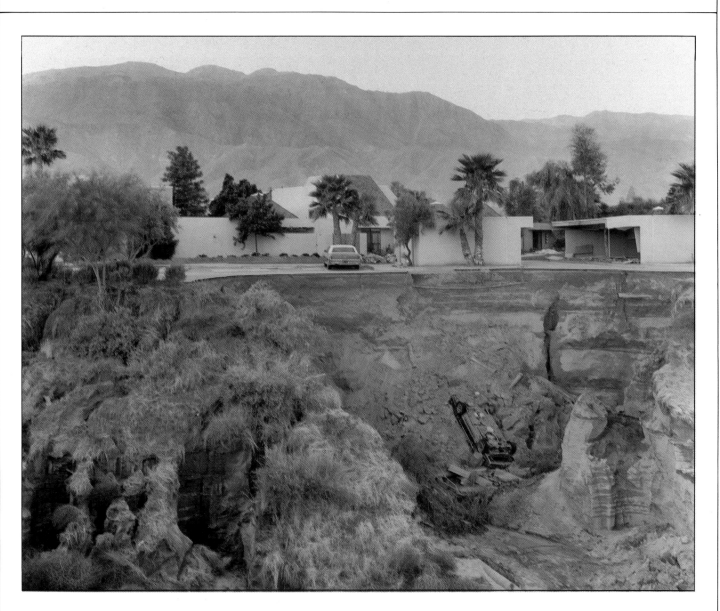

control. The photographs of the Formalists — and, indeed, many of the examples used in this chapter to illustrate basic design elements — represent something of a minority condition: their visual dynamics are largely the result of the photographers' intentions. It is, however, small coincidence that many of the subjects that responded well to such deliberate design are, in a sense, passive and unassertive. As we see photographers attempting to apply the same design techniques to more fluid, uncontrollable situations, the results are generally more haphazard. Whereas, say, the still-life photographer can reasonably expect to fashion an image how he wants, someone at the other end of the scale of control — a street photographer — is usually struggling to balance the image. Indeed, in news reporting, events dominate the assignment, and if the conditions conspire to prevent a powerful composition, then it is just too bad. For example, to discuss the famous photograph by Nick Ut of a Vietnamese child burned by napalm (page 85) in terms of its compositional qualities would be an irrelevance: the content of this picture overwhelms all other considerations. This, naturally, represents the other extreme; in most photography composition and content exert dynamic influences upon each other. Content can suggest composition, composition can help to tell the story.

Above After a Flash Flood, Rancho Mirage, California, *Joel Sternfeld, 1979. A quiet, understated composition is more effective here than a design that actively pointed out the wrecked car would have been. Indeed, the humor in the picture comes from the delayed realization that this is more than an ordinary, workaday shot of someone's house. The flat, unrich colors in the original are another aspect of Sternfeld's wry style.*

CHAPTER 3

Primitive Rites

'The photograph is a memento from a life being lived.'
John Berger

'To photograph is to appropriate the thing photographed.'
Susan Sontag

Judging by the quantity of film sold, more than 20 billion pictures are taken each year. This represents an impressive visual record of the earth and its inhabitants and is evidence that, for an activity which is hardly fundamental in terms of survival, photography certainly provides strong gratification of some kind. There is, of course, no mystery about the subject of such relentless picture-taking — self, family and places visited on holiday account for nearly all of it — but the reasons why it should happen on such a scale perhaps go deeper than the casualness with which such pictures are snapped. On the grounds of sheer quantity, the motivation for all this personal photography, most of it unpretentious, deserves some attention, but there is another reason for taking it seriously: if so many people practise photography themselves, it must influence their demands and expectations of professional photography.

Most people never question why they take personal pictures; it is a kind of record-keeping — a visual diary of life, experiences, events. The motives are always taken for granted as is the pleasure of looking over old photographs and reminiscing. It is important here to distinguish between two kinds of amateur photography. One, in the minority, is a technological hobby, advertised heavily and supported by wonderful equipment that performs tricks. The other, very much larger, and the starting point for this chapter, is concerned only with images of personal interest; most people who use cameras are not interested in the technology beyond expecting it to perform flawlessly and without attention. Snapshot imagery of this kind may be derided by serious photographers, and there are certainly few hidden treasures tucked away in the world's family albums, but it is of consuming interest to the individual. As such, it is not only an important social phenomenon, but one that has a direct effect on photography of more critical interest, chiefly because the audience is familiar with and participates in the same activity.

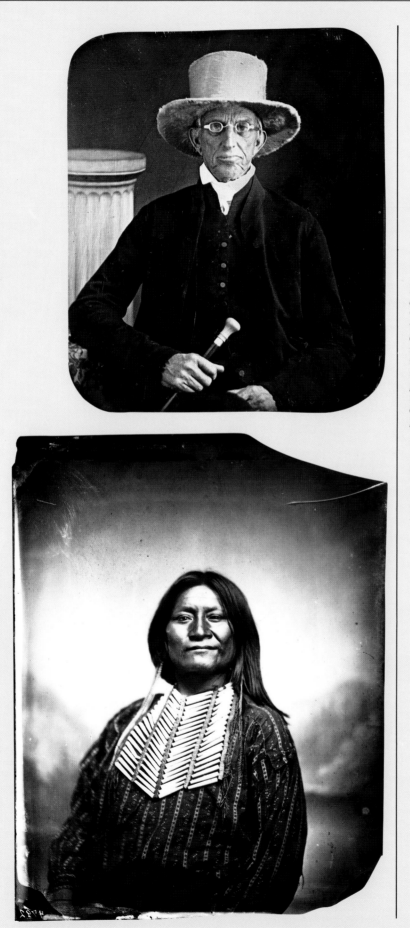

Left *No information is available about this arresting portrait of a Massachusetts Quaker, except that it was about 1845 when he sat in this studio (the mock classical column behind was a typical nineteenth-century studio prop). Unlike many sitters he is not in the least diffident in front of the camera: the direct, upright pose (we presume an indication of the man's character) make this a refreshing example of portraiture performed for personal use.*

Left *An equally strong display of character — but of a quite different personality — is this poorly documented portrait of Heap Wolves, an Esa-Dowa chief killed by an Osage in 1872. This confident confrontation with the camera suggests a subject certain of his own superiority.*

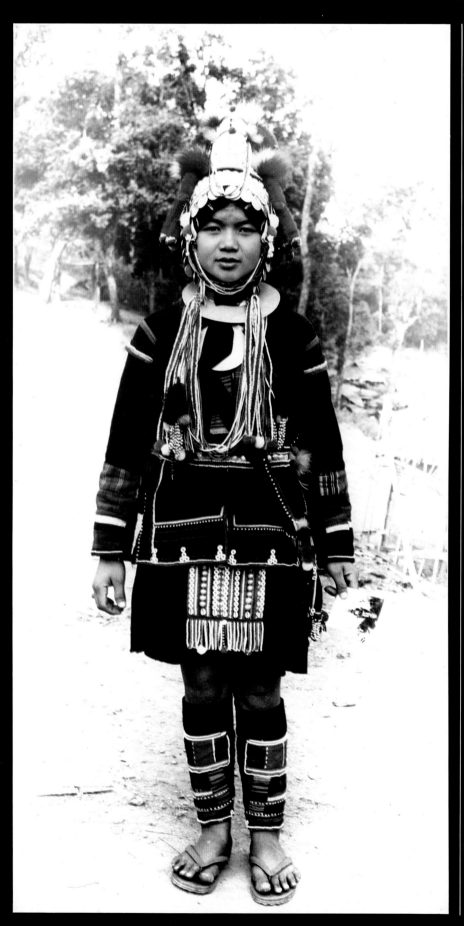

Photographing the Akha

These photographs provide a study in contrast between the expectations of different audiences. The direct and distinctly formal photograph (left) is the only type of portrait composition acceptable to the members of this Southeast Asian hill tribe. Reminiscent of Victorian portraiture, it shows the entire figure in a dignified pose. The tribeswoman is holding a Polaroid picture of herself, given to her by the photographer. Such gestures are important strategies for winning confidence and good will. The other five photographs were part of a picture essay on the same people for the consumption of a Western audience. Individually less descriptive, these pictures are more interpretative and evocative, semi-candid shots that show scenes from daily life.

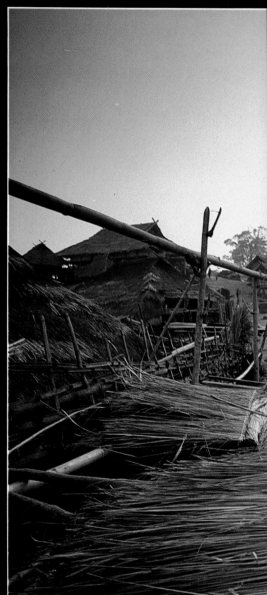

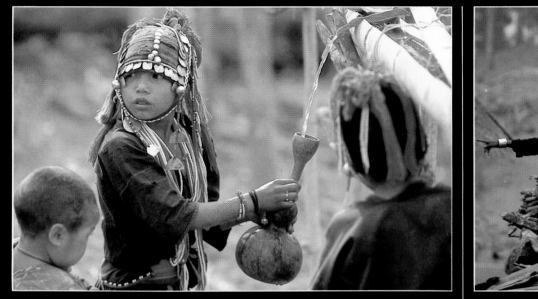

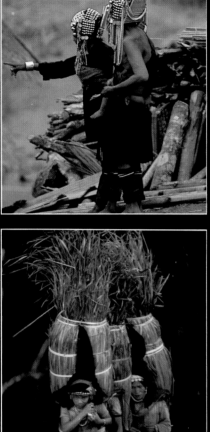

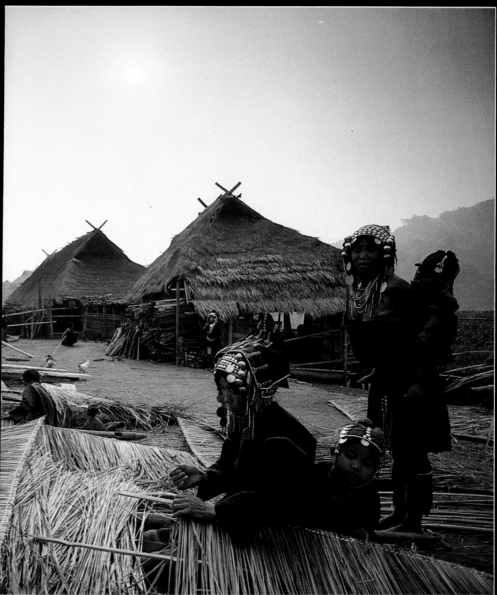

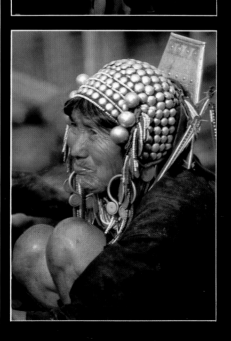

Given that photography has been startlingly successful as a popular activity and commodity, the inescapable conclusion is that it fills an older, universal need. When photography was invented, the publishing media may have been rather slow to use it, but the public loved it from the start. The *carte-de-visite*, a pictorial calling card introduced in Paris in the 1850s, was economical enough to become widely used. In the United States, the cheap imitation daguerreotype, known as the tintype, was extraordinarily popular. Much of the demand, naturally enough was for portraits.

Patented in 1856 by Hannibal Smith, the tintype's success was due to its speed of production (using new solutions that processed quickly) and its low cost (the support for the image was a thin sheet of metal rather than coated glass). Large numbers of commercial tintype photographers emerged to take advantage of this new process, and they sold the idea to the American public, hundreds of thousands of whom posed for their portraits. Even though the results were often crude, being performed by photographers who tended to be opportunists rather than artists, the quantities bought attest to the tintype's popularity.

From the point of view of these consumers, a photograph was simply a more realistic, speedier and cheaper version of making a likeness, and whatever the creative differences that we can appreciate between photography and other graphic arts, they are largely unimportant in this area — an uncomfortable conclusion, perhaps, as such photographs are definitely in the majority. Whereas pre-photographic portraits demanded skills learned in a long apprenticeship, were consequently expensive, and so were mainly acquisitions of the rich and socially significant, the camera performs the same function for anyone. It may not do it as well in the hands of amateurs, but for most people's purposes it does not need to. Photography has democratized one of society's perpetual needs.

For the people who sit for these portraits, what exactly are the criteria for success? The usual critical and creative judgements are likely to be misleading in this instance, for they reflect an outsider's appraisal. Personal portraits are performed for the sitter's benefit, and, from that point of view, a good portrait is one that catches a reasonable likeness, flatters the physical appearance, and if possible elevates the status of the subject.

The two pictures on page 63 are from the golden age of photographic portraiture, when the demand was already high but before cameras were available to the mass amateur market. Both these examples have been chosen for being more than just a successfully performed service (at least, we can assume that both the subjects *should* have been pleased with the result; the record does not say). They are also interesting to a general audience because of what they show us of another society and because some complexities of character can be glimpsed in both faces. This may seem to conflict with what has just been said — that personal portraits should by rights be judged only on how well they perform the immediate task of satisfying the customer — but without this extra dimension, other people's views of themselves would unfortunately seem dull to the rest of us.

While the criteria mentioned previously — a good likeness, a degree of flattery and enhancing status — are universal requirements, different societies naturally have different ideas about what is proper. How different opinion can be is amply demonstrated by the pictures on pages 64-5, all taken in the same Asian hill-tribe village on a professional editorial assignment. For a Western audience there is little doubt which are the more interesting photographs. It is just these types of close, semi-candid pictures that are popular in magazines; the viewer is given a glimpse of natural expression and actions in an exotic situation. The same, however, is by no means true for the subjects of these pictures. The photographer spent sufficient time living in this Akha village to be able to overcome any self-consciousness among its people (this is a pre-requisite for any assignment that hopes to look at a society in depth), and had complete freedom in shooting. However, when it came to providing the Akha with a portrait for themselves, the only acceptable one was the extremely formal picture.

Naturally, a portrait session calls for dressing up — no surprise there — but to the Akha only a full-length, unsmiling pose is thought to be dignified. Closely cropped pictures that truncate limbs are as obviously wrong and silly to the Akha as such clichéd mistakes as lamp-posts emerging from heads are to us; nor does a candid or relaxed moment have much appeal. This frozen formality is not a legacy of the small-town photographers' studios occasionally used by the Akha, and the moments before and after the shutter was fired involved some horse-play. A portrait is *always* a serious matter.

In camera-using countries, what constitutes an acceptable portrait is quite different. Most people would complain that in a head-to-toe photograph the face appears too small to reveal expression. The face is important for us because it displays personality and this is a requirement because Western society stresses the value of the individual. Concentrating on the face alone is not sufficient, however; the sitter should appear relaxed and, if possible, smiling, in other words, casually confident and at ease with the world — qualities of modern rather than universal importance. As both the Akha portrait and these examples show, creative success in this area of photography is less important than the fact that the pictures obey certain accepted rules.

While magazines and books encourage us to view photographs only as images — pictures to look into, with no physical substance — personal portraits tend to be treated as more tangible items. Once taken, the image is not simply a representation of a person, but an object in its own right; in fact, a kind of icon. If this seems rather too grand and metaphysical, look at how these photographs are used.

Lockets and frames are the simplest treatment that portrait pictures receive, but they are a clear indication that their owners regard them as special objects. In some ways, it is a pity that the old *non*-reproducible processes were quickly superseded by negatives and prints, for the very fact that there could only be one copy of a daguerreotype or tintype suited the personal portrait to perfection; here was a unique, solid object. The closest modern equivalent is the integral instant print, pioneered by Polaroid; obviously popular because immediate, it is also valued at least partly because its sealed, neatly packaged image has some of the qualities of a miniature. But of all the processes, the daguerreotype has the most distinct character, for it can be seen properly only at certain angles to the light and against a dark background because of its silvered surface. As reproduced here (page 73), the portrait of the Hiller family in the 1850s unfortunately has none of the physical properties of the original, although the typical gilt frame is included to give some sense of its physical presence. A daguerreotype has to be handled and moved to be seen, and its metallic sheen and patina give a special, elusive visual quality of its own.

As an icon is an image that merits special display and has a distinct presence, so the photographs decorating the antique camera of a photographer at the Acropolis and those displayed in the precincts of Rangoon's Shwe Dagon Pagoda have distinct ritual overtones. At such monuments, to which a visit is an occasion of some importance, a photograph is for many people a necessary act. Without becoming too fanciful, it could be said that such iconographic photography establishes a note of permanence in people's lives. The array of Chinese portraits, softened and diffused by their ceramic base, has just such a function: these are memorial plaques for the deceased, in a temple in the New Territories.

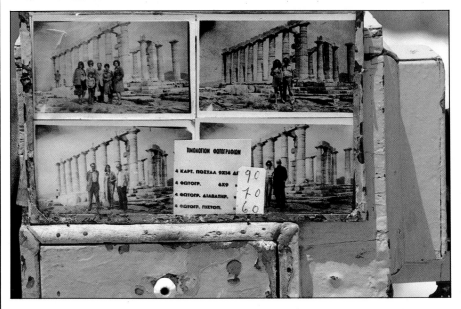

Far right above *Photographers fill an important role in Rangoon's major place of worship, the Shwe Dagon pagoda. For visitors who have come to worship, having a simple portrait taken with the temple in the background is both a remembrance of the visit and a tangible link between person and place.*

Far right below *In contrast to the Western tradition, which favors engraved markers and headstones, the Chinese way of death makes a prominent use of photographs. Remembrance is a more literal affair, and these permanent portraits on ceramic plaques, here in the New Territories, become, in time, the reality of the deceased for their descendants.*

Right *This portrait camera, decorated with examples of the photographer's work, provides on-the-spot proof of a visit for tourists.*

Even though only a minority of portrait photographs are treated in such intensely ritualistic ways, these uses suggest that similar influences may be at work more widely, if less obviously. The idea that the soul can be captured in an image — whether a mirror or a photograph — is perhaps an over-quoted piece of anthropological lore, yet certain people actually believe it. To give one example, the Akha hill-tribe to which the woman on page 64 belongs does not object to being photographed (which is surprisingly reasonable, considering that these people are a natural target for the occasional tourist's camera) However, photography of pregnant women is genuinely taboo. This is not simply to do with invasion of privacy by a stranger at an intimate time, but reflects the Akha's sincere belief in the spiritual power of a photograph — for them, it is the opposite of a talisman. Such a reaction is more likely among people with animist beliefs, but it is by no means absent in what most people would choose to call sophisticated Western society. In point of fact, the Akha, like most tribes that remain culturally distinct, are primitive only in popular imagination. Taboos about imagery cannot be dismissed as awe of the products of an advanced society; most of the tribal peoples who still exist do so because they have strong, supportive societies and have resisted absorption into the more amorphous culture of the West. They are generally perfectly familiar with standard technology, and photography is no special mystery — a generation of Polaroids has seen to that. What is displayed here is a fundamental attitude towards portraits that in the West has been obscured by sophistication. The most reasonable explanation for the appeal of these pictures is that they play a ritualistic role.

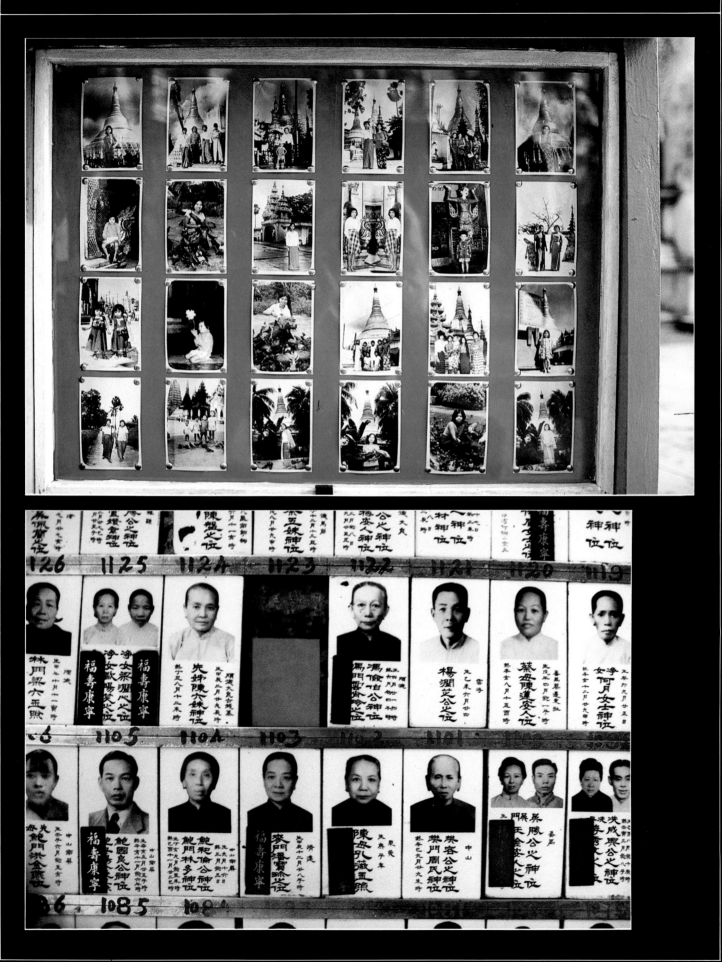

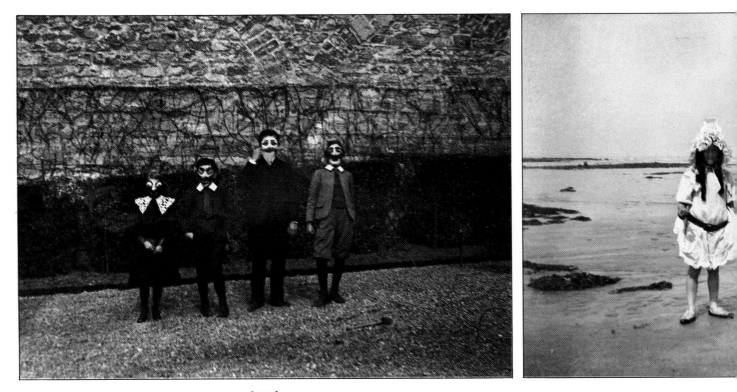

The ritual of photography goes further than the production of portraits. Cameras are so easy and quick to use that they have opened up a much wider range of possibilities in personal photography Indeed, just owning a camera creates a kind of compulsion to use it, and the result has been new ritual uses. Weddings and other social ceremonies are occasions for a specialized form of portrait; travel and holiday pictures have a different function again. Postcards capture a place more efficiently than most people can, yet are no substitute for a personal snapshot, however ineptly produced. It is not that the Eiffel Tower, Monument Valley or the Egyptian Pyramids actually need to be photographed any more, but they, and countless lesser sites, hold particular memories for the people who visit them, and it is this that the camera helps to pin down. A photograph of a place is a proof of visit.

The special quality of a photograph being put to use here is the realism that it confers. This may often be a spurious selected version of reality, but in personal photography it satisfies the needs of the moment. The psychology of holiday travelling is complicated enough, but there is one universal requirement — the need to show that the trip was performed and the itinerary completed. Photography is ideally suited to fulfil this need and, if the pictures brought home are often accompanied by excuses for not capturing the true feeling of the journey, they are no less effective.

Although personal travel pictures are usually offered for display to friends, they are not taken primarily for the benefit of an audience. No one, after all, is likely to disbelieve a trip to France or Arizona in the absence of photographic proof, and the pictorial quality of such pictures is not usually compelling (enthusiastic amateurs apart). The only people who really benefit from such travelogues are the picture-takers themselves. As such, they do not need proof of a visit so much as a means of making something more out of the experience, and this is where photography can really become a ritual activity.

In our society, much is made of the individual and the accumulation

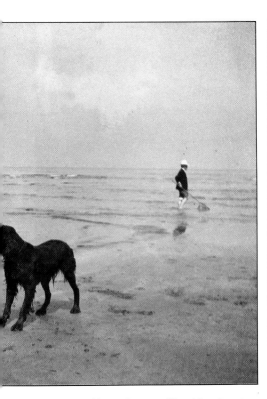

Above *Jacques-Henri Lartigue has benefited from two particular advantages: he had a privileged childhood, which gave him both the means to indulge his interest and a rich source of subject matter for his camera, and he was a naturally gifted photographer. He began photographing his family, friends and society at the age of seven, in 1901, delighting in the incidents and odd humor of life around him. Two examples are shown here:* Mardi Gras avec Bouboutte, Louis, Robert et Zissou, *1903 (left) and* Villerville, Simone, *1904 (right). Commercial restraints never entered into Lartigue's work, and he had an unprejudiced attitude towards photography, both of which resulted in a general lack of contrivance in his work. Like all true amateurs, this work was done without the knowledge of or recognition by the serious world of photography — it was 'discovered' when the best of it was complete, more than 50 years later. If Lartigue's stature in photography today is a result of 'discovery', what other private collections of similar merit remain to be recognized?*

of personal experience. The camera, which records scenes from the life of its owner with consummate ease, is the perfect instrument for detailing experiences. An album of personal pictures is the visual equivalent of a diary — easier to amass and better suited to a visual culture. Travel, as a common means of acquiring new experiences, highlights this type of use. For many people, photography is a means of focusing their own attention on an itinerary. Taking pictures is both a constructive activity with a tangible end-result and a system of punctuation for the journey. One of the problems with travel is that it can easily become rather aimless. A camera solves this by giving a kind of purpose.

When used to focus experience, personal photography can have strong, positive qualities. It develops visual sense and encourages a visual interpretation of life. However, seeing life through the camera can come to have a rather odd effect on perception. The typical procedure that it tends to promote is a cursory investigation of a scene — checking for a likely subject — followed by picture-taking that is, by comparison, elaborately performed. The viewfinder reduces a real situation to the conditions of a picture and, in a modern electronic camera where this image is surrounded by information displays, the total effect is to distance the photographer from the view. The way in which the image is projected through the eyepiece overlays it with technology. The excitement of the occasion is linked to the anticipation of taking a new picture.

Professional photographers are particularly prone to this two-dimensional view of life; a photojournalist quickly develops the habit of looking at any potentially interesting subject through the camera. Eventually, this becomes second nature, so that all visual experiences are treated as images, with part of the photographer's attention always directed towards picture-making. A practised photographer tends to analyze any situation in terms of its picture possibilities.

Paradoxically, then, while photography increases sensitivity to the visual aspects of life, it can also desensitize the photographer to other feelings. It is not even difficult to reach a stage, with prolific shooting, where the photographer has to wait for the developed film in order to see the events clearly. This is not necessarily because the photographer was guessing at the time of taking the picture, but because attention to the visual aspects of a scene can be quite seriously distracting. In general, this distancing from reality is not something that worries professional photographers a great deal — it is simply part of the job — but in certain situations when the photographer ought to be fully aware of what is going on, it can cause a disturbing dislocation.

George Rodger, a highly regarded English freelance photographer of the Second World War, was one of the first to enter Belsen concentration camp with Allied troops in 1945. He began work immediately, taking pictures of the bodies, treating the occasion as a source of pictures rather than reacting to the horror around him. When he realized what he was doing, he decided that his days as a war photographer should end. In an admittedly extreme situation, Rodger understood what many professional photographers do not — the distancing effect of the camera.

If perceptions are altered while people are actually using cameras, the photograph itself may come to have an unusual relationship with the real scene. As the memory of an event, imperfect to begin with, fades, the photograph becomes more and more the real version. Just as the pictures in a family album gradually begin to stand in for these fading memories, when a photographer has reached the stage of seeing life as a string of pictures, there *is* no other tangible experience. The more familiar we become with photographs, the easier it is to believe that these permanent images are the true representation of the ephemeral experience that we were trying to capture. Taken to extreme, personal photographs can become a substitute for experience.

Whereas these attitudes arise as by-products of taking pictures regularly, when photographers do begin to look deeply into the way they see the world, the results can be more self-conscious. The extreme case is when photographers treat their cameras as a means of introspection, moving towards symbolic representation.

Using the camera for personal exploration is an extremely popular approach, especially for photographers who do not have to meet the demands of clients. But photography has a special difficulty with this type of self-expression, because the *means* remain so realistic. Certain objects or situations may evoke powerful associations for the photographer, but there is a danger that an observer may either take them at face value or find different meanings there.

A perfect example of this is the notion of 'equivalents', first articulated by Alfred Stieglitz towards the end of his photographic career, and later developed fervently by Minor White in his work and teaching. Stieglitz, a major influence on photography for half a century, coined the term 'equivalents' to describe certain of his own photographs that were essentially analogies for his own feelings. He photographed such common and available subjects as clouds, the sun and trees as a means of conveying more complex human emotions. His cloud pictures were, to him, 'revelations of a man's world in the sky, documents of eternal relationship'.

Such oblique personal exploration was taken to fresh heights by Minor White who, while working in the straight, craftsmanlike manner of Edward Weston, intended his photographs to be seen as evidence of 'the intangible'. Occasionally he would give clues in the titles, such as *Empty Head* for a photograph of a bulging shape formed by ice on a windscreen, but more often he preferred a more mystic approach. One sequence of pictures taken in 1949 appears to be a pleasant study of rock patterns at Point Lobos, California (holy ground for the followers of Weston and Ansel Adams). To White, however, 'the subject of the sequence is not the rocks'; it is instead his upset emotions following the collapse of a love affair. Not surprisingly, such an approach was controversial, and few other photographers, even among his students, have embraced his philosophy wholeheartedly. Carl Chiarenza, who teaches photography at Boston University, recalled that White's classes 'could be excruciating', and that one body of opinion held that 'it was just artificial, that this guy was off the wall with all his spiritual stuff'.

While such an approach is as valid a way as any of personal creative development, it runs into difficulties when the photography is put on display. Whether Minor White wanted it or not, his pictures have certainly become public photography. As such, they have become widely admired and enjoyed, but not always for the reasons for which they were taken. Although this type of presentation alerts the viewer to the photographer's broad intentions, the full meaning of the pictures may depend on a background story to which the observer may be denied any access.

There are, then, two kinds of personal picture, both to do with capturing and enshrining some part of the photographer's life. One is the formal record — the image that shows what people or places or

Far right *Although produced with more difficulty and at greater expense, which therefore limited its market, the daguerreotype has much in common with the modern Polaroid. Both are unique images, individually mounted, appealing as objects and as pictures. Turning a daguerreotype in the hand reveals a changing display of tones caused by the reflective metallic surface.*

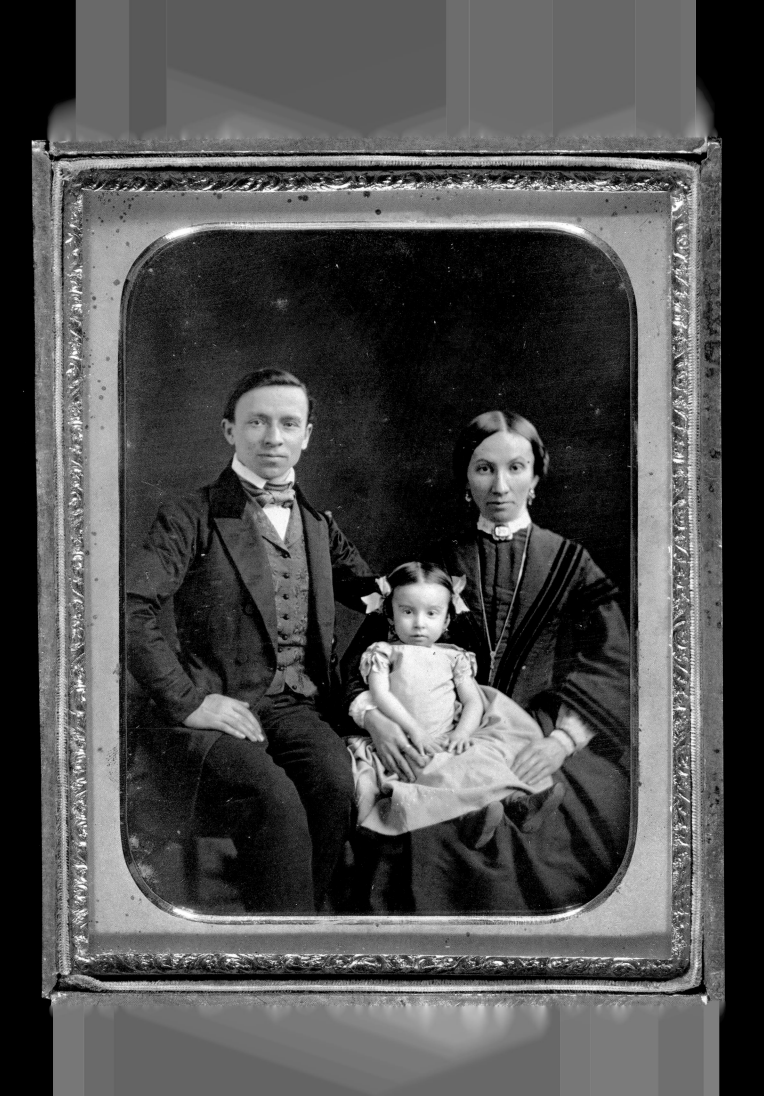

events look like, and which can come to *represent* what it shows. The other tries to capture something much more intangible — the photographer's private feelings — and does so by means of picture elements that may be too subjective to be appreciated fully by anyone else in the way it was intended.

Documentary photography could be seen, at the simplest level, as the public equivalent of the private photographer's personal record, preserving its subject matter of people, events and artefacts in the same way as pictures in a family album preserve the private lives of those who take and keep them. As might be expected, however, a closer examination reveals all kinds of ways in which the 'record' can be distorted. The distortion is not necessarily intentional and may not even be recognized by the photographer, but if anything this can make it more insidious.

Documentary photography began to be articulated as a distinct idea in America in the 1930s, in reaction to the more contrived forms that were popular. The manifesto of the Photo League, formed in 1936, was in part concerned with the duty 'of recording a true image of the world as it is today'. The League's task was 'to put the camera back in the hands of honest photographers'. This approach embraced photography of people and issues as well as places and events.

Since we began this chapter with portraits, it may be interesting to compare those that aim to please the sitter — an obvious interpretative treatment — with the type of 'documentary' picture perhaps best typified by the series of portraits made by August Sander during the 1920s and 1930s. Sander's *People of the Twentieth Century* is a series portraying ordinary German people between the wars, with no attempt at artifice. Since Sander naturally did not have personal relationships with his sitters and was fulfilling no commercial brief, we could take his aim as being to show and record the individual character of ordinary people, in other words to be as 'objective' as possible about his chosen subject matter. But here the essentially public aspect of such photography — its context — reveals an important difference between public and private, or 'subjective', pictures. Sander's seemingly uncontentious work was considered 'anti-social' by the Nazis and banned. For some audiences, cool detachment is itself an editorial position.

The portraits by Irving Penn in his book *Worlds in a Small Room* were made in a portable daylight studio that was carried, often with difficulty, to a number of remote locations. On the face of it, these pictures seem to be in direct line with Sander's documentary pictures (and, in fact, Penn was taught by Sander). Penn has even simplified the surroundings by providing his own tented backdrop, so surely this must focus attention even more clearly on the subject? Certainly, every physical detail is recorded with extreme accuracy, and frontal poses suggest directness and honesty in the approach. However, these images were arranged with infinite care by Penn, and reflect *his* view of the subject. While Penn's early ambition was to make an enduring record of cultures that were fast disappearing, he soon realized that his attempts to show people in their natural situations would fall short of his own expectations. In an effort to make his task more manageable, he isolated his subjects from the props and supports of their surroundings, arranged them with care, and imposed his own viewpoint. Recognizing fully the effect this would have, he said: 'Taking people away from their natural circumstances and putting them into the studio in front of a camera did not simply isolate them, *it transformed them.'* As he saw it, his subjects were presenting themselves to him in a new, unaccustomed way. Now, if this is true, is it only the portable backdrop that has wrought the change? Cannot a similar question be asked of Sander's seemingly exact, uninterpreted pictures?

No photographer of talent simply allows the sitters to do as they please, or restrict his or her own role to providing lighting and setting and to firing the shutter at an appropriate moment. In order to capture the personality of his subject, the photographer has first to decide what he thinks it is (itself a highly subjective process), then to present or develop this view by choosing a certain relationship with the sitter. While a viewer's intuition suggests Penn's portraits do manage to probe the character without contrivance, there must still be an act of faith in the standards and fairness of the photographer or sympathy with his point of view.

With Richard Avedon's somewhat savage style of portraiture during the late 1950s and early 1960s, our faith may be more strained, particularly if such aggressive treatment is no more than a reaction against the regular, pleasing style of portrait. It is hard to imagine some of Avedon's sitters actually liking the results; perhaps they bravely approved such treatment for being uncompromising. Avedon has said: 'The photographs have a reality for me that the people don't. It's through the photographs that I know them.' Avedon further supports his case for interpretative treatment by saying that he believes people come to be photographed as they would 'go to a doctor or fortune-teller — to find out how they are'. In other words, people *expect* the photographer to interpret or reveal aspects of themselves that they themselves cannot see. They do not, of course, always enjoy visits to doctors or clairvoyants — it depends on the results.

Certain subjects offer fewer opportunities for interpretation. The techniques of architectural and wildlife photography are certainly different, but what both have in common is that a large proportion of work in these areas is concerned with record-keeping.

Both the photograph of a South American cayman on page 76 and the massed shot of pelicans at Lake Manyara in the East African Rift Valley (page 77) are typical of a whole body of work that is both popular and uncontentious — appealing pictures not only because they are effective pictorially but because they portray subjects most people find interesting. The two treatments differ: one verges on the impressionistic, with limited colors and limited focus, the other uses the technique of a long-focus lens to enhance the real spectacle of an enormous flock, but both perform the same basic function of showing animals in their natural surroundings to an audience that is unlikely to see the same thing for themselves. Wildlife photography today performs exactly the function that travel photography of the nineteenth century was intended to have: in the words of John Thomson, it 'affords the nearest approach that can be made toward placing the reader actually before the scene which is represented'. This honourable, if straightforward, job is likely to belong to wildlife photographers well into the future and, while this field is perfectly susceptible to creative ability, the inherent interest of the subject matter and the ecological fragility of much of it, keep documentation high on the list of priorities.

While the subject matter is generally more accessible, the service that photography can perform for architecture is, as the art historian

Right *Another aspect of wildlife photography's documentary nature is the display of the spectacular. Certain features of the natural world, such as large congregations of animals, are inherently impressive, yet understandably not common. Massed images such as this photograph of white pelicans on the shores of Lake Manyara, Tanzania, are always imposing. To enhance the impression of great numbers by producing a compressing effect, a long telephoto lens — 600mm — was used.*

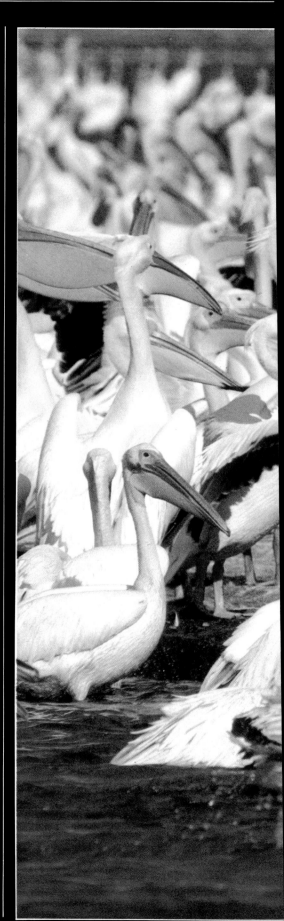

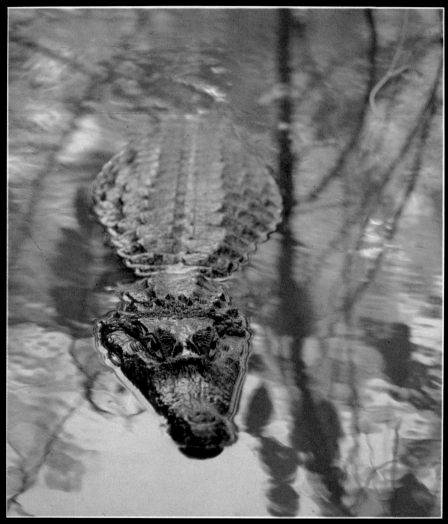

Above *A large part of the appeal of wildlife photographs lies in the relative inaccessibility of the subject matter. Close views, particularly of animals that are potentially dangerous, are outside most viewer's own experience, and the camera provides, among other things, a vicarious experience. Although this head-on photograph of a black cayman in an Amazon swamp has pictorial qualities that are themselves of interest (the directness of the composition and the simplicity of the two-color design), it serves for most viewers a documentary function.*

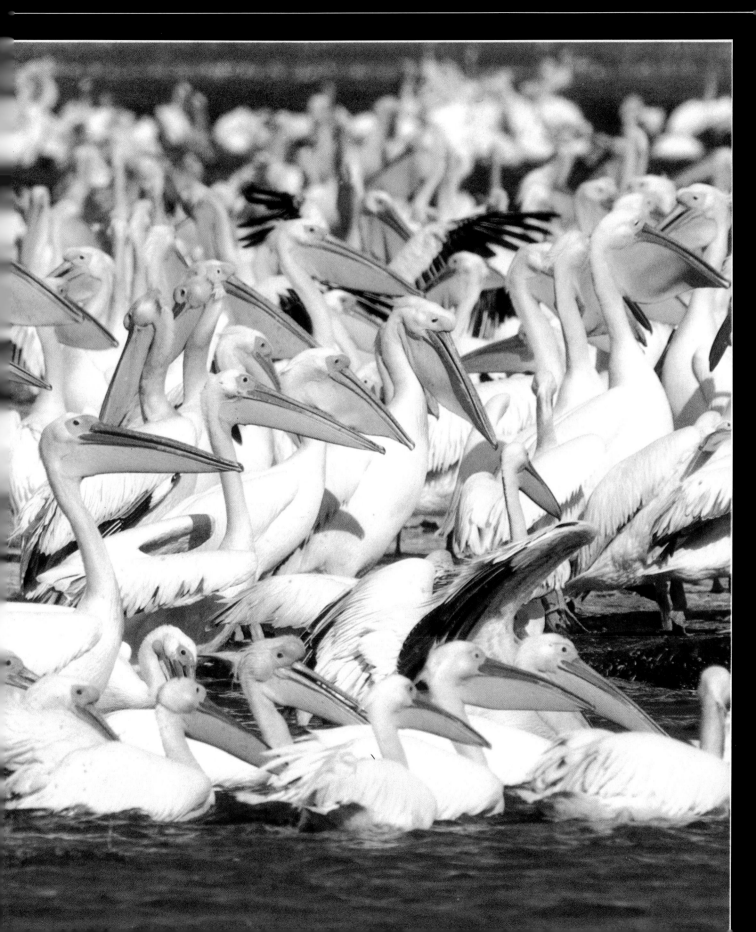

Kenneth Clark said, to 'discover values which would otherwise remain hidden'. An architectural photographer is, or should be, sympathetic to the work of another artist, namely the architect. Given that the subject, such as St James's Palace (right), is already a designed work, there is some further obligation to be faithful to the subject. With time, this approach acquires an historical importance. The photographs of monuments by Frederick Evans and Eugène Atget (*see* below and right) are different in treatment, but both share these qualities of sympathy and exactness of detail. Although Evans was less interested in documenting architecture than in rendering the qualities of light and volume, part of the value of his pictures and of Atget's for us is that each is an unsurpassed record of the material furniture of past times. None of these views of Lincoln or Paris is the same today, and Atget was certainly aware of the need to document a Paris that was already changing. To a later generation, with no experience of these places at the turn of the century, such photographs *are* the reality. Even more than the private record in a family album, these images now represent their lost subjects.

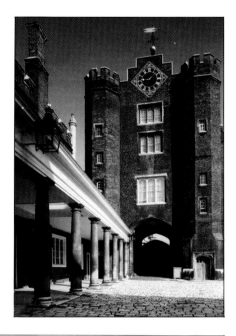

The photograph of a kitchen wall in Hale County, Alabama, by Walker Evans is also documentary in style, but is motivated by a social

Right *Although Frederick Evans was very much concerned with the pictorial element in architecture (he titled one of his most famous pictures, of Wells Cathedral, A Sea of Steps), on the occasions when he photographed the exterior settings of buildings he left an unrepeatable record of the historical context. The contrast of religious and secular architecture in most cathedral towns has diminished over the years, as the skylines increase and change. This view of Lincoln at the turn of the century gives a vivid impression of soaring, unassailable architecture.*

Above right *Formal architecture encourages a formal photographic approach. To convey detail and proportion in this view of the courtyard and clock tower of St James's Palace, London, a large-format camera has been used, both for the ability of a large sheet of film (4 x 5in) to record and convey fine detail and graduations of tone, and for the facility of camera movements, which in this case have been used to shift the lens panel upwards so there is no convergence of verticals. In a fixed-body camera, with a regular lens, the only way of achieving this view would have been to aim up, making the image of the tower appear to lean back. With a view camera, the flexibility of the bellows means that the camera can be leveled (to give straight-sided verticals), yet the upper part of the image can be slid into frame. Such corrective measures in photography are part of the documentary ethos.*

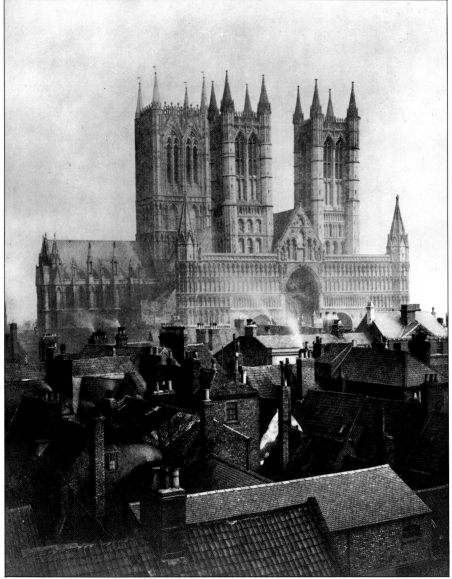

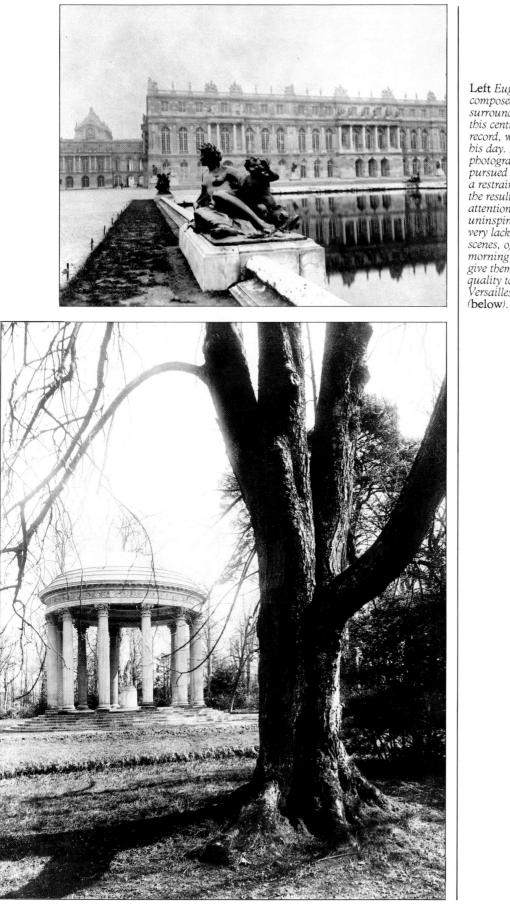

Left *Eugene Atget, whose neat, carefully composed photographs of Paris and its surroundings in the first three decades of this century now form an invaluable record, was virtually unacknowledged in his day. He did not begin to take photographs until the age of 42, but then pursued an independent course, working in a restrained and unaffected way. Although the results, had they been given any critical attention, might have seemed plain and uninspired to Atget's contemporaries, the very lack of mannerism in these unhurried scenes, often photographed in the early morning to avoid the intrusion of people, give them an important documentary quality today. These two examples show Versailles (**above**) and the Petit Trianon (**below**).*

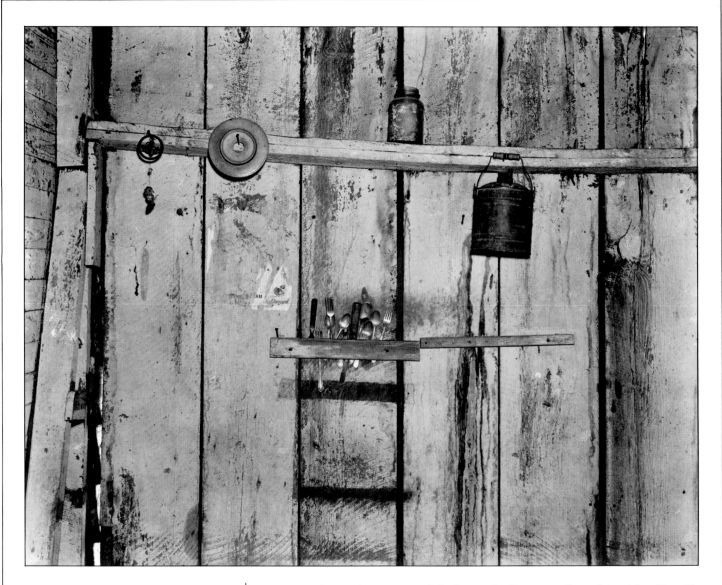

Above *Photographed as part of the Farm Security Administration project to record its activities during the American Depression, this direct, unsentimental image of a kitchen wall in Hale County, Alabama, is typical of the work of Walker Evans. Composed as a kind of still-life, its very simplicity focuses attention on the minutiae of life — details that are strikingly poor and make an eloquent comment on the effects of the Depression.*

purpose. One of a group of dedicated photographers hired by Roy E. Stryker of the Farm Security Administration, Evans set out to photograph the lives of sharecroppers during the years of the Depression.

The formal, even plain, approach that Evans took may seem at first unenterprising, undramatic (*see* above). Far from lacking artistic skills, however, Evans chose to use no technique that would distract attention from the subject. The plainness of the composition and lighting is a clue that the interest lies in the subject matter and not in the cleverness of the photography. The pitiful array of possessions, arranged in puritanical order on the rough board wall, is clearly not the American dream of the 1930s, and Evans wanted the people who saw the picture to realize that this was how many Americans were actually living. Many other photographs also taken for the Farm Security Administration show more obvious signs of social commitment — for example, Dorothea Lange's photograph of sharecroppers (*see* right) employs drama to make the same comment — but Evans used the restraint of a documentary approach to deliver a more subtle blow.

There are no hidden distortions in Evans' photographs. He set out to record, not to construct, leaving the conclusions up to the viewer. Undoubtedly, he was helped by his subject matter — poverty with a specific cause. Not all documentary photographers have been able to

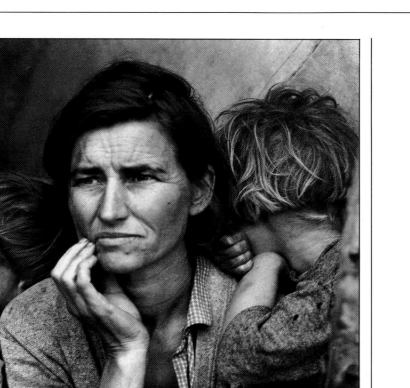

Left *In contrast to Evans' straightforward treatment is the emotional and evocative work of Dorothea Lange, who also photographed for the FSA. Probably her most famous photograph of the period is this, taken in 1936 and entitled* Migrant Mother, California. *Much of Lange's work conveys the misery of the Depression through the defeated and subdued expressions and postures of her subjects.*

interfere so little, in spite of what they probably felt were good intentions.

In the 1860s, John Thomson set out to record scenes from the life and landscapes of China, riding on the wave of interest in exotic travel. Since international tourism was not yet established on a popular scale, and photography was so new that most places were still virgin territory, the role of the travelling photographer was uncomplicated: to show what exotic places looked like.

Thomson visited China for a total of five years in the 1860s, with the intention of producing a photographic record that would be as informative as possible. He was not outwardly concerned with self-expression or 'art'. The photographic historian Beaumont Newhall considered that the work contained 'that sense of immediacy and authenticity of documentation, which a photograph can impart so forcibly'.

On closer examination, however, we can see that this is true only up to a point, and that authenticity, for a Victorian photographer, often involved some compromises to overcome technical limitations. If Thomson had had access to camera and films that allowed rapid shooting, we might indeed have seen a good deal of the candid depiction of Chinese life that Thomson wanted. But, given the materials of the day, the only way of showing people in close-up was to pose them, which

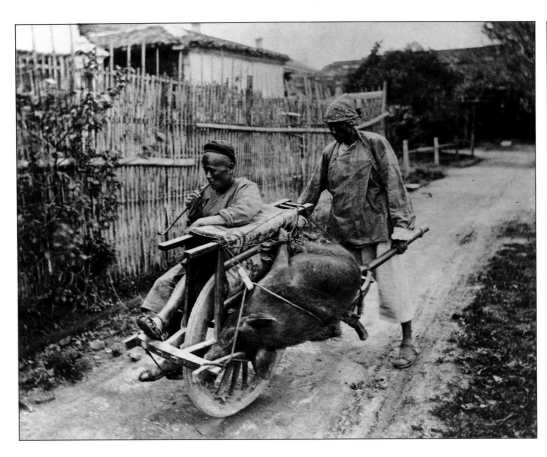

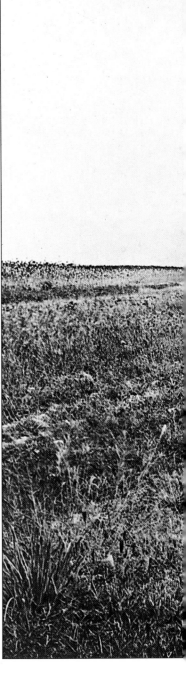

Thomson appears to have done regularly. He did this conscientiously, for he was not out to distort the record, but he did it inevitably with his own eye for the way things should be. The barrow is evidently at a virtual standstill (above), while in other scenes individuals pose 'naturally' beside monuments. A Victorian reader might be forgiven for thinking that picturesque Chinese were forever meditating in impressive landscapes. These quaint arrangements may not be so harmful but it is fairly clear that we are receiving the questionable bonus of Thomson's own class prejudices.

The danger for the viewer, obvious in principle but hidden in specific images, is that photographs which may seem to be essentially documentary, whether they are records for public or private consumption, are often influenced by other attitudes — both towards the subjects of the pictures and towards the photographs themselves as objects. Atavistic though this may seem, most of this kind of photography has some kind of ritual, both for those who make it and those who use it.

Below left *and* **below** *John Thomson's pioneering efforts at recording life in China in the 1860s and early 1870s and street-life in London in the following decade have earned him the reputation as a founder of documentary photography. The close, almost candid shot of a boar being transported on a barrow in northern China* (**below left**) *seems remarkably modern for capturing an everyday action, yet the materials and equipment with which Thomson worked placed limitations on what*

he could shoot without planning. Given the overcast light in this scene, and the normal speed of action, it seems certain that Thomson must have set about a re-enactment, in slow motion. In more favorable conditions, with bright backlighting and more moderate movement, Thomson was later able, in some of his London scenes, to work with shutter speeds as fast as one second. Here, this would have been out of the question. In the photograph (**below**), *taken in about*

1865, white limestone sculptures of camels are seen flanking the Avenue to the Ming Tombs north of Peking. Here, there is no movement to create a problem, but the posed figure, although serving a purpose in showing the scale, displays the controlling hand of the photographer. John Szarkowski calls Thomson's approach 'similar to that of an ornithologist who is genuinely fond of birds' and believes it encouraged 'precisely accurate description'.

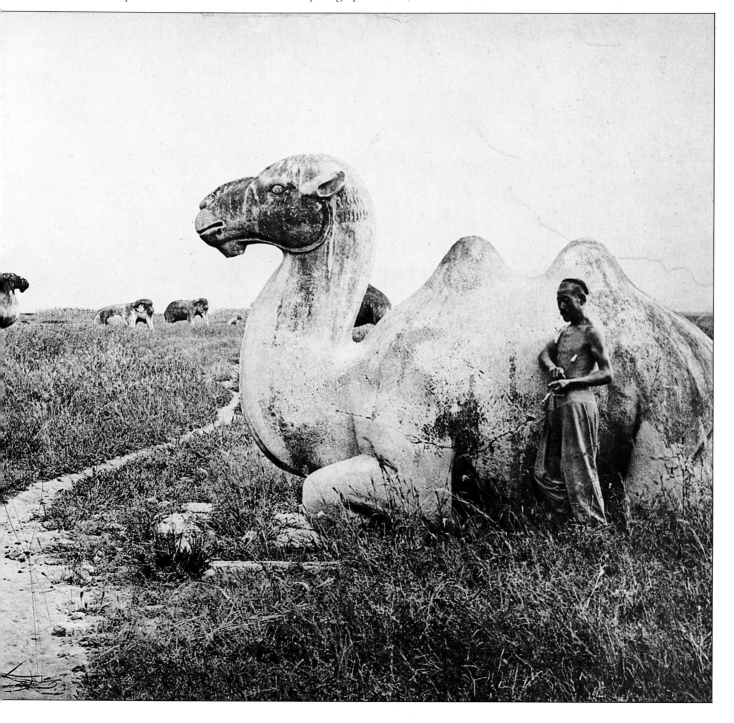

CHAPTER 4

Codes
of
Conduct

...each time I pressed the shutter release, it was a shouted condemnation, hurled with the hope that the pictures might survive through the years.
W. Eugene Smith (Second World War)

'To get the best picture of a captured prisoner, you have to get him just as he is captured.'
Horst Faas (Vietnam war)

An event without a picture suffers a problem of identity, a fact well understood by both newspaper editors and censors of all kinds. A striking image can enhance the impact of a newsworthy occasion and give it the kind of archival permanence that even an eloquent description cannot; the *absence* of pictorial evidence, on the other hand, can make the event seem vague and insubstantial in the public's mind. Famines, for instance, have regularly plagued the Third World, yet somehow it is the few that have generated powerful photographs that have registered their horrors with the Western public. One of the most shocking events of 1983 was the shooting down of a Korean airliner by a Soviet fighter; there were no pictures, and it is tempting to think that, if there had been, the memory and substance of the event would now be stronger than it is. *Life*, in their year-end issue, recognized the need to *show* something of the incident and assigned photographer Michael O'Neill to portray the pitiful debris of recovered possessions — the only answer for a picture magazine under the circumstances.

Similarly, the place of wars in the public consciousness depends very much on the extent of the visual record. After the American public relations disaster in Vietnam, in which an open-house policy for journalists resulted in an uncontrolled barrage of comment and criticism, several governments have relearned the value of close censorship. The British involvement in the Falklands, that of the French in Chad and of the United States in Grenada were all conducted without the dubious benefit of any significant battlefront photography, and from the point of view of the three governments, the result was an unqualified success — the events were less memorable, and so arguably less criticized, than they would otherwise have been.

As soon as newspapers and magazines acquired the printing technology to use photographs rapidly — this happened after the reproduction process known as half-tone was perfected in the late 1880s — the camera was destined for reporting. While a picture of a news event can be cropped, emphasized in different ways and subtly manipulated, it cannot be substantially reworked in the way that a sub-editor can alter raw copy. It also scores two major points with the audience: rightly or wrongly, it has a head start in believability, and it is easily grasped in an instant. Text takes longer to understand, and more effort to remember.

Despite the inevitability of photojournalism, it is, by any standards, an extremely ambitious task. One of the great successes of photography is the way in which it can simplify its subject matter. While this may be marvellously convenient for popular news presentation, accurate reporting usually calls for thoroughness and balance — qualities not easily found in single images. In the way that news is gathered and reported, the issues *may* turn out to be simple enough to present in one short statement, but not necessarily. Unfortunately, when the style of presentation is decided in advance, the temptation is to make any report fit into a simple form. In other words, once the decision has been taken to cover a news situation by means of photographs, they are likely to be used even if, in the event, the story proves to be too complicated for a simple, pictorial treatment. Some stories need simplification to make the issues

Below *Nguyen Kong (Nick) Ut's famous photograph of a girl (Phan Thim Kim Phuc) accidentally napalmed by South Vietnamese aircraft in 1972 is one of the most enduring images of war and suffering, and has played a part in fixing the nature of the Vietnam conflict in the memory of the Western public. The circumstances are, in a sense, unimportant to the power of this image — the suffering is obvious.*

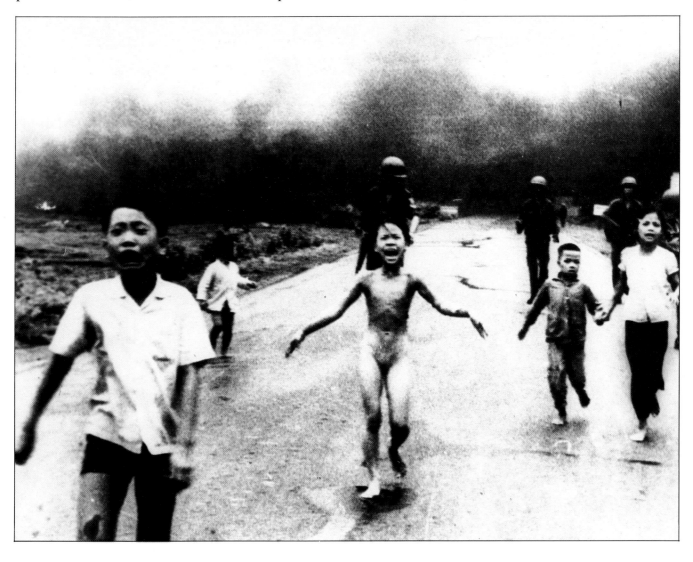

clear; others need to be elaborated because they are not as straightforward as they might first appear. Photography, which works at an immediate, sensory level, is not an instrument for debate and argument and, while it can simplify beautifully, is more likely to be misleading if it accompanies a story that needs direction.

While this is the *potential* difficulty in photojournalism, in the early days of photographic reporting, it did not seem to be much of an issue. A photograph was just an additional means of documenting events, and on the face of it *less* susceptible to subtle trickery than writing; innuendo, satire, omission and other editorial weapons seemed to have no counterparts in what was imagined to be straightforward visual recording. Journalism for a mass audience is, however, a relatively young activity, and its effects and successes as a whole are still under review. Photography, quite simply, has turned out to have had a huge impact, largely due to the ways in which skilled photographers can manipulate it. Techniques of design and composition provide enormous scope for altered versions of events and situations.

The reason why the question of interpretation is so crucial to photojournalism is that any type of reporting implies a point of view: important stories are *presented* to the readers rather than displayed as flat documents. Unlike documentary photography, which attempts to be detached because it sets out to present an accurate record for the future (even then, a selective one), reporting is concerned with the immediate. It is designed for immediate consumption, and *actively* tackles its audience. An effective news photograph and text waste no time; they press their information on the reader in a fundamentally opinionated way.

What makes fair reporting possible in those countries with a free press is the *variety* and consistency of the media. In any individual instance, however, there may be no clear-cut standards of 'fairness'. Richard Nixon's views on what was fair comment were not the same as the *Washington Post*'s. Many stories involve such considerations to some degree, and most significant stories, human conflict in particular, are dangerous editorial areas.

Questions of fairness also arise when photography is used for reporting like text, yet its effects and the tactics used by photojournalists and picture editors are more difficult to pin down. As an extreme case, libel is very hard to prove in a photograph, while it remains a basic hazard for most newspapers in their text reporting. The paparazzi photograph of Lauren Hutton (*see* right) is very unkind and highly intrusive. Imagine, however, what a writer would have to say in order to convey the same effect; remember that, just as the photograph does not qualify or compromise in its extremely unflattering view, the words would have to be just as brutal. Even if an editor could think of a good reason to say what the photograph shows, no one would dare print the description for fear of a libel suit. This kind of invasion of privacy by the camera is possible simply because the law cannot define the effects of photography with any precision. There are regular rows over such invasive photography, but ineffective censure is the usual result, because pictures can often defy vocabulary. Many photographers have recognized this fact; John Heartfield, who savagely satirized Hitler and the Third Reich in a series of photo-montages, began by assembling parts of different illustrations during the First World War, in his own words, 'to say, in pictures, what would have been banned by the censors if we had said it in words'. Though the means may be more elusive, there *is* a photographic equivalent of innuendo.

The paparazzi photograph is, admittedly, an extreme example, and it represents the outer reaches of photojournalism. It does, nevertheless, forcibly demonstrate just how biased a view photography can give, although pictures that are really outrageous carry their own warning about accuracy; the public may be titillated, but also knows that it is seeing what amounts to a piece of distortion, an exaggeration designed to entertain rather than report.

Below *Lauren Hutton, looking quite unlike her* intentional *public self when groomed for cosmetic advertisements, reacts to paparazzi photographer Alan Davidson with a frontal assault, while her friends have more success in preventing another photographer from taking pictures. The word* paparazzi *comes from a character*

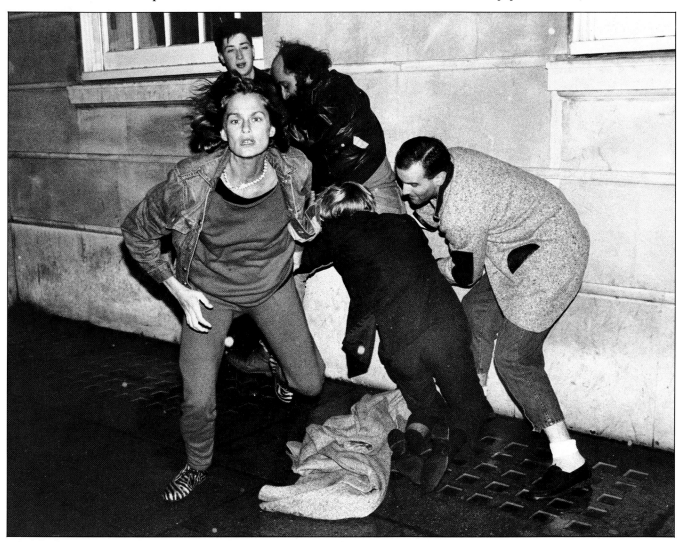

Most manipulation in photojournalism is more subtle than this and is not necessarily objectionable, any more than is an article written with a point of view. The more skilled a photographer is in design, the more able he is to influence the audience's reaction to a news picture and, in practice, basic journalistic training encourages him to decide what the facts are and then to make the most of whatever he uncovers. On assignment, a photojournalist does the same kind of groundwork as any reporter, one of the aims being to distil and clarify the information. This process is necessary just to get to the position of being able to shoot; it is not surprising that a photographer would then follow through and use his abilities to make the point appear as clear and definite as possible in the picture. Jill Freedman's photograph of a protest march on Washington in 1968 (page 88) combines, very effectively, the two major ingredients of such occasions: the marchers themselves and their police guard. However, the manner of the juxtaposition

invented by Fellini for his film La Dolce Vita — *an annoying photographer, Paparazzo, whose name reminded Fellini of a similar Italian word for gnat, a buzzing, annoying intrusion. Writer Anthony Burgess, introducing a collection of similarly unkind and intrusive photography, identified the cruel pleasure that such pictures inspire: 'No rise without a fall, and the gods demand punishments not from the mediocre but from the ambitious. . . . The extraordinary are revealed as terribly ordinary, and there is no diviner punishment than that.'*

Right *Jill Freedman's photograph of the archetypal components of a 1968 protest march to Washington uses a photo-journalist's experience to make a comment. The camera position and the wide angle of view (from a 20mm lens) present the policeman's truncheon as dominant and threatening. Other possible viewpoints, say a foot or two to the right, could easily have been more neutral in comment, but probably less dramatic.*

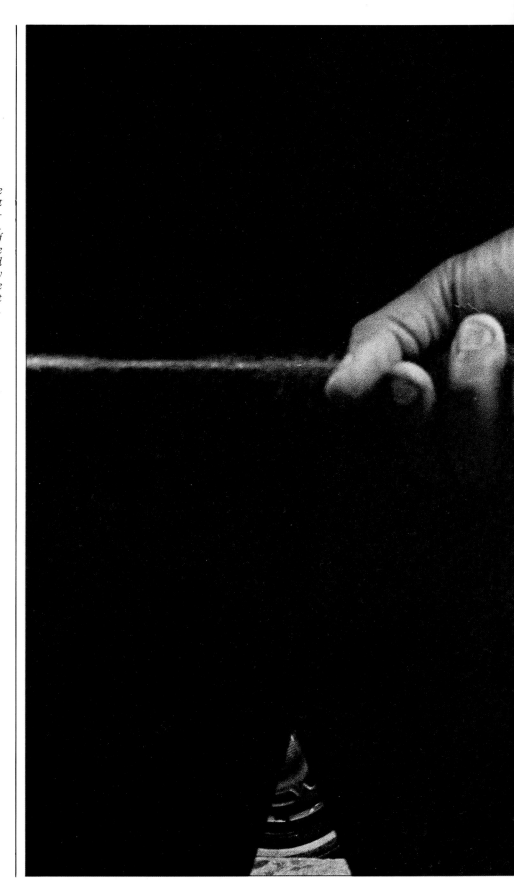

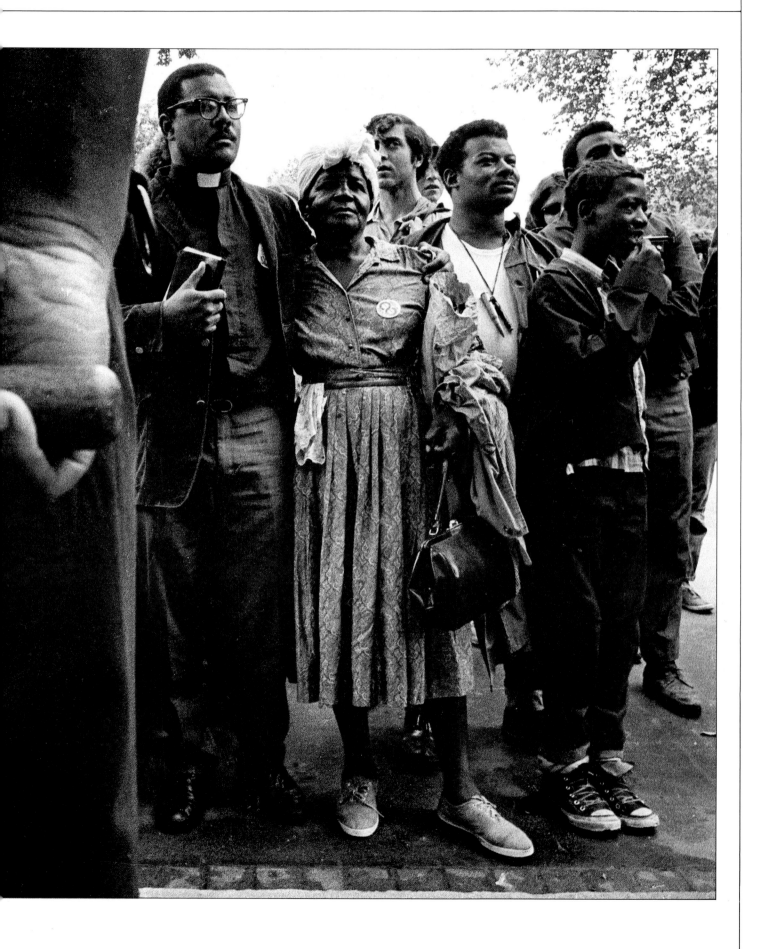

has some distinct implications. On the right of a picture that is divided clearly down the middle, stands a group of reasonable, well-behaved people, mostly black, and confirmed for our eyes as basically decent people by the presence of a preacher. On the left, looming large through the camera's viewpoint and wide-angle lens, is that symbol of all that is worst in faceless authority, the fist and truncheon. Whether or not the truncheon was used to break open any of the heads of this group of protestors, confrontation and oppression is clearly implied.

The methods used here to highlight a journalistic issue are by no means unusual. Indeed, there is a kind of repertoire of techniques that is used quite regularly to dramatize and to concentrate attention. These techniques are not always put to work in a deliberately calculated way; some of them have become standard tactics. They include the associations of grain, contrast and monochrome film, the use of special lighting, cropping, and timing.

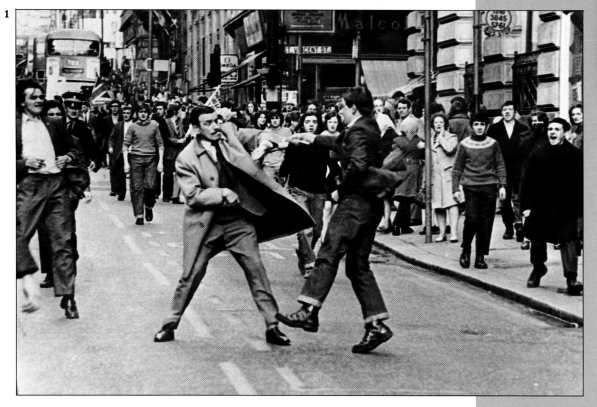

Cropping a news photograph *This news photograph of a street fight which took place during the course of a Glasgow demonstration is fully descriptive in its original form: the fight itself occupies the center of the frame, the demonstration is shown in the background, people intervening in the dispute and the reactions of uninvolved spectators are at either side (1). Different ways of cropping the image emphasize different aspects of the event. The first treatment places the fight at the right hand side of the picture, and adds weight to those intervening at left (2). Cropping in tightly to show the fight in isolation loses context and hence interest (3). The third cropped version displays the full range of reaction from the spectators — from aggression to anguish (4).*

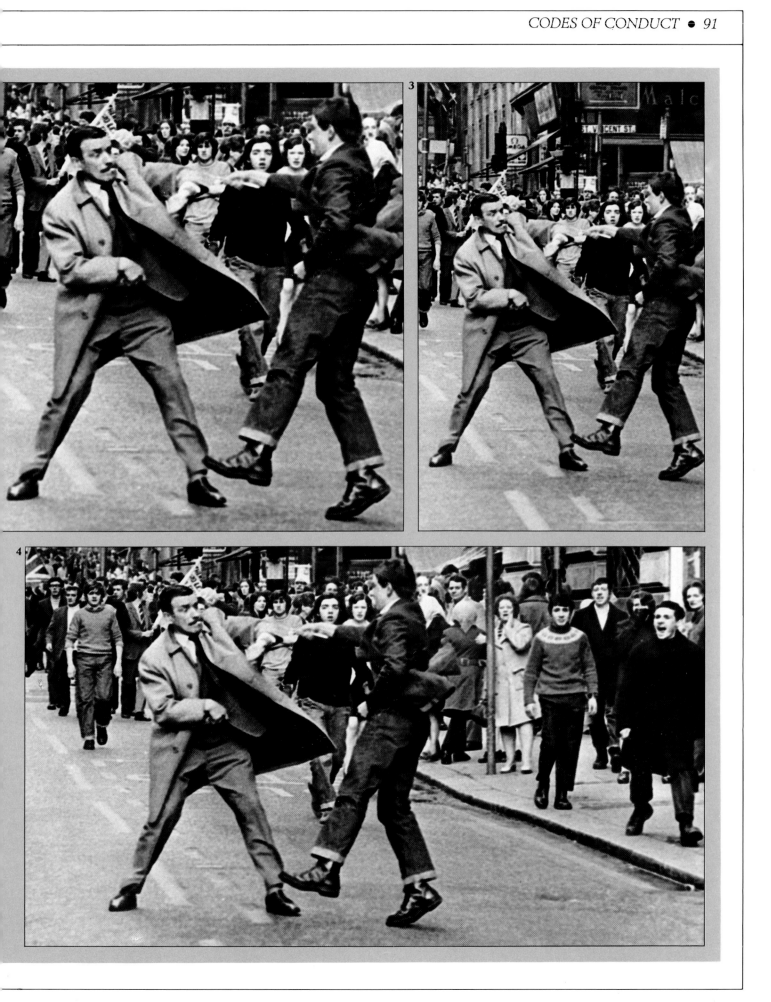

Below *The caption, in full, reads:
'Kennedy shot, Dallas, Texas: U.S.
President John F Kennedy (right) slumps
forward into the arms of his wife Jacqueline
seconds after being shot by a sniper as his
motorcade travelled through this city
yesterday. November 23d, 1963.' Both the
terse language of agency news reporting
and the inevitably coarse grain of a picture
enlarged to its maximum are now
themselves the hallmarks of hard, dramatic
news.*

Until color film became the more usual stock for reportage photography, the two basic variables of image quality — grain and contrast — gave a useful and simple choice of treatment. Graininess varies according to the speed of the film and to the type of developer used; how obvious it appears in the picture depends on the size of the enlargement. Contrast also varies with film speed (the faster, the lower the contrast), but can be controlled even more during the printing by selecting the grade of paper.

From a purist point of view, grain and high contrast interfere with the

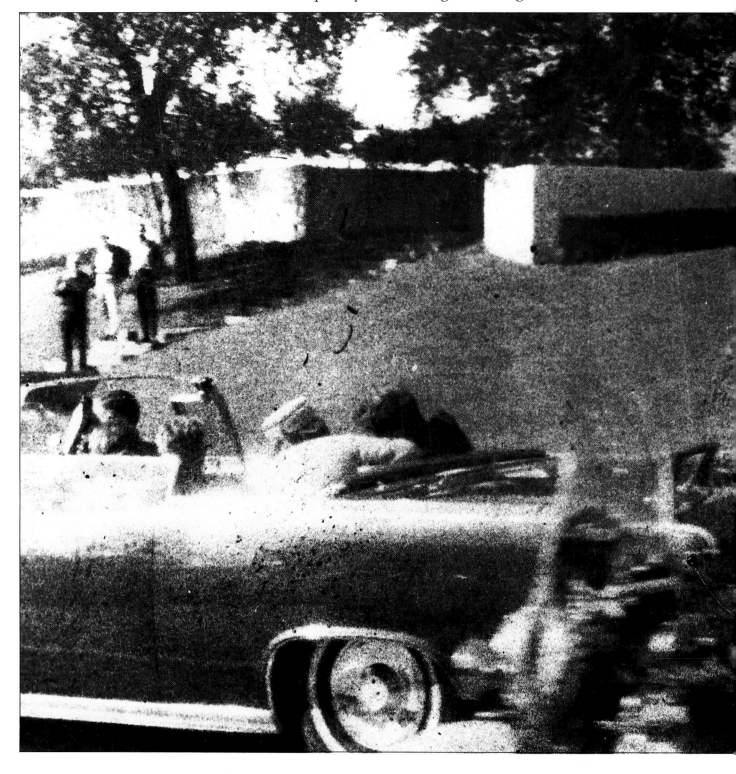

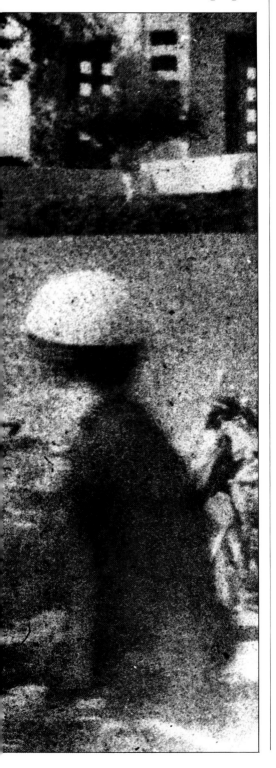

picture; they make the processes of the medium visible and, if extreme, begin to break up the image. However, this is actually what makes them valuable for certain kinds of photojournalism. Grain gives a picture a rough-edged look, and high contrast gives it a stark quality.

But something more than simple graphic association is involved here. Modern films are much better than early emulsions, and the degrees of graininess and contrast can usually be chosen by the photographer. Several decades ago, however, hard, gritty images were the result of the deficiencies of the technology and reflected the difficulties of photo-

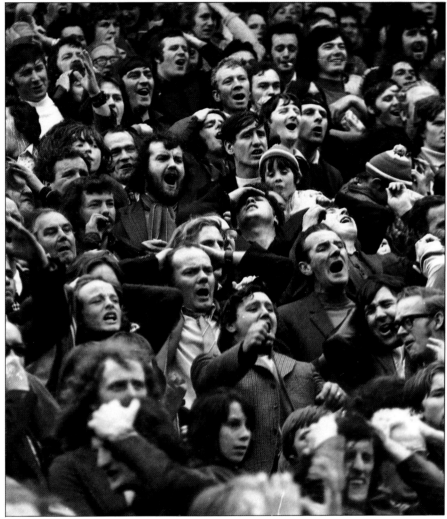

graphic reporting. To an extent, when photographers exploit grain and contrast to make pictures seem more urgent, they are in effect making a kind of pastiche of those earlier images.

The grainy, indistinct print of the Kennedy assassination (*see* right) shows the typical effect of enlargement, a gritty quality that, over the years, has come to be associated with the dramatic news event. The reason for such enlargement is obvious enough — our desire to peer into the picture as closely as possible and extract every last detail of an event, a desire that picture editors have generally attempted to meet by enlarging the image to the point where the only remaining details are the clumps of silver grains in the film. This has been done so often, out of necessity, that it now carries certain implications: it signals drama.

Today, more and more photojournalists work with color transparency film to suit the needs of magazines. International news journals, for example, include at least some color pages, but much of the layout, naturally, is left until the last minute. At this stage, picture editors like to have the option of using a picture in either color or black-and-white.

Occasionally, however, magazines that normally use color throughout will assign a picture story in black-and-white just because the 'hard' associations of monochrome are felt to suit the subject matter. Typical examples include stories about mental institutions, cancer wards and other bleak human areas. In such cases, the editors and photographer together rely on a certain carry-over from the past to emphasize a mood. While this is certainly still an effective technique, its days are probably numbered. Color does not always beautify and need not detract from the strength of a dramatic situation, as is shown by Romano Cagnoni's photograph of the Soviet invasion of Afghanistan on page 97. Taken with a hidden camera and high-speed film, the picture's limited range of colors and green-tinged shadows, far from being pictorially attractive, actually help to convey the grimness of the situation — Russian tanks in a Kabul winter. As this non-beautifying use of color becomes more generally accepted, through repetition, the associations of black-and-white will diminish.

According to the type of reporting, there may be a choice of lighting. When this is under the control of the photographer, it can be an important and forceful component. In 1963, Arnold Newman was asked by an American magazine to photograph the powerful German steel magnate Alfred Krupp (*see* right). Newman was unwilling to perform the assignment, for he considered Krupp, who was a convicted war criminal because of his use of slave labor, to be nothing less than the devil. Eventually, when he was persuaded to go ahead by the editorial department, he decided to portray his subject as the criminal he felt him to be. One difficulty with this was that the man looked, as Newman described him, 'like a nice, distinguished gentlemanly human being'. Undeterred, Newman chose to rely on a basic technique of using two low lights aimed upwards towards Krupp's face, something he acknowledged to be 'the usual cliché'. Even so, like many clichés, it did the job. What completed the diabolical effect was Krupp leaning forward towards the camera. Newman hid the exposure-test Polaroids that he was taking, for Krupp naturally could not imagine the visual effect that the lights were having, and would have terminated the session had he known.

These strategies may or may not work according to the photographer's intentions, because in journalism there are other people and processes involved. In 1981, the German magazine *GEO* published in its national and American issues a series of photographs of giant pandas — claimed by the publishers to be a journalistic scoop and billed as 'Pandas in the Wild'. The American issue went on to say that 'for the first time ever' a Western journalist had been allowed to photograph the animals in their wild, natural setting, in Szechuan Province. Giant pandas being rare, attractive and the symbol of the World Wildlife Fund, have a public importance, hence the fanfare for the pictures, one of which, from the same series, appears on page 97. Hence also, however, the attention that the article drew from a number of naturalists familiar with the *actual* conditions — a secure enclosure of about two acres that is part of the breeding center in the Wolong nature reserve. Natural setting certainly, but wild certainly not. The photographer, Timm Rautert, had access to this enclosure, where he took pictures of captive pandas that were part of the breeding programme carefully *not*

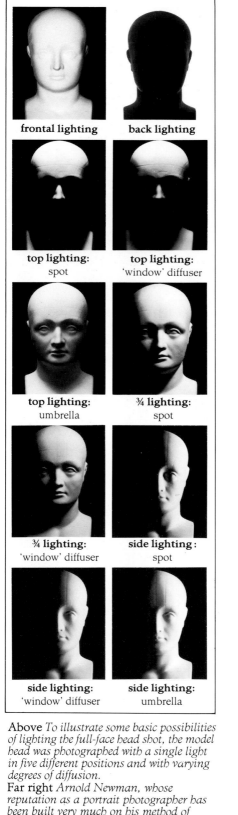

frontal lighting	**back lighting**
top lighting: spot	**top lighting:** 'window' diffuser
top lighting: umbrella	**¾ lighting:** spot
¾ lighting: 'window' diffuser	**side lighting:** spot
side lighting: 'window' diffuser	**side lighting:** umbrella

Above *To illustrate some basic possibilities of lighting the full-face head shot, the model head was photographed with a single light in five different positions and with varying degrees of diffusion.*
Far right *Arnold Newman, whose reputation as a portrait photographer has been built very much on his method of showing his subjects in the context of their life or activities, made this menacing portrait of the German industrialist Alfred Krupp in 1963. Newman's deliberately unsympathetic treatment earned his subject's enmity.*

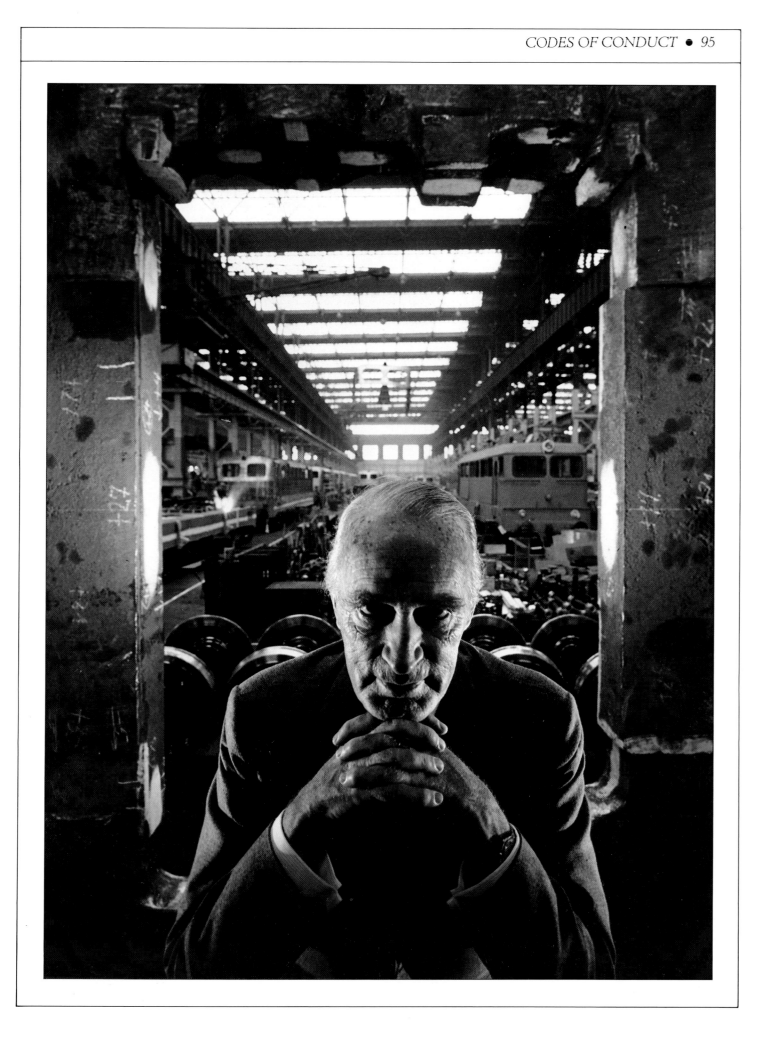

showing any fences or other evidence of captivity. There was nothing at all wrong with that, but somewhere between perfectly legitimate photography and publication something went very wrong editorially. Exactly what is not clear, for in the nature of such embarrassing matters there was a certain amount of self-justification and recrimination. After the earlier trumpet-blowing, in which *GEO* claimed that these were 'some of the most extraordinary wildlife photographs ever taken' (they would have been — giant pandas are hardly ever seen in their natural habitat, let alone photographed), later issues carried a correction and the photographer was dismissed. Where and from whom the misrepresentation came is any outsider's guess.

The text and captions that accompanied these pictures clearly made all the difference to their significance, yet this copy was added after the photographs had been taken. It is revealing that the American editor considered that the heading 'Pandas in the Wild' made only a 'technical difference'. It does, but such a difference can, in many areas of photography, be crucial for the audience.

Just as the way a picture is cropped or edited, in or out of the camera, can imply a different context, so the style of shooting can be suggestive. As a crude example, if the basic technique seems to be careless or hampered, the subtle inference could be that the photographer was working under pressure — in other words, that the situation was difficult and even dramatic. 'Subjective camera' is a term more commonly used in cinematography — it is a combination of shooting techniques that puts the viewer in the place of the camera and emphasizes the presence of the photographer in the scene — but it has a definite place in photojournalism. Azel's picture on page 15 is a perfect example of this treatment, with the camera, fitted with a wide-angle lens, appearing to dive into the crowd.

Finally, timing can be absolutely decisive in determining the point that a photographer decides to make. In Françoise de Mulder's photograph of a car bombing (page 100), timing was essential to the *structure* of the image, as opposed to Brigitte Dahm's picture of an explosion (page 20), where timing involved catching the critical instant. In the de Mulder example, timing has been crucial in producing a highly detailed photograph that asks to be read carefully. Such a situation is usually full of incoherent action but, while the confusion may impress itself on an observer, when translated into an image it is more likely to dissipate attention. What de Mulder has done is to choose a moment that is *visually* coordinated, to imply action and busyness. The photograph is not, of course, in any sense orchestrated, but fine anticipation on the part of the photographer results in a picture that has something of the tableau about it. Inappropriate though it may seem, the photograph has some balletic qualities, which make an odd, perhaps poignant, contrast with the ugliness of the event.

An underlying assumption in all these examples, and in photojournalism in general, is the need to stress the point. From a journalistic stance, it is absolutely reasonable, yet even this has attracted criticism from certain quarters. Sally Eauclaire pushes forward the cause of art photography by arguing that disasters are the province of 'photojournalists willing to serve up sweeping summaries for immediate, vicarious delectation and voyeuristic consumption'. She uses these words in discussing the work of Joel Sternfeld who, as we have already seen on page 61, deliberately avoids stressing any of the obvious newsworthy aspects of a situation. For an interesting comparison, look at the two photographs on pages 98-9. Both are of the same event, the

Below *At the start of the Soviet invasion of Afghanistan in 1981, Romano Cagnoni arranged to enter the capital, Kabul. Working surreptitiously, he traveled the streets of the city with his camera concealed under clothing, operating it with a rubber bulb by remote control. The cold, subdued colors in no way prettify this example of* photojournalism — *a charge frequently leveled at color film used in situations which many people are accustomed to seeing treated in black-and-white. In fact, such a bland, deliberately restrained use of color emphasizes the tension and harshness of the situation, while satisfying the needs of news magazines.*

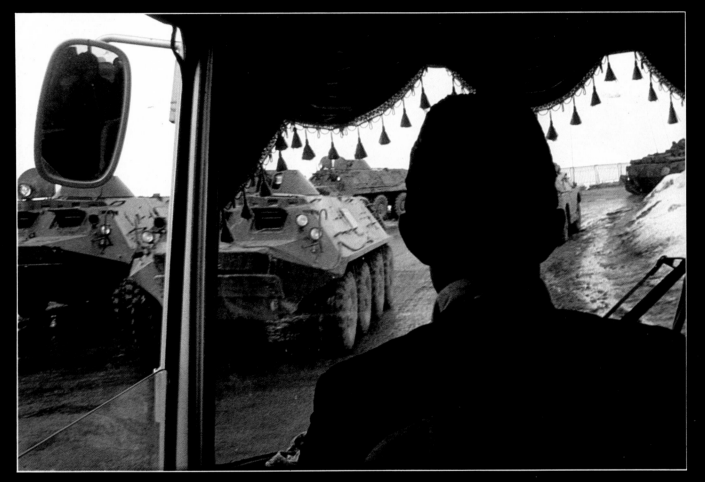

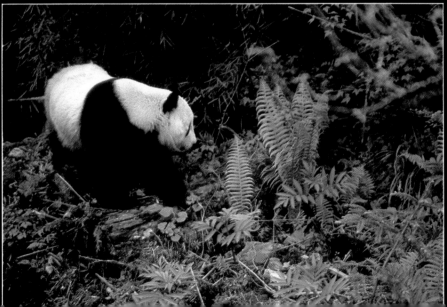

Left *One of a series of pictures taken by ex-GEO photographer Timm Rautert, this naturalistic view of the rare giant panda is perfectly legitimate as captioned on the transparency, but this series caused a furore when it was presented by* GEO *magazine as having been taken in the wild. The surroundings are natural, but enclosed, a fact which made all the difference to the use and reception of the photographs. In photojournalism, captions matter.*

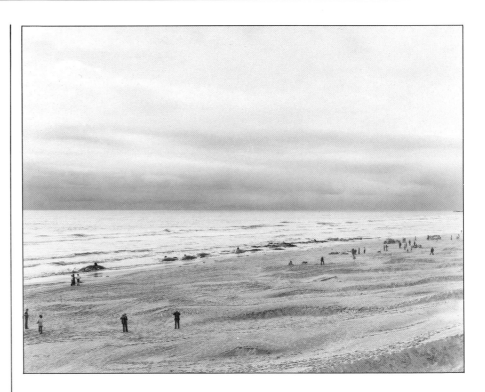

unexplained beaching of 41 whales on an Oregon beach in 1979, but what a difference there is in the photographers' intentions. Charlie Nye's closely cropped view shows the detail of the tragedy — a man listening for sounds of life from one of the large, helpless creatures, already sinking under its own weight into the sand. It is a classic photojournalistic treatment, providing the essential visual information coupled with human involvement. Sternfeld, on the other hand, gives us a view that is almost perverse in its understatement of the occasion. It is the view which any of us would have had if we had walked towards the shore and did not yet know what was happening; the difference is, of course, that Sternfeld *does* know, and is being deliberately unsensational; his picture may be odd for an audience accustomed to photojournalistic techniques, but it does demonstrate that news photography is not the only vehicle for treating unusual events.

The more skilled the photographer, the easier it is to use these techniques to increase the persuasiveness of pictures. This brings in its wake a responsibility not always appreciated, even by photographers themselves. Clearly, there are many reporting situations that can be manipulated very little, and no moral questions are raised. In others, however, the very existence of manipulative techniques tempts their use. The danger, of course, is misinformation, and it depends very much on the motives of the photographer. In most news reporting the photographer is mainly concerned with fulfilling the assignment and producing an unambiguous picture point. When an image does become misleading, it is often a case of a photographer going too far — imposing his own beliefs and feelings. In other areas, opportunities for telling a lie with a camera are greater.

Photography abounds with cases of faking, but most of these understandably remain unpublicized; nor are all of them serious. Some areas are more prone than others, through easier opportunities and greater editorial pressure for results. Wildlife photography has a

Left *and* below *Two versions of the same event — the unexplained beaching and stranding of 44 whales on the Oregon coast in 1979 — demonstrate not simply different manners of working, but different interpretations of the notion of an event. For Charles Nye, who took the photograph* below, *it was a reportable event in a news context,' and he treated it accordingly,* *showing plenty of relevant information and including a figure in the foreground to indicate scale and direct our interest. Joel Sternfeld, however, chose to question the idea of newsworthiness itself, and relegated the dying creatures and their attendant humans to elements in a landscape — the very opposite of the urgent, buttonholing approach of most press photography.*

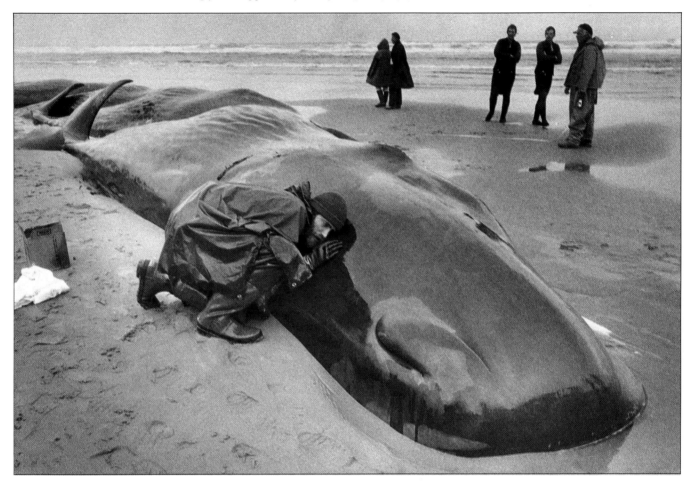

particularly checkered record in this respect, with all kinds of faking being presented to a non-expert audience (and non-expert editors) as the real thing. One major picture agency has even circulated dramatic animal silhouettes prepared from card cut-outs in the studio (with real skies added by copying), while another outrageous technique involves artfully placing stuffed animals in real natural surroundings. The case of the *GEO* panda mentioned earlier is simply an example of people going too far and attracting sufficient attention to be caught out. Similarly, natural enclosures for animals are common — in many zoos, for example — and a surprisingly large proportion of published animal photographs are taken in just such captive, or semi-captive, conditions.

The problem is to draw the line between legitimate reorganization of the circumstances and outright fakes. Staying for the moment with the field of nature photography, it is certainly indefensible to photograph one live animal being deliberately fed to a predator and then to publish the picture as if it were a natural event, as has happened. Nor is it acceptable to claim unequivocally that any photograph taken of an animal in captivity was actually taken in the wild. Below these cases, however, are

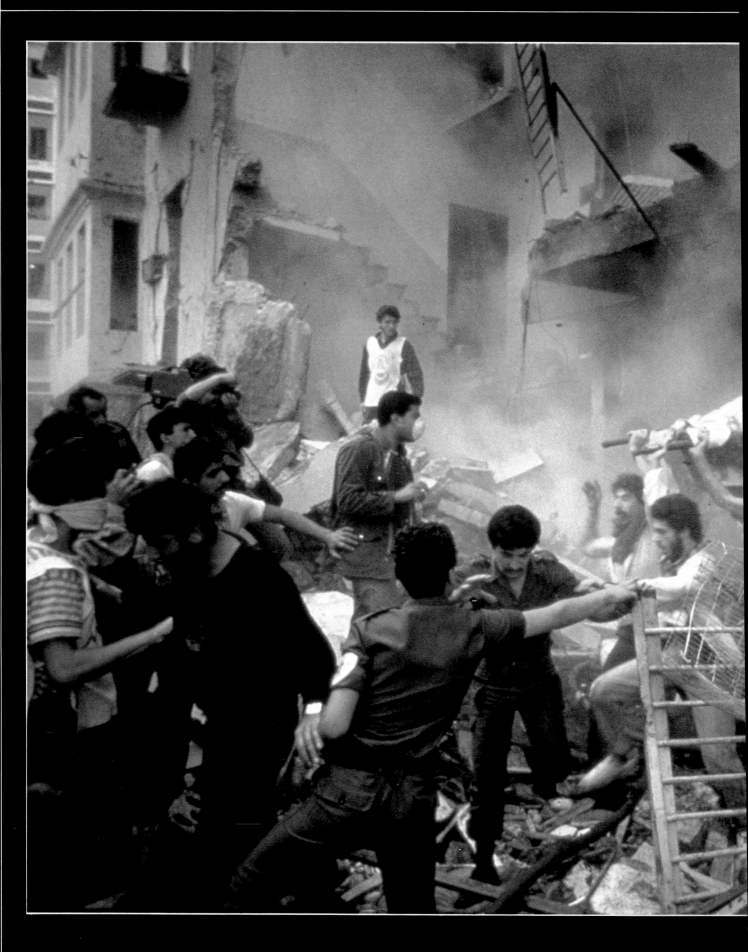

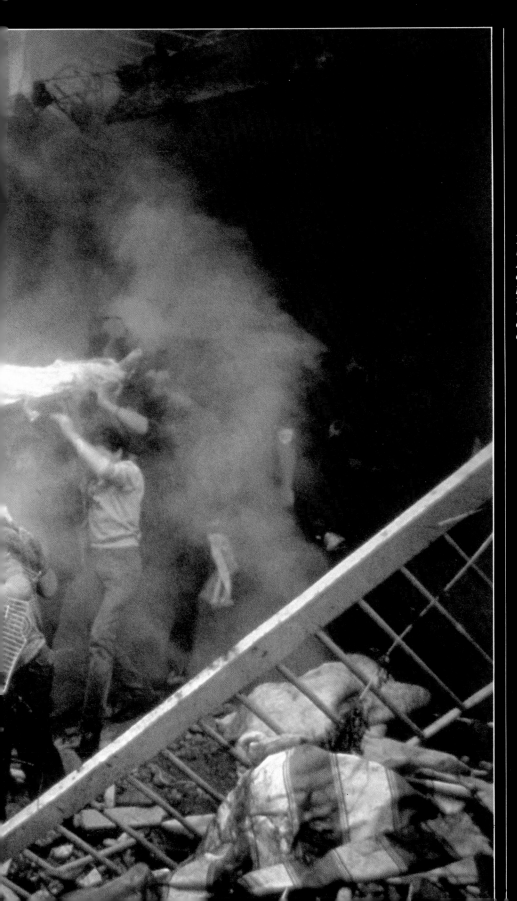

Left *From the wreckage of yet another bombing in Beirut, in 1983, Françoise de Mulder has made, through alert timing and positioning, a surprisingly cohesive photograph. The action is clearly described, no easy matter under such circumstances, but a result of the photographer's experience of working in difficult conditions.*

Below *In a theatre of war noted for its lack of battle photography coverage (British War Office policy did not encourage freely interpretative journalism during the Second World War), Sergeant Lenart Chetwyn's vital and atmospheric photograph of Allied troops attacking through a smokescreen is probably the most well-known and well-used from the Western Desert. It does, however, have a pedigree suspected by many, for Chetwyn's photographic unit was known to recreate battlefield situations.*

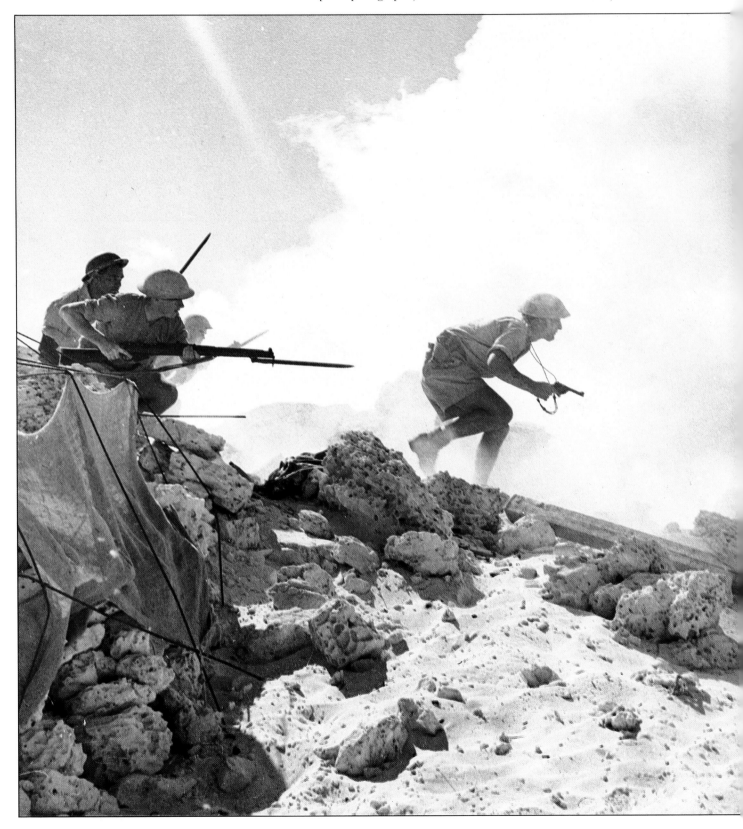

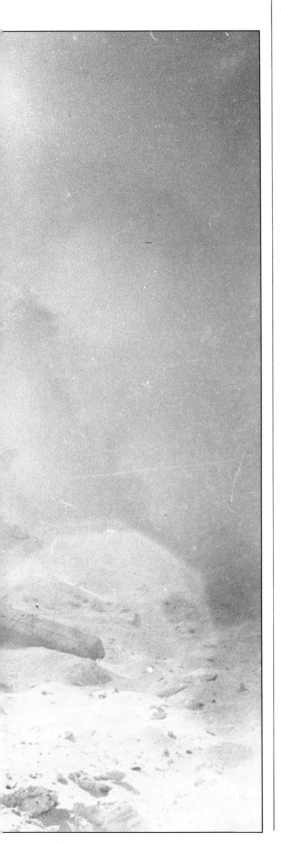

infinite shades of gray. What about a photograph of an insect, taken in a studio but among vegetation gathered from its natural home? Surely, there is nothing wrong here; in fact, a large number of published insect photographs are taken in this way, for technical control. The argument for legitimacy — a perfectly acceptable one — is that as a complete portion of the animal's environment has been transferred to the studio, there is no essential difference from photography on location. In any case, any wildlife photographer sufficiently capable of dealing with insects is also acquainted with their basic behavior, and is not likely to misinform. A caption declaring the controlled conditions would be virtually superfluous.

Why should the case of the panda be different? The principle is exactly the same; but what sets the two cases apart is the greater importance of pandas, which makes the *fact* of one having been photographed in the wild the sole issue. How well the picture was taken is not so important. To take another example, if the interest of a captive, photographed animal lies in its behavior rather than its appearance, how can the viewer judge whether this is natural? Photographs of defensive reactions in small animals are not uncommon in picture libraries — and for a good reason. In many cases the animal is simply reacting to the photographer's attempts to prod it into action. The only way to legitimize this would be to declare the circumstances in a caption.

Here lies the biggest practical loophole for fakery and misinformation — in all areas of photography. Between an innocently taken photograph and a misleadingly captioned published image is a chain of command that can involve a picture agent, editorial department and caption writer. In haste or through laziness, pictures are often captioned without consulting the photographer, sometimes with appalling inaccuracies. Many of these cases are simply mistakes but this loophole in the publishing system has also been used deliberately as a kind of excuse for allowing misinformation to slip through. It is, after all, easy enough for the photographer, and quite tempting, to omit details supplied with a photograph that might harm its sale, and allow picture editors to make whatever they want of it. By the nature of things, if a photograph looks good and fits the specifications, the editorial department of a magazine or book publisher *wants* it to be accurate in all essential ways, and so is susceptible to skipping over embarrassing details. This is the type of situation where, as Harold Evans says, the camera is used as 'an accessory to untruth'.

This type of 'untruth' begins to matter considerably when the subject matter is as important as, say, war. During the desert campaign of the Second World War, one of the most active of the British army photographic units was known as 'Chet's circus', led by one Sergeant Chetwyn, who was previously a Fleet Street photographer. He was responsible for the dramatic and frequently published picture (*see* left), in which Allied soliders are seen advancing into battle. *Time-Life* Books, for one, took the picture at face value, running it as a cover image and chapter-opener for a book on photography and captioning it as 'Australian troops advancing on a German strongpoint at El Alamein, 1942'. But Jorge Lewinski, in his admirable book *The Camera at War*, provides a very different background. Partly because British official policy discouraged front-line journalism, and partly because inactive troops were frequently available for 'exercises', reconstructed events were not uncommonly photographed. Lewinski quotes a British cameraman, Ian Grant, as saying that 'Chet's circus' were '...bribing the support of some of the troops who were relaxing with bottles of whisky.

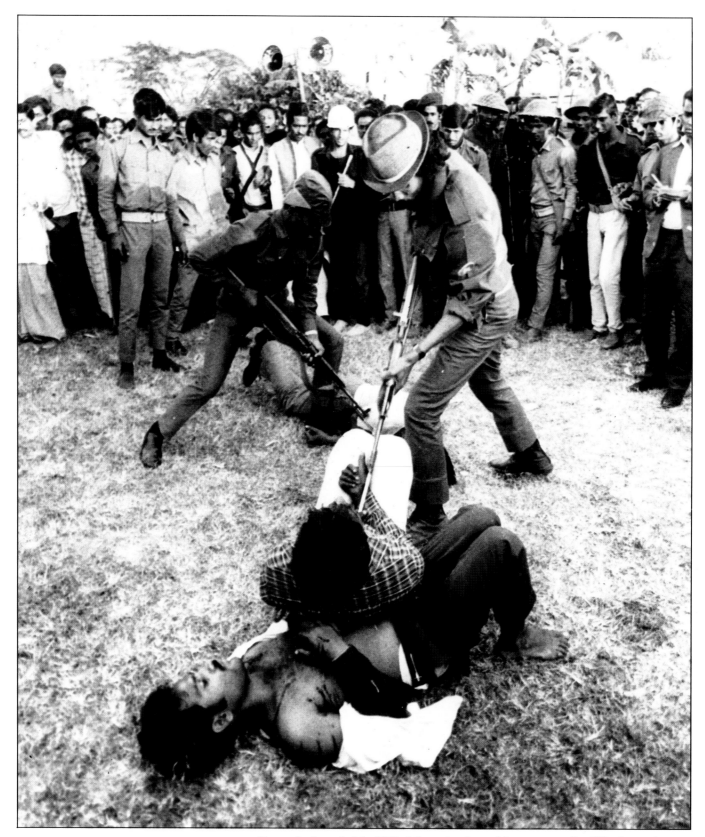

Above At the end of the 1971 civil war in East Pakistan, these Bihari prisoners were executed in Dacca's football stadium in front of Western cameramen. The taunting that preceded this killing gave the journalists warning of what was to come, and for many posed a difficult moral question — to record the atrocity or to try to defuse the situation by walking away. Some, including Marc Riboud, refused to use their cameras. Others, including Horst Faas, who took this photograph, did their job.

Then they created their own little battle sequences. You got things like Chetwyn sitting on the top of a tank with maybe a couple of tanks riding out in echelon in front out of the frame of his camera. They would charge forward. In front he would have a box of hand grenades and he would lob the grenades in front of him while he was filming. This was approved by the War Office, but a lot of photographers did not like it.' Understandably, Chetwyn himself does not agree with this interpretation, but Lewinski, who has interviewed other photographers, has no doubts: *his* caption to this photograph in his book reads: 'Desert war photograph, staged 1941.'

The temptation to overstep the bounds of legitimacy in pursuit of a strong image is not the only moral issue that faces photojournalists. Because we are so familiar with the camera in its role as recorder, apparently working passively from the sidelines, it is easy to forget that sometimes it can influence events as they happen. Photojournalists themselves also fail to appreciate this on occasion, becoming used to viewing the world through the eyepiece of the camera.

In the world of publicity, events are often staged specifically for press coverage. Known as 'photo opportunities', they regularly cover, for example, actors at the opening of a new show, heads of state at stops on a tour, and so on. Good staging ensures good pictures, and these are then more likely to be published. In less pleasant circumstances, however, such publicity-consciousness can have disturbing results. In moments of undisciplined violence, the very fact that press photographers are around, waiting for action, can encourage their potential subjects to special performances.

A famous, and disturbing, example of this occurred in 1971, at the end of the Bangladesh civil war. In the Dacca football stadium, a Bangladeshi leader had just finished a speech when he saw four captive Biharis. In the presence of a number of foreign photographers, who were given a front-line view of the performance, he then, after some showmanship and taunting, bayoneted the prisoners to death. Some of the photographers, anticipating what was about to happen, refused to take pictures on the grounds that the Biharis' lives might be spared if there were no publicity. Others did shoot, and the resulting pictures were widely published; some were even awarded prizes.

The questions that this event raises are indeed disturbing. Was this a show, at least partly staged for the press? Would a complete boycott by all the photographers present have made any difference? Was a photographer's obligation under these circumstances to try to prevent the killing or to show the horror of it to a wider audience? There are no easy answers.

Such moral dilemmas have increasingly become an issue in photojournalism. A landmark was Cornell Capa's exhibition and book *The Concerned Photographer*, in which the idealism that had been taking shape among such photographers as the members of the Magnum Agency was expressed coherently. Capa wrote, 'I have struggled for some time to define in words what I mean by "concerned photography", but as it often happens, the present is often defined in terms of the past. Lewis W. Hine, an early humanitarian with a camera, may have stated it best. "There were two things I wanted to do. I wanted to show the things that had to be corrected. I wanted to show the things that had to be appreciated." ' The tradition of social awareness in photojournalism, which reached a kind of peak in the late 1960s when

Below *Werner Bischof, whose most productive period was from the end of the Second World War until his death in a mountain car crash in Peru in 1954, had a natural, unaffected manner with children.*

This portrait of a Hungarian child in 1947 is one of the most well-known of several memorable pictures, and demonstrates the Swiss photographer's knack of producing images that capture general sentiments.

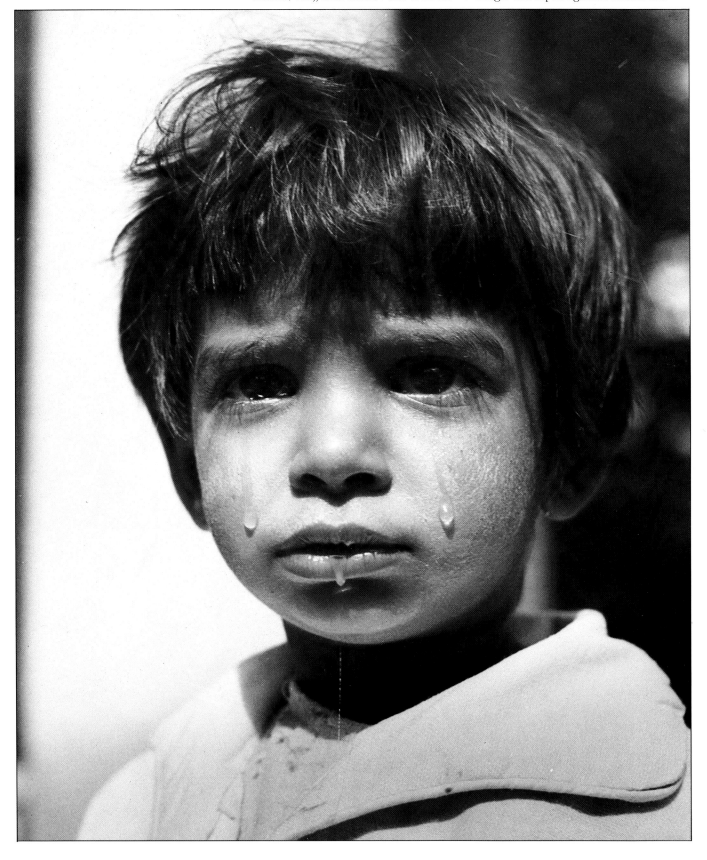

civil rights and the Vietnam war were major concerns, remains, although there is less editorial space today allocated to uncomfortable issues. In Cornell Capa's view, 'The concerned photographer finds much in the present unacceptable which he tries to alter. Our goal is simply to let the world also know why it is unacceptable.' The social and political views of those photographers who are 'committed' have for the most part been liberal rather than conservative, anti-establishment and concerned with the basic rights of the individual. Jill Freedman's photograph of the protest march (page 88) displays these attitudes as does Werner Bischof's compassionate photograph of a Hungarian child in 1947 (see left), although in a more general sense. Dan Weiner, whose work was exhibited in *The Concerned Photographer*, expressed the sentiments shared by such photographers when he wrote: 'The thread of humanism has greater vitality than ever, even if abused today.'

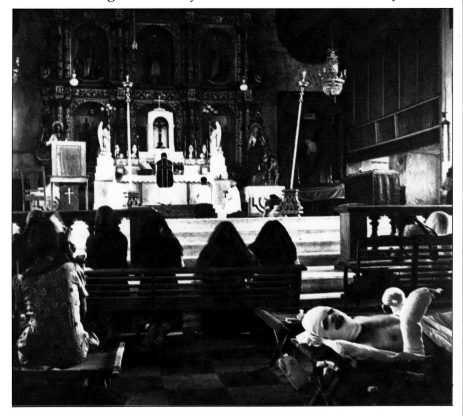

Left *Few photojournalists have had as great a sense of commitment to their work as W. Eugene Smith, who believed that if his photographs of war were sufficiently strong they could actually help to prevent other wars. In many of his best pictures, Smith's commitment is presented more as outrage. The power of this photograph of a badly wounded man in a Spanish church (from the* Hospital on Leyte *series, November, 1944) comes from Smith deliberately contrasting two worlds; the composition appears to favour the peace and order of the church, until we see the bandaged head and think about the man's disfiguring wounds and his suffering. His position in the frame suggests that he has been ignored — a reasonably accurate prognosis for war casualties.*

Wars are such an extreme human condition that they have drawn some of the best photojournalists to explore and comment. Such classic images as that of Eugene Smith's picture of a badly wounded man in a Spanish church (see above) bring home the personal misery and horror of human conflict. No one could disagree with the point being made here — war is evil. Where the stance of the photographer is so universally acceptable, there are usually no problems. Difficulties arise when the approach stops being broadly humanitarian. To say that war is wrong is one thing: to take sides in a particular way is another.

In photojournalism, the Vietnam war had a special place. As in no other war, the theatre of conflict was thrown open virtually to all comers. Provided that a journalist could show some accreditation, the American military would generally provide all the facilities, an open-house policy that, because it eventually backfired on the United States, is never likely to be repeated. Moreover, this was the 1960s and photography was

Far right *This well-known and harrowing image from the Vietnam war is, as we can see here, the work of two of the conflict's more famous photographers, Tim Page (**below**) and Philip Jones-Griffiths (**above**). A 12-year-old, killed by automatic fire from a US helicopter during the Mini-Tet offensive in Saigon, 1968, lies stretched out in a pick-up truck while her young brother weeps. The two photographs were taken within an instant of each other, both with wide-angle lenses. Tim Page was standing just to the left of Philip Jones Griffiths. To any photojournalist, it is natural that certain circumstances should inspire the same reaction from different photographers. Such convergence calls into question the all-too-common tendency to label photojournalists: Griffiths and Page are generally considered to have had quite different approaches to the Vietnam war.*

booming as a new, fashionable career. In the wave of youthful reaction in America and Europe against traditional social values, photography had a freewheeling appeal and could be picked up almost as quickly as a camera itself. Vietnam saw the arrival of countless first-time photographers ready to try their luck, in addition to the experienced professionals.

The result, photographically, was an onslaught. Often, the same scene was recorded nearly simultaneously by more than one camera. The two pictures (*see* right) of a boy, crying in anguish over the body of his dead sister lying blood-soaked in the back of a truck, are often mistaken for each other, yet are the work of two photographers whose reputations were made in Vietnam: Philip Jones Griffiths and Tim Page.

The remarkable similarity of this pair of images is not an isolated example, and helps to illustrate the density of reporting in Vietnam. At this instant, Griffiths and Page were together in a situation that provoked the same journalistic response, but the body of work of each of these photographers is actually quite different. Page is probably best known for his own personal part in the mythology of Vietnam, mainly through Michael Herr's book *Dispatches* and through a characterization of him in the film *Apocalypse Now*. He became, as William Shawcross put it, a 'war groupie', hooked on the appalling mixture of high technology, savagery and military bungling. When asked to produce a book that would end once and for all the glamour of war, he replied, 'Take the glamour out of war! I mean, how the bloody hell can you do *that*? Go and take the glamour out of Huey go take the glamour out of a Sheridan...Oh war is *good* for you, you can't take the glamour out of that. It's like trying to take the glamour out of the Rolling Stones...I mean, you *know* that, it just can't be done.' Among his photographs of the death and misery — common currency in Vietnam — are those that capture the cowboys-and-indians glamour of military hardware, the excitement of young GIs playing with deadly toys.

How different is Griffiths' attitude to the same war — much more in the tradition of the 'concerned photographer'. The anger in his book *Vietnam Inc.* is unconcealed, and he was eventually banned from returning to the war. To many people, Griffiths' uncompromising moral stance must seem the only valid one, but Page's coverage shows another side of Vietnam — and echoes the feelings held by a large number of the participating American forces. It is an aspect of photography's peculiar relationship with reality that two photographers with very different views of the same issue can at times come up with exactly the same image.

One of the conclusions that anyone should be able to draw from the examples in this chapter is that the photographs with the most immediate effect are those that need no explanation. For many people, the test of greatness in a picture is to remove it from its immediate context; according to this view, it should still have power when time has dissipated its newsworthiness.

As a result, in serious photojournalism a great deal of store is set by what could be called universal images. These are the pictures that avoid the specific event and the personalities of the moment, and show instead the basic emotions and conditions — joy, hunger, pride, misery, and so on. That, at any rate, is the ideal, although in practice it is not always easy to find simple images that tread the line between universality and stereotype. From the point of view of any photojournalist, this

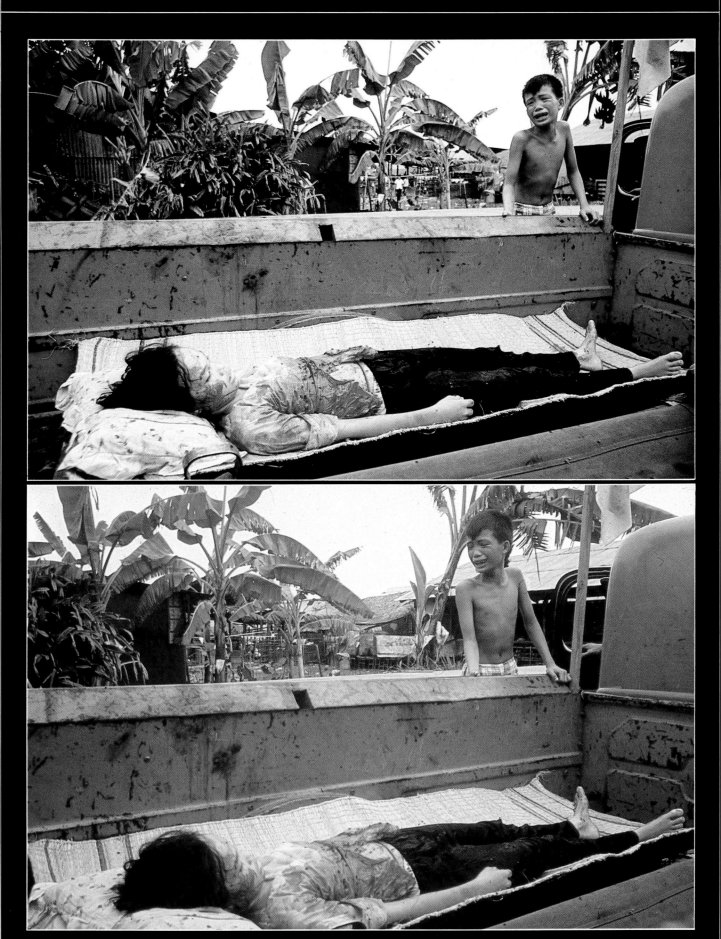

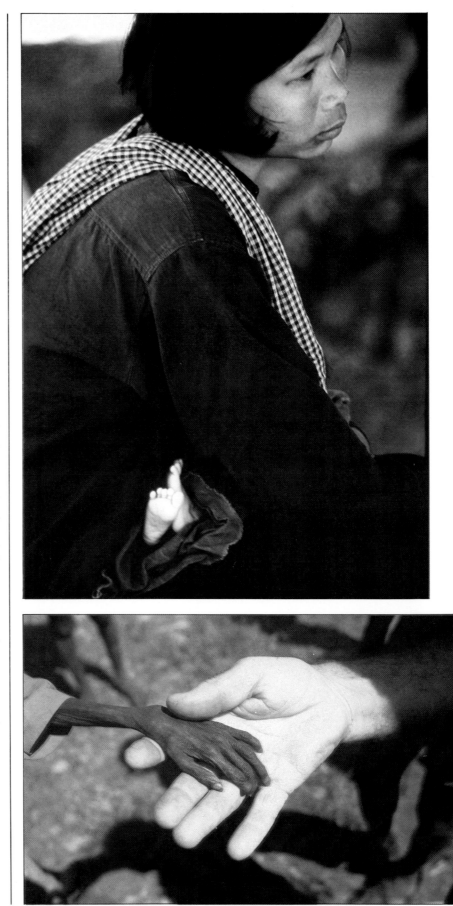

Above right *A picture that eloquently summarizes a news situation, this photograph of a Cambodian refugee mother and child, taken by David Burnett in a camp just inside Thailand, won the American 'Best Magazine News Photograph of 1979' award. The fragility of the refugee's plight is contained in the tiny feet — all we can see of the young child. As an example of the ethos of the single compelling image, this is perfect. Burnett says, 'I've always believed that if you stay behind your camera long enough, quietly and patiently, the subject will do something interesting, even amazing.'*

Below right *This horrifying close-up of a starving child's withered hand, photographed by Mike Wells, illustrated a story on hunger in Africa, run by the German magazine* Stern *in 1980.*

type of image is worth striving for, because this wide, instant appeal ensures that they are used prominently and frequently.

David Burnett's prize-winning photograph of a Cambodian refugee mother and child (*see* above left) is one such well-known example. The universality of the image, with the child's half-hidden feet implying vulnerability, has ensured its wide use, not only to illustrate features on the Cambodian situation, but to represent the general condition of refugees. That there is no background to tie the picture to a specific time and place is important. An even more powerful image, in the same vein but much more horrifying, is Mike Wells' photograph of the intimate effects of famine (*see* above right), combining, in the simplest and most effective way, the meaning of Third World starvation and the implication of Western aid.

It is tempting to say that photography is really in its element with such one-shot emotional images. They deliver their punch quickly, and all at once. Certainly they bear an extended look, but prolonged study is not likely to yield any surprises. Unlike, say, the complex structure of Françoise de Mulder's Beirut picture (page 100), these photographs have in common a simplicity of both idea and design. Symbolism is an important technique — the withered hand is so shockingly alien precisely because it appears in close-up.

These are classic images because they exploit photography's most effective quality — its ability to simplify everything. There is, however, something of a trade-off involved, for in distilling the situations into very basic images, they avoid closer involvement. While this in no way detracts from their worth, it means that the kind of reportage photography that makes sense only in its context has a harder time. In Joseph Koudelka's photograph (*see* below) there is clearly something

Below *This 20-year-old man has been convicted of killing his 18-year-old commonlaw wife, mother of their three children. He is at the scene of the killing at Jarabina, Slovakia, being watched by the residents and the police. So runs the caption to this photograph taken in 1963 by Joseph Koudelka and from his study of gypsies in Czechoslovakia. Like many pieces of photographic reporting, this picture is intriguing by itself, but needs its caption to be fully appreciated.*

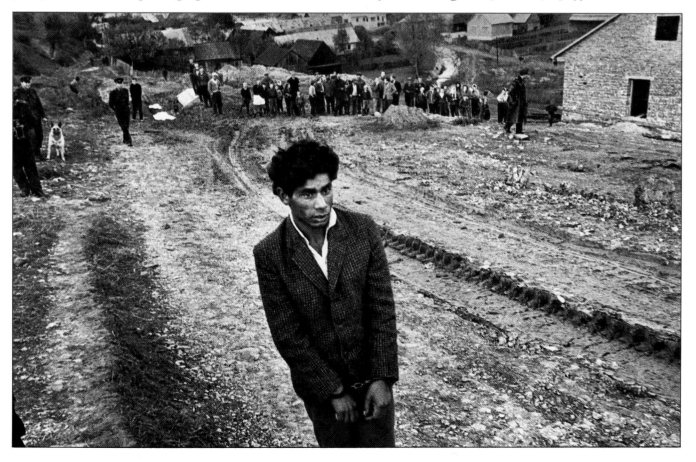

unpleasant afoot, but exactly what is impossible to be sure of without being told something of the context. The handcuffs and the uniformed figures in the background suggest that the man is a criminal, but the real story we can only tell from a fairly lengthy caption.

The photograph at right shows a beaming Harry Truman in 1948, holding what appears to be anything but reason for celebration. The story is that Truman had been faring badly in the polls, and the Chicago *Daily Tribune* had taken a chance in order to beat its rivals to the newsstands and anticipated the results before the last votes were entered. Truman, in what turned out to be a victory, had fun at the expense of the newspaper, and the result is a moment that is photographically well known. Without background *and* explanation, however, the effect of the picture is virtually unintelligible.

The need for explanation handicaps these two strong pictures — at least when compared with the broad use and acceptance of the other symbolic images. To appreciate the full effect of Koudelka's picture, for example, takes time, and the extra information required in a caption saps some of the immediate drama. Unfortunately, such thoughtful photographs tend to win less critical approval from most audiences.

This prejudice represents something of a confusion about photography's different roles. Photojournalism has the immediate concern of reporting events, not of seeking a place in the archives. In other words, because its circumstances are different then, if photojournalism must be judged, it should be judged within its own context, not as potential gallery photography. Wilson Hicks, the first picture editor of *Life*, coined the term 'third effect' to explain the synergy of photograph and caption, in which each is supposed to enhance the other. But the caption furnishes only one context for a news photograph; the photograph may be one of a series in a picture essay, or accompanied by a full written account, or displayed nakedly, without text. In many instances, it is not so much that the 'third effect' occurs because a caption improves some photographs, but that other photographs suffer from the *lack* of a caption.

This issue of the *context* of a news photograph has a direct bearing on the ultimately important question for serious photojournalism — does it have a measurable effect on its audience? A straightforward piece of reporting can be judged quite easily on how well it informs its readership, but whether the type of images that illustrate this chapter can actually influence public opinion is open to question. The more factual and down-to-earth a news photograph, the more likely it is to succeed in its admittedly limited task. But as soon as photographers begin to look for universal visual truths, they run the danger·of producing either images that no one could possibly disagree with, or else, if the image is genuinely shocking, of numbing the audience.

Photographers such as Eugene Smith have used their talents in the hope that some social good might come out of showing cruelty, inequality and suffering. Most editors also believe that there is a social service to be performed, although this may be tempered by the commercial needs of selling a newspaper or magazine. Indeed, social value is the only morally unassailable argument for photographing the bleaker side of human life. The record of effectiveness, however, is not at all clear and probably never can be. Just as, in the commercial world, it is difficult to prove that advertising actually increases sales by a measurable amount, so the effect of serious photojournalism on both the moral

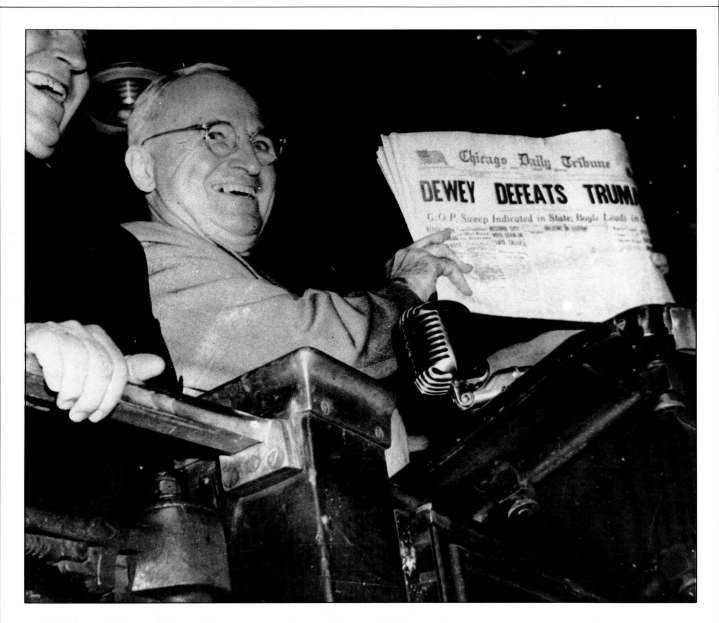

sensitivity of the public and on events themselves will always be a matter of opinion. Julia Scully, the editor of *Modern Photography*, in looking for evidence of pictures that ever had any effect on the progress of a war concluded that only Ronald Haeberle's photographs of the My Lai massacre in Vietnam played any significant part in turning public opinion, and added, 'but that seems almost negligible considering that photographers have been documenting wars since Roger Fenton went to the Crimean front in 1855'. John Szarkowski is in no doubt about *his* opinion, claiming that 'photography's failure to explain large public issues has become increasingly clear'. His argument is that photo-journalism has bitten off more than it can chew, and is inherently too superficial to deal with complex events.

John Berger is more cautious, but still pessimistic about the effect that photographs of agony and violence have on the public; in an essay on the war photographs of Don McCullin, he comes to the conclusion that any really shocking image merely brings out in the viewer a sense of his own moral inadequacy. As for the photographers themselves, however, the fact that there are those like McCullin who continue to take the risks argues even more strongly their opposite belief.

Above *An AP photograph from 1948, this odd piece of humour shows President Truman at St Louis' Union Station, holding up for the crowds a copy of the* Chicago Daily Tribune, *published a little too early on election night with the wrong guess. 'That', Truman told the crowd, 'is one for the books.'*

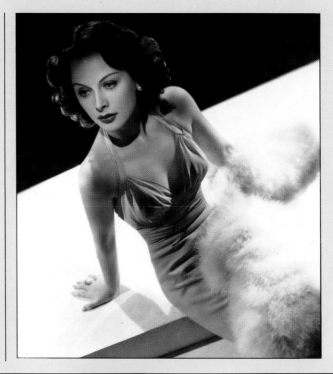

Right *and* **below** *Two portraits from the heyday of Hollywood glamour photography, one of Jean Harlow in 1935 by George Hurrell (**below**), the other of Hedy Lamarr by Laszlo Willinger (**right**), have one single objective: to present the star subjects as seductively and alluringly as possible. The Harlow portrait was made to promote her film Reckless, and so had more overtly sexual aims. The manner of most Hollywood promotional photography of the period was luxurious, three-dimensional and dramatic in its use of lighting, pose and settings. Large numbers of Klieg lamps were commonly used, each picking out a particular line or feature, but as both of these successful photographs show, 'It's not how many or what kinds of lights you use, but how they are placed,' as Horst, one of the leading romantic fashion photographers of the day, said. Strong diagonal lines were another method of conveying drama and theatricality, achieved in the Lamarr portrait by a combination of tilted camera on a geometric studio set, the pose, eye-line, and high angle of the back-lighting.*

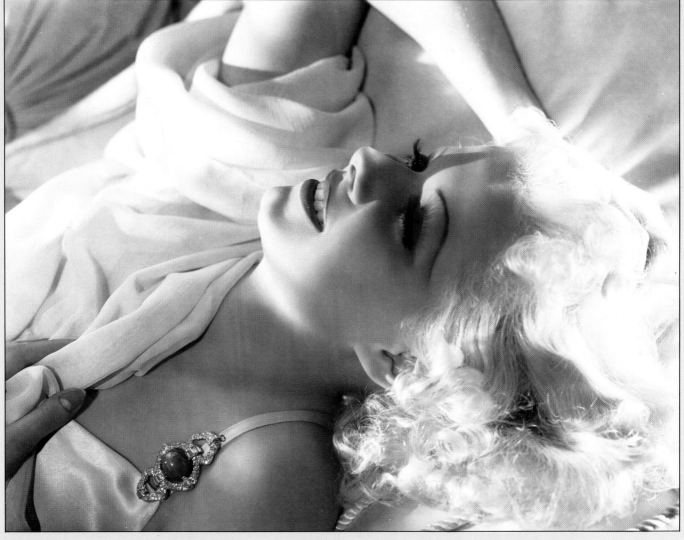

CHAPTER 5

Improving on Reality

'If you just take a straight picture of what's there
it destroys the mystery, the magic.'
Art Kane

'Add sunset here.'
Advertising agency's note to retoucher

Two scenes from the American west. The first is in the tradition of the grand vision, established by three or four generations of large-format photographers and a number of Hollywood films; the view, of a delicate arch in Utah, has been selected with care, the shot timed for the precise moment of the day when shadows would race across the fore-ground slope of rock, the colors rendered richly and the sky deepened for contrast with a filter (page 117). This is the spectacular treatment, the approach to landscape photography that searches for the splendor and then treats it in the most striking way. The second scene, by comparison, is subdued (page 116). The lighting is flat, spreading pollution filters the air and reduces the panorama, and there is no awe-inspiring natural feature to focus the viewer's attention. Nature here is not particularly grand, and the photographer, Robert Adams, is an articulate environmentalist who has preferred to show the average condition rather than the special.

Both photographs are 'real' in the sense that no manipulation took place (aside from the filter), but one shows the kind of landscape that we would most enjoy seeing, while the other shows what we are more *likely* to see. On a tour of the American wilderness the spectacular scene would be a destination; Adams' view from Lookout Mountain would be an all-too-typical stop along the way. Adams' intention in this respect is, of course, deliberate.

It is no surprise that most photographers should prefer beauty of subject or treatment to plainness. Given that even the least competent can choose to treat a scene in different ways, the easiest option in terms of approach is to show the subject at its best. For most people, indeed, an attractive image is its own justification. This natural tendency to make things look good is just what Robert Adams and a number of other

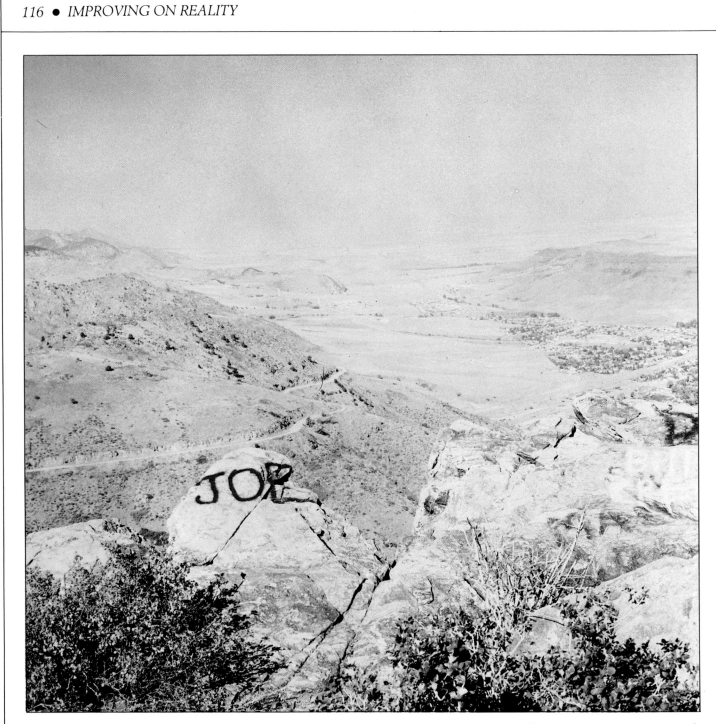

modern American photographers are challenging, pointing out with some justification that such a cosmetic view of life is itself a kind of cliché. This may be a legitimate argument, but to a mass audience, the contest is already rigged — luxuriant, elegant images are the ones most in demand.

For most art critics, a blatant commercial motive in a picture is hard to swallow and, as beautifying photography is basically aimed at pleasing its audience, it has had something of a rough time in the galleries. The basis of critical disapproval for the kind of images that grace the pages of the *National Geographic*, amateur photographic magazines and a large proportion of consumer advertisements is principally that the photographer has taken the easy way out, and opted to perform a standard treatment for the subject rather than look for an original approach. To an extent, this is true; while glamour may not be easy to achieve, it is at least an obvious direction for those unsure of how to portray their subject.

Left *Robert Adams, a college teacher who began taking photographs full-time in 1970, aims deliberately for a neutral, restrained approach to the American landscape. This view of modern America was taken in 1970 with a large-format view camera, and is entitled* From Lookout Mountain — Smog, No.7, *a description that reveals Adams' environmental concerns.*

Below *This late afternoon view of Delicate Arch in eastern Utah is a celebration of the great beauty still to be found in the wild places of America. There has always been a conflict of opinion among those concerned with protecting the environment as to whether the cause is better served by showing the beauty that remains or the ravages that have been wrought — to inspire or warn.*

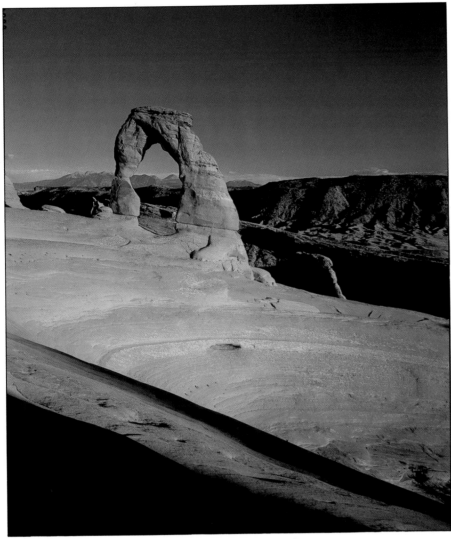

Lack of direction is responsible for sapping more photographic energy than anything else, and the pursuit of the visually ideal is one kind of solution.

On the face of it, then, photographers who beautify may seem to be uncritical of their subjects, even lazy. In commercial work — advertising in particular — even how the picture should look has already been decided by the client, and the job that remains for the photographer is one of execution. Nevertheless, these criticisms are somewhat superficial. High moral stances on motive and treatment may sound very satisfying in a critical essay, but there are no good grounds for denying an audience photography for entertainment rather than edification, particularly if the result of such an intellectual approach is to produce pictures that are visually dull.

Moreover, as the examples show, the processes of beautification are quite complex, and extend further than the techniques employed. In order to beautify a subject well, rather than in a stereotyped fashion, a photographer must be sensitive to all its qualities, and capable not only of analyzing it objectively — how different types of lighting will affect it, for instance — but also of reacting to it subjectively. Success depends quite heavily on being able to identify what other people will respond to — finding an original enough treatment to arouse the viewer's interest, but one which is not so eccentric that it leaves the audience behind. Having an eye for beauty and the skill to display it are no mean abilities for any photographer.

When such cosmetic photography is performed with little talent, the

Below *Timing, viewpoint, and of course the selection of a dramatic subject, characterize travel photography of the exotic. Taken just after sunset, on the evening of the Burmese Buddhist festival of light, this picture of the Shwe Dagon pagoda in Rangoon makes the maximum use of color to convey a sense of spectacle.*

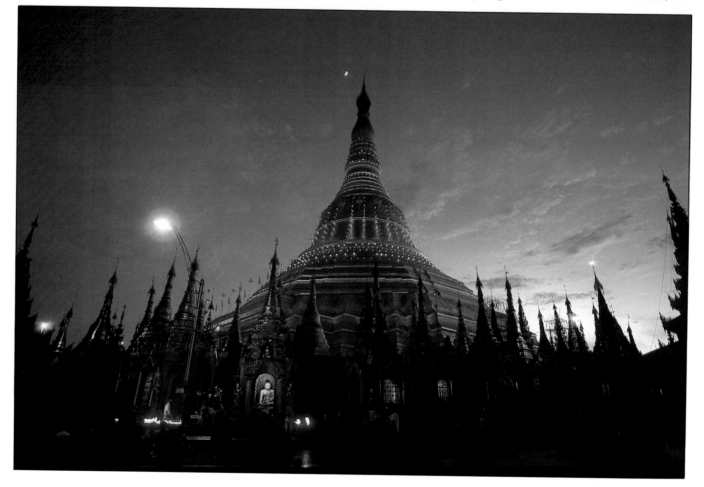

results are, naturally, shallow and cloying. This, however, reflects the degree of ability and is not inherent in the *notion* of adding glamour to a picture. Although the average level of skill in this area is not high, including as it must most amateur photography, it would not be fair to judge all such imagery by the worst of picture postcards. The best photographers in this field put at least as much effort into exploring their subject matter as do those gallery photographers who assume a less 'commercial' point of view; the difference is that in glamourized photography that effort is turned into pictures that appeal to a wide audience.

One of the most natural targets for the beauty treatment is travel, in its exotic sense. Among the earliest uses of the camera was to bring the oddest and most spectacular corners of the Earth back to a domestic audience. In the beginning, photographers such as John Thomson (pages 82-3) could be content with a relatively documentary style — the

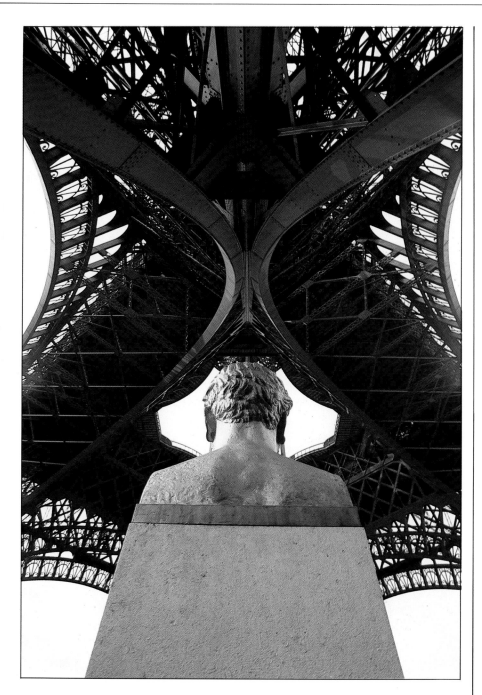

Left *A new view of a heavily photographed subject, this picture of the Eiffel Tower by Axel Lenoir relies on a careful exploration of the subject and a striking, symmetrical design to create a different treatment. For the next photographer who attempts an original view, this is one more possibility crossed off the list.*

subjects were sufficiently unusual that they spoke for themselves. More recently, however, with foreign travel within the reach of a large part of photography's audience, such plain treatment no longer excites. Even so, the legacy of exotic adventure still persists, and it is quite widely accepted that the more distant or strange the place, the more dramatic it should seem. Exotic, of course, is relative, and while the photograph of the Shwe Dagon Pagoda (*see* left) is full of visual splendor, the drama of seeing it for the first time is transient. A place is only exotic for a visitor,

Another way of looking at this is to reiterate the truism that it takes a fresh eye to find the best visual qualities in a scene. If forced to consider the Eiffel Tower as a picture subject, most Parisians would probably claim that they were sick of the sight of it. Axel Lenoir's treatment of the subject, however, conveys a new enthusiasm for one of the world's most over-photographed sights (*see* above).

8

Photographing the Parthenon

The working process of finding a flattering treatment for a subject often involves a logical succession of moves, assessing the problems and then exploring the permutations of viewpoint and lighting. The object here was to photograph the Parthenon, an important tourist attraction, in the most attractive way. To do this, the photographer had to find a viewpoint that excluded modern Athens and the jumble of street furniture at the base of the Acropolis (1, 2 and 3). A further complication was that part of the Parthenon was covered in scaffolding. Low light conditions at dusk and dawn (4, 5, 6 and 7) helped to obscure the unwelcome detail and add color and interest. The final result, taken with a telephoto lens from a nearby hill exploits the dawn light to hide the scaffolding (8).

1

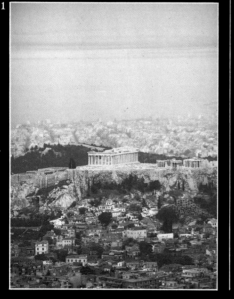

2

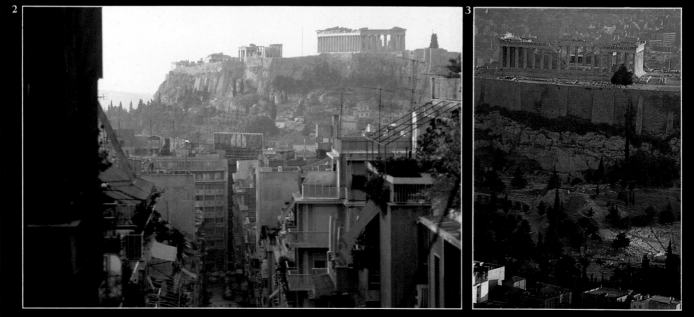

3

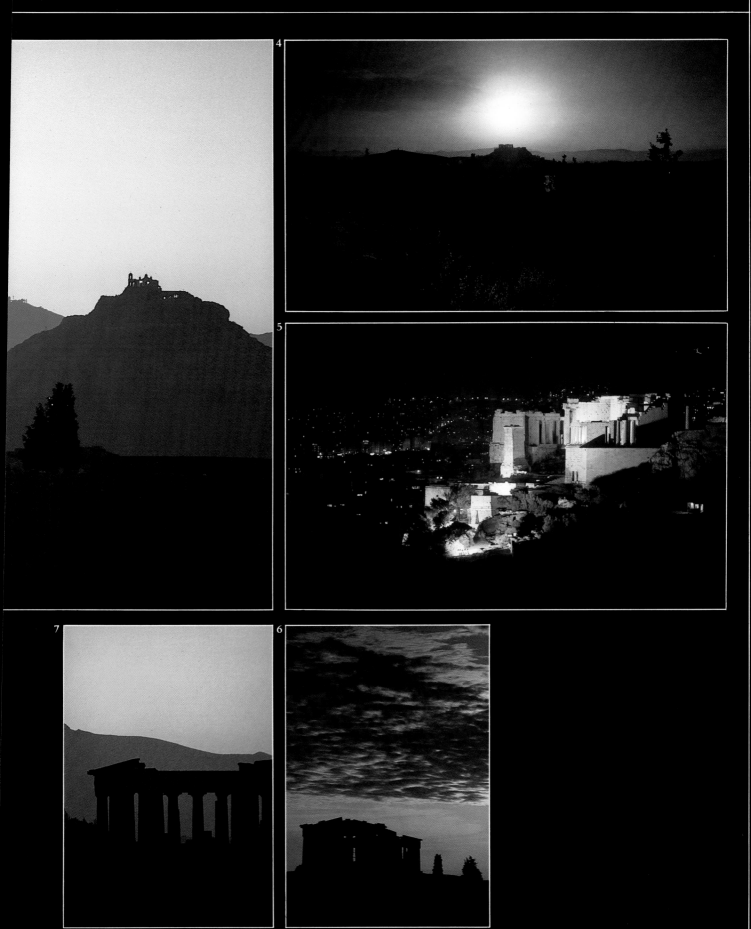

side from this quality of freshness – upon which, after all, all original work depends – there are also a number of more practical strategies photographers can use to 'improve on reality'. One of the most fundamental is to reorganize the content of the shot, excluding by whatever means the parts of the view that are unattractive, unharmonious, distracting — the frayed edges of a scene. This can be done not only by cropping in to remove, say, telegraph wires and garbage cans, but by examining all the possible viewpoints with the full permutations of lenses, and by shooting under certain lighting or weather conditions. Mist, for instance, can mute unwanted elements as effectively as the most elaborate retouching. An example of this reorganization is the treatment of the Acropolis (pages 120-1). Athens, as the first photograph shows, from street level, is not on the whole a beautiful city, yet the object in this case was to produce an attractive photograph of its major visitor attraction, the Parthenon. The working method was to look for a high viewpoint that would exclude both the foreground street furniture and

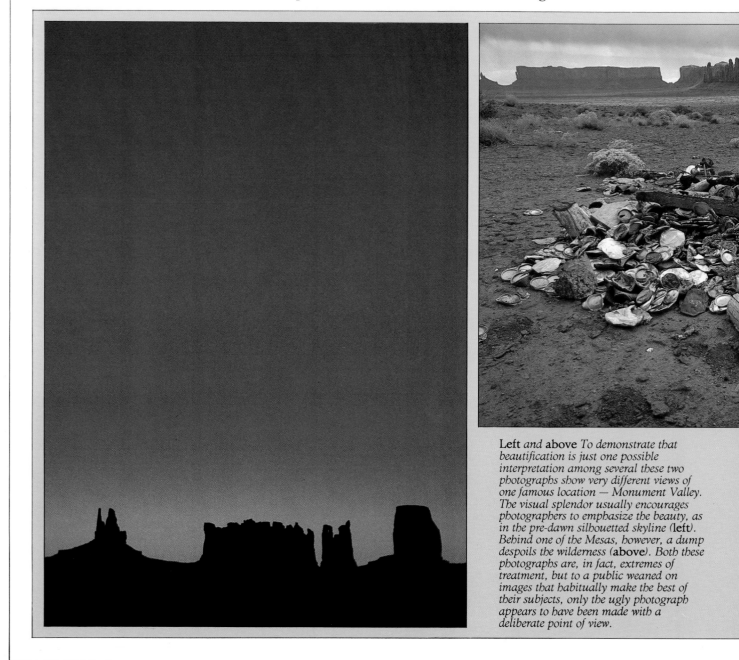

Left *and* **above** *To demonstrate that beautification is just one possible interpretation among several these two photographs show very different views of one famous location — Monument Valley. The visual splendor usually encourages photographers to emphasize the beauty, as in the pre-dawn silhouetted skyline (*left*). Behind one of the Mesas, however, a dump despoils the wilderness (*above*). Both these photographs are, in fact, extremes of treatment, but to a public weaned on images that habitually make the best of their subjects, only the ugly photograph appears to have been made with a deliberate point of view.*

background apartment blocks. The assignment was complicated by the fact that scaffolding was erected along one side of the building. In the final version, the camera position was a nearby hill-top, the lens a telephoto to exclude reminders of the grimy city, and the lighting a dawn silhouette to hide the scaffolding. The sequence of eight pictures shows the work in progress — a methodical examination of how the Parthenon appeared at the beginning and end of the day from each of the surrounding hills.

Timing, particularly in scenic photographs, is an essential consideration, and an hour or two either side of dawn and dusk are especially favored periods. The warm colors, interesting skies, and possibilities of including the sun and its reflections in the design are obvious advantages, some of which are clearly in evidence in the photograph of the arch in Utah (page 125) and that of bird's nest collectors in Thailand (*see* below). A further reason, however, is that such times generally have romantic connotations for most viewers. Another popular choice for

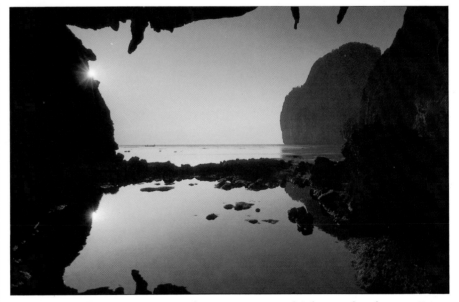

shooting is the storm-spectacle — moments which are clearly transitory and special.

Color is, as Maurice de Sausmarez says in *Basic Design: the dynamics of visual form*, such 'an intimately subjective field of experience' that it has a central role in conveying what the photographer considers to be 'beauty', itself a subjective response. The expressive function of color can work in many different ways, but richness is probably the quality used most often, with such spectacular results as Yoshikazu Shirakawa's photograph of Mount Everest (page 124). The time of day, as we have just seen, is one important control; another, used here, is filtration. This can be performed in a variety of ways, at the time of shooting, in a duplicate, or in making a print, with filters that tint the entire image, or a graduated part of it (as in the photograph of Monument Valley, *see* far left), or a part of it that has been polarized. Even the reciprocity characteristics of the film can be used for their color sensation, as in the photograph of a night storm in Rangoon on page 30. It is just such maximum use of hues against which the proponents of the New Color movement rail: the critic Max Kozloff condemns such treatment as being concerned with 'not the sensations, but the sensationalizing of colour'.

In certain conditions, the graphics of the view can be exaggerated, or at least stressed by manipulation of color. The fantastic shapes of desert

Below **right** *In photographing outdoor scenes, and natural landscapes in particular, there are certain standard techniques that, if not always guaranteed to beautify, will at least put a good face on the subject. Here, the photograph has been timed for the enriching colors of sunset, a wide-angle lens used so that the sun can be included in the picture without overwhelming it, and water surfaces exploited for their mirror-like reflections.*

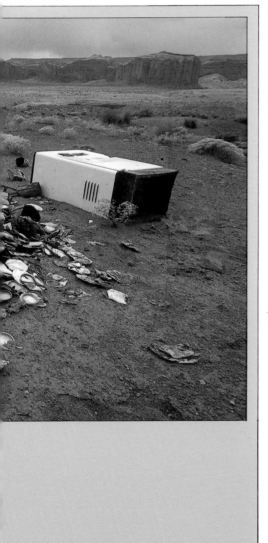

Below *Filtration applied to an already dramatic view — of Lhotse in the Himalayas — has produced a landscape that appears almost unearthly. Japanese photographer Shirakawa, known for his painstaking and strenuous approach to the world's most impressive landscapes, has here pulled out all the stops to produce an image that sacrifices realism for drama.*

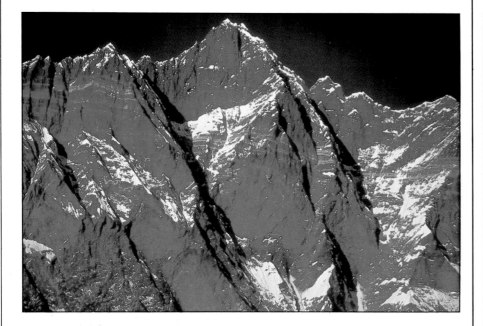

arches in Utah in the photograph on page 125, is a tempting candidate for this approach.

One of the great difficulties of the cosmetic approach to photography is the need to temper the use of standard techniques — the formula methods of lighting, camera angle and so on. They are tried and tested, but can also become clichés. It would have been easy, for instance, to include the large orange ball of a setting sun in one of the Parthenon pictures on pages 120-1, but this is a dangerously overworked type of image.

Similarly, in photographing people, a soft-focus lens will hide blemishes, make skin texture look better and provide a more soft, seductive aura, yet, though it works technically, it is a little too sugary for most modern tastes. While it is possible to get away with being obvious and imitative, in order to have any *positive* success with a glamorous photograph, some originality is crucial. In other words, while it may be tempting to be lazy and go for a stereotype, the result is likely to be acceptable to the audience but not stimulating. Nevertheless, as these examples have shown, there are some standard beautifying techniques and not to use any of them would simply be perverse.

Commercialism is never far from this area of photography, for under-standable reasons. Because glamorous images appeal to a sizeable audience, they are by definition very marketable. Glamour can be used

Below *One method of suggesting the exotic in a landscape is to use techniques of abstraction, in order to create an unusual graphic image that conveys little of the real-life nature of the scene. This view of a natural rock arch uses a direct view of the sun and close cropping to create a silhouette that is at first difficult to decipher.*

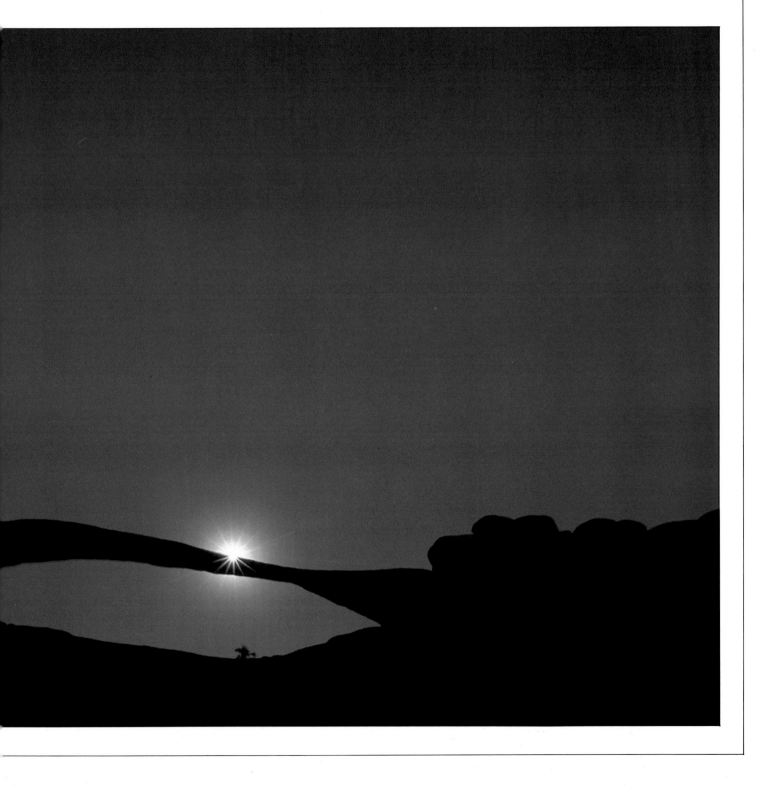

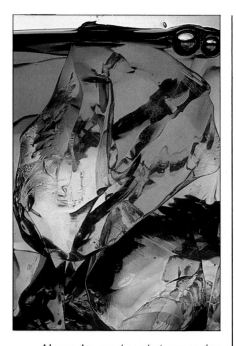

Above *Among the techniques used to imbue the commonplace with glamour and visual interest are close and unusual viewpoints, and studio lighting that enhances the richness of color and tonal variety. In this enlarged view of a full whisky glass, the framing has been chosen to exclude the obvious (the edges of the glass or the setting) and to concentrate instead on the subtle shifts in color as the liquid is seen through different thicknesses of ice cube. The lighting is purely from behind.*

Right *Although familiarity with the brand name and product is a precondition for the success of such images, this close view of condensation on the outside of a bottle of gin conveys, without any extraneous clutter, two important sales features of the advertised product — it is refreshing, and it is pure. The information is carried sensually rather than literally. The obliquity in this advertisement (the word 'gin' does not even appear, nor does any actual gin) is justified by the fact that this version had been preceded by a long-running campaign that had already built up consumer awareness.*

to sell the photograph itself, in a picture magazine, or to sell its subject matter, in advertising and public relations. The techniques for creating glamour have not only been used in the commercial world, but have been actively developed and encouraged by it. The most sophisticated of this photography has been nurtured within the advertising industry, and this in turn has had an influence on what is acceptable in other, non-commercial subject areas. One of the strongest examples of this is the elevation to pictorial stardom of quite humble still-life objects. The highest advertising budgets are for consumer products, and many of these are as mundane as can be. Nevertheless, they have attracted the greatest creative effort, with considerable success. In the eye of the public that absorbs these images, ski-boots, glasses of whisky and perfume bottles have actually become fit subjects for attractive pictures, every bit as much as landscapes and people.

Another great crucible of photographic glamour was Hollywood. The end of the star system removed the impetus for carefully engineered portraits to enhance, build or even change the image of an actor but, in its hey-day, Hollywood glamour photography reached some remarkable peaks of success in presenting its subjects at their very best (page 114).

Today advertising is the greatest patron of photography, bar none.

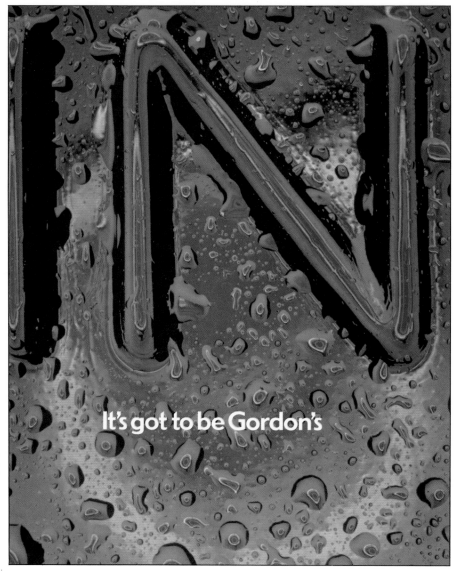

It's got to be Gordon's

Although the best work in this area is highly sophisticated, astute, and performed to standards of quality and technique that are far ahead of other fields, the commercial motives (and the high financial rewards) have worked against its critical acceptance. Most advertising photography is indeed prosaic, because it must suit the needs of creatively undemanding clients. Further, the layout of an advertisement nearly always precedes the photography; if the design calls for a straightforward product shot, for example, there is little room for imagination. But when a photographer is given a little creative freedom, even unlikely subjects can be the basis of elegant or imaginative pictures, photographs that transcend the immediate task of selling a product, such as those by Lester Bookbinder, shown below.

With such images, advertising has contributed to the creative development of mainstream photography in two interesting ways. The first, already mentioned, is that it has broadened the range of acceptable subject matter. The second is that, with so much orientation towards the presentation of products, advertising has encouraged the exploration of the visual qualities of an object. In product photography — still-life for the most part and the foundation of advertising illustration — the subject is given; the job is to make it look good. This ability to extract interesting

Below *Even the least prepossessing of subjects can be given visual interest if sufficient photographic flair and imagination is exercised. Indeed, a subject as inherently unexciting as a stack of magazines might be said to need photographic help. Illustrating 10 years of publication of the magazine* Management Today, *Lester Bookbinder has used both filtration and differential focus to produce a simple, elegant design that does not try to fight or overwhelm its subject.*

Below left *The commission, from* Vogue, *was to portray something intangible, but commercially important — smell. Lester Bookbinder's imaginative solution was to simplify and to avoid being visually literal. He juxtaposed sprigs of flowers and herbs (fresh country smells) with a sensitive, shadowy image of a woman. Optical distortion helps the juxtaposition, suggesting clouds of perfume, and contributes to a delicate image — in keeping with the subject.*

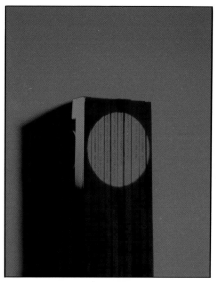

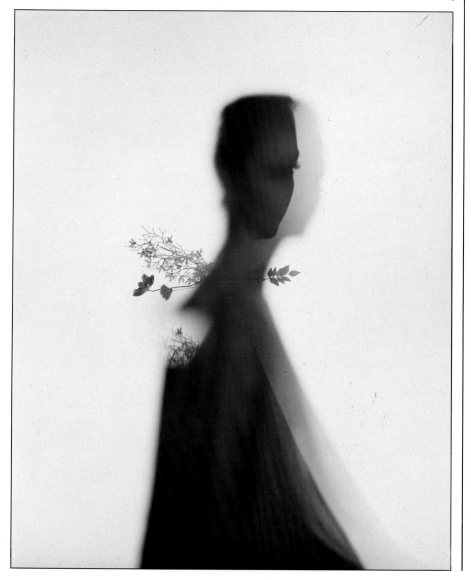

Below left *and* **below** *These two photographs for Citroën cars by John Claridge show the vehicles in evocative scenery. On location, a photographer working with cars has the dual problem of needing to find an attractive large setting and finding or providing broad area lighting that will show the form of the car clearly without distracting reflections. Most vehicles have several brightly reflecting surfaces. Here, Claridge has used high viewpoints so that the upper parts of the cars are prominent, and has then photographed them under smoothly toned cloudy skies. A neutral graduated filter on the photograph* (**below**) *reveals the tonal differences in the clouds to the camera (their reflections in the car are much brighter), while a blue cast to the photograph* (**below left**) *helps the unify the picture.*

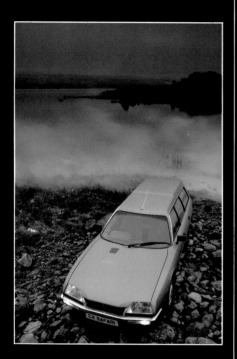

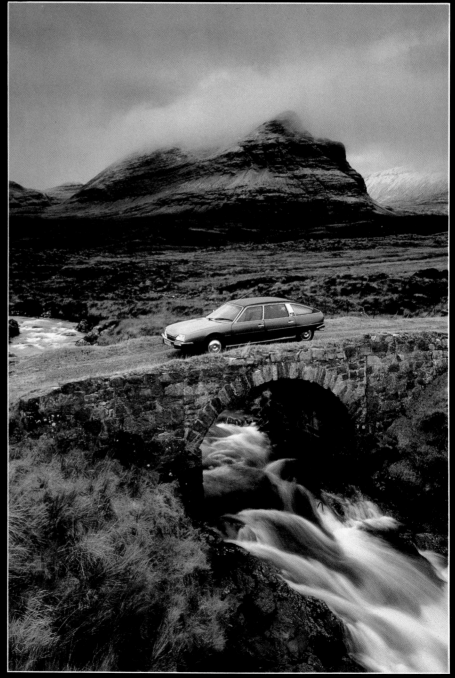

images out of almost any subject has come in useful when applied to non-commercial art photography.

A more specific task of advertising photography is to develop one particular quality of a subject as far as possible; often it is a non-visual quality — a smell, taste or texture — and this makes the problem more interesting. A prime example is the specialized area of food advertising. While much commercial food photography is relatively uninspired — concerned mainly with presenting specific dishes or products as attractively as possible — the best express the sensuality of eating. A virtually universal aim is to present the food in as appetizing and decorative a manner as possible, but as much of food's delight comes from the sensations of taste and texture, lighting and composition are even more crucial considerations than they are normally. Robert Golden, whose work is shown here on pages 130-1 says: 'If you create a mood, then you create a sense of life, and within that sense of life you create the relationship between people and their experience of food. This is all a sensual experience; food *is* an integral part of the sensuality of life, just like sex. I don't think they're a far cry from each other, in fact.' Part of Golden's technique for conveying this sensuality is a sophisticated use of filters to soften the image and so both help to blend the elements together and hide 'unseemly detail'.

Such product photography, however sophisticated, is nevertheless fairly straightforward in principle. Advertising does have many more complicated strategies for attracting attention and for persuading. One of the biggest developments in the industry in recent years has been a determination to entertain the audience.

Conservative advertising philosophy says that the only sensible, cost-effective approach is simply to sell the product by saying loudly and clearly what it will do for the customer; if the resulting advertisement is irritating and unstimulating, the justification is that this sales technique works *despite* the audience's reaction — brash car salesmanship applied to a mass market. The counter-view is that pummelling the audience alienates them, and that advertising should engage the public's attention by other means — in other words, by providing entertainment. The merits of these two opposite positions is not the issue here, and their differences are unlikely to be resolved, given the difficulty of isolating the effect of advertising from all the other factors involved in selling products. What *is* important for photography is that the entertainment philosophy in the advertising industry has created an enormous opportunity for imaginative pictures.

The main surge of the entertainment strategy occurred in the 1960s; despite falling in and out of favor with various branches of the industry, it is still one of the liveliest areas of commercial work. Certainly, the various annual industry awards favor entertaining advertisements quite heavily and this provides a clue as to why they continue in force. In the general absence of agreement on why and how any advertising works, personal opinion is prominent. Research and marketing departments will always claim to be able to measure the effectiveness of advertisements, and their methods often show that the dullest ones work quite well; copywriters and art directors, on the other hand, argue even more strongly that effectiveness cannot be pinned down, in order to preserve their right to work as freely as possible.

The result of all this is that photography (copywriting also, but that is not our concern here) has more exciting opportunities than perhaps it

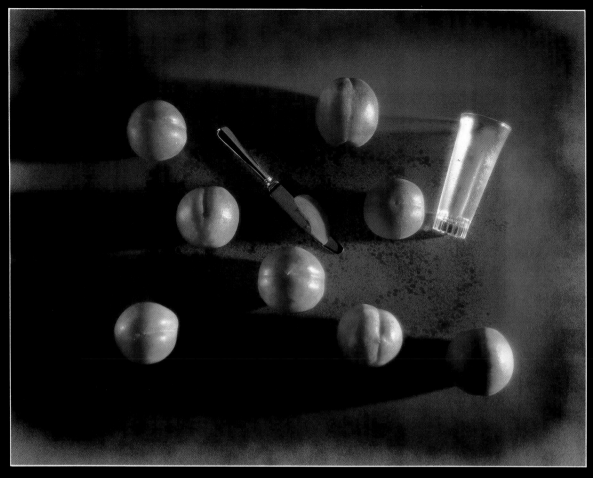
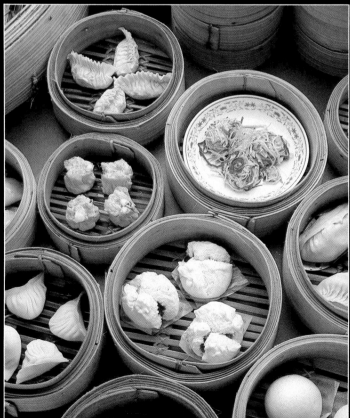
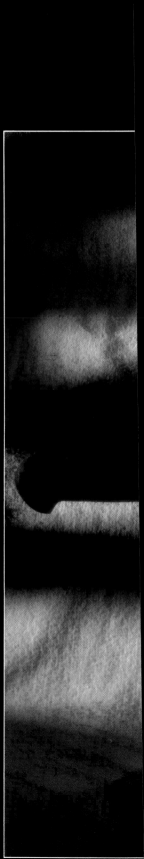

Food photography *In both of the atmospheric studio photographs (**left** and **below**); taken for a self-promotion calendar by Robert Golden (a specialist in food photography), the lighting has been set up with great care and subtlety. The chiaroscuro is important to the evocation of mood, and is in part a reaction to what Golden sees as the dull standardization of most studio lighting techniques. The delicately flared highlights are achieved by combining diffusing filtration over the lens and a concentrated distant light source.*

Low lighting angles have given the photographer opportunity to experiment with shadow shapes as positive elements in the composition. Despite such premeditation in the arrangement of these studio pictures, Golden still acknowledges the role of intuition and accident: 'No matter how you bring intellectualism and technique to bear in your photography, there is nevertheless a peculiar kind of magic that occurs between yourself, the camera, the objects that you are photographing, and light itself, of course in conjunction with

*color. In the end, something results that is far beyond the mere capacity of any of these separate elements, the complete picture is a summation in this sense, containing as it does part of the unconscious as well....I often see the picture as somewhat of a surprise!' An alternative approach to beautification is to allow the setting or origins of the food to speak for it, as demonstrated by this picture of dim sum in bamboo baskets (**below left**).*

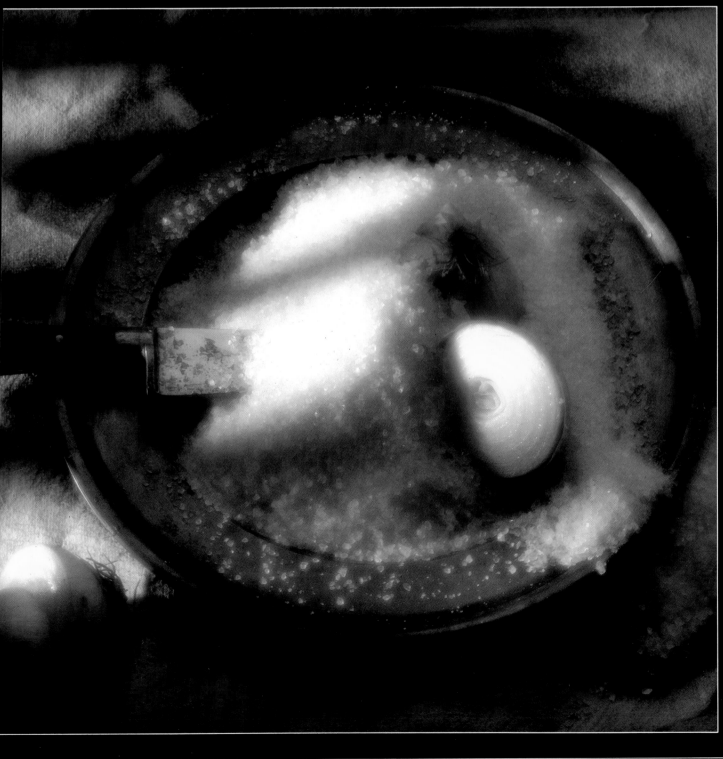

Setting up a studio still-life *The brief was to produce a conventional still-life arrangement to illustrate an article on herbal medicine. Preliminary sketches* (below) *show the main elements of design, arranged in alternative layouts, together with notes on lighting and general treatment.*

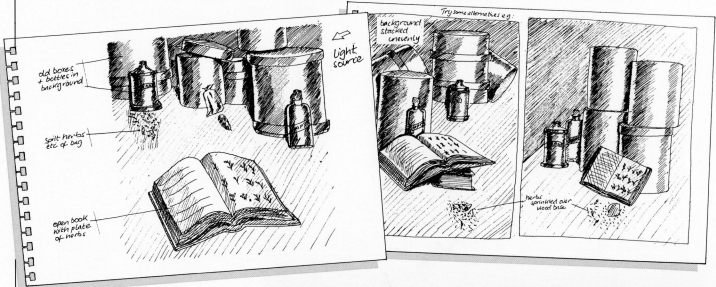

Right *The final shot has been refined to a coherent image by repositioning some of the containers in the background and the lid of a tub in to occupy empty space in the lower right-hand corner. The diagonal position of the book adds compositional interest; herbs scattered in the foreground and salt spilling out of the back in the background give a more casual feeling. To avoid vertical distortion, a perspective-control lens was used.*

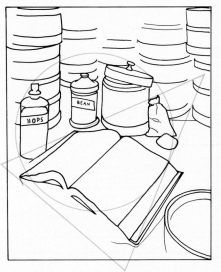

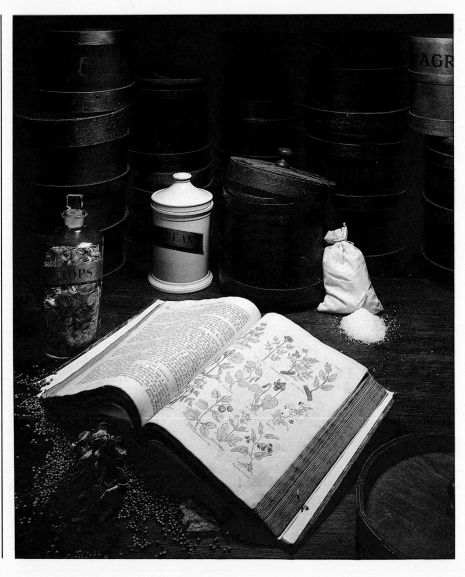

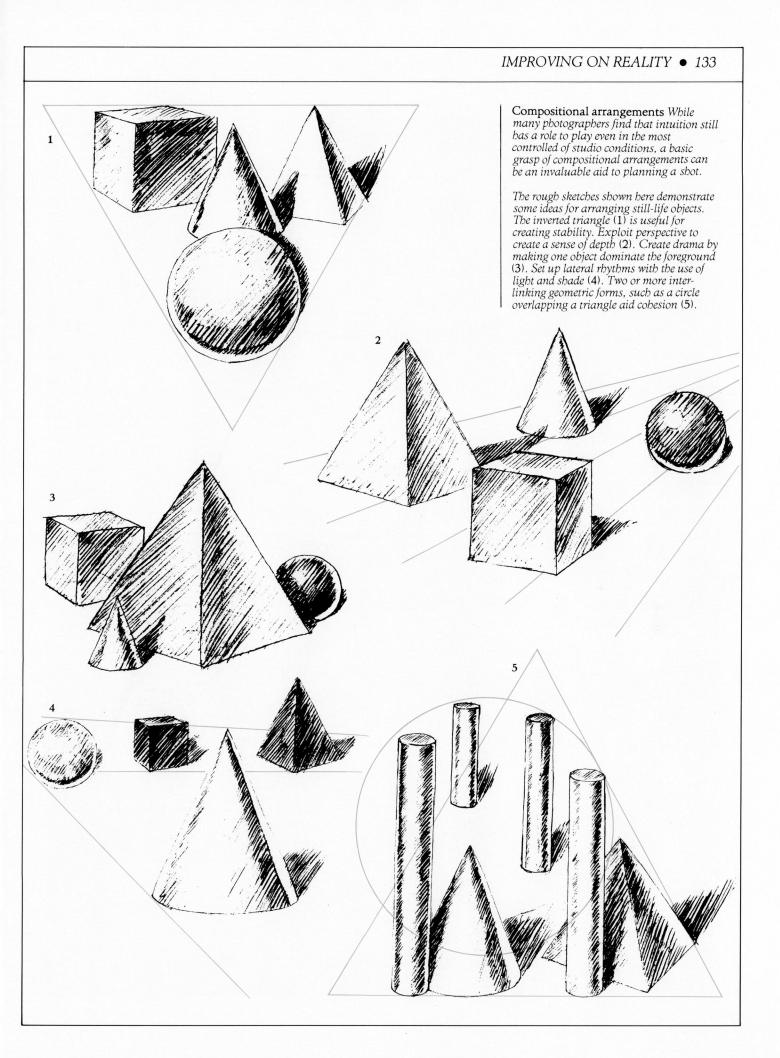

Compositional arrangements *While many photographers find that intuition still has a role to play even in the most controlled of studio conditions, a basic grasp of compositional arrangements can be an invaluable aid to planning a shot.*

The rough sketches shown here demonstrate some ideas for arranging still-life objects. The inverted triangle (1) is useful for creating stability. Exploit perspective to create a sense of depth (2). Create drama by making one object dominate the foreground (3). Set up lateral rhythms with the use of light and shade (4). Two or more inter-linking geometric forms, such as a circle overlapping a triangle aid cohesion (5).

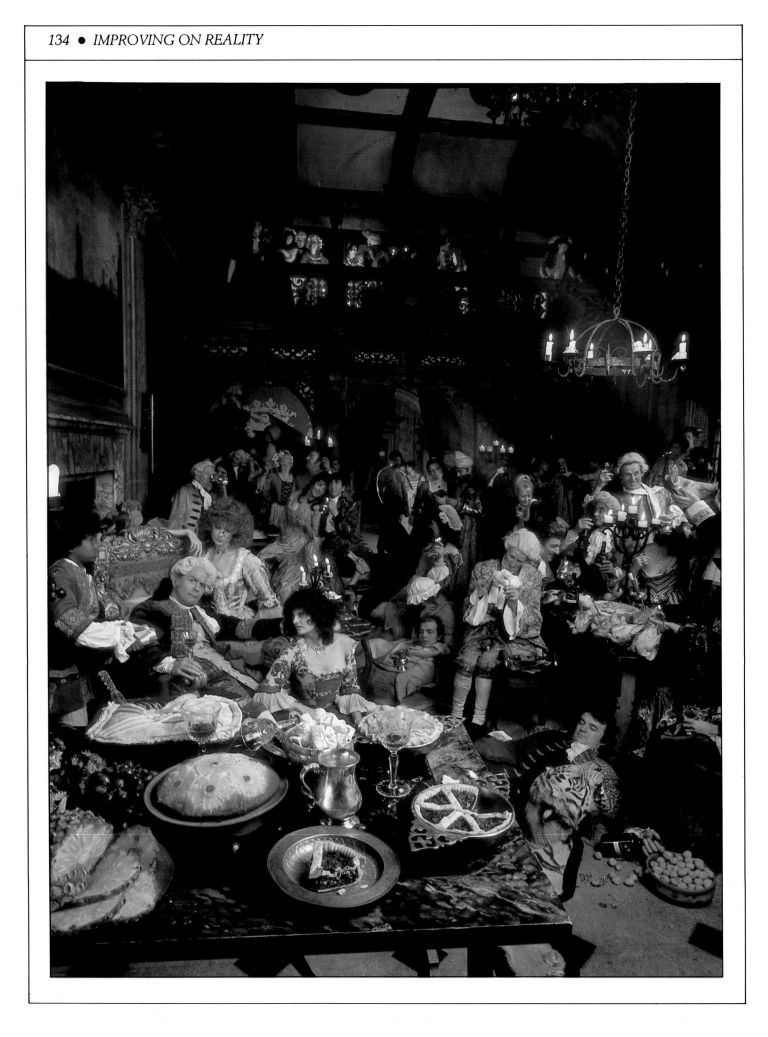

Left *and* **below** *In Michael Joseph's carefully staged tableaux a special virtue is made of the great effort and planning needed. Particularly in the period banquet scene, an advertisement for port, the viewer is invited not only to examine the minutiae of expression and action, but also to admire the photographer's organizational ability.*

Bottom *This illustration for a record cover is patently false. Because the viewer is virtually being shown where the trickery takes place, authenticity was important. The two images — naked hand and gloved hand — were shot separately on large-format film, with an extra reference shot of the background hidden by the arm. The photographs were assembled by a masking and duplicating technique known as photo-composition and printed as a dye-transfer. A retoucher blended the images carefully and painted in the inside of the glove. Even the glove's stitching becomes flesh-colored as it merges with the hand.*

need have. The advertising industry attracts very talented art directors and no one, least of all agency creative departments, illustrators and photographers, like to waste talent; consequently, considerable effort is channelled into advertisements that set out to intrigue, amuse or stimulate the audience. The award-winning cigarette advertisements for Benson and Hedges(pages 198-200) are such an example. A cigarette pack is a mundane object, yet modern advertising regulations in Britain prevent manufacturers from showing virtually anything else; certainly, suggesting that smoking is *enjoyable* is completely out of bounds. Within the tiny area left for maneuver, the Benson and Hedges campaign has been particularly successful. The advertisements draw attention to the gold pack by placing it in situations where it replaces or mimics other, expected objects. The incongruity, which displays little logic but great visual sophistication, provides the entertainment and the humor.

Where a strong link with the product is maintained — that is, where the *function* of the product can be fully explained — the entertainment value consists of idealization. Sometimes this is of the product itself, if it is inherently interesting, such as a luxury item, but more often it is the setting and ambience that is idealized.

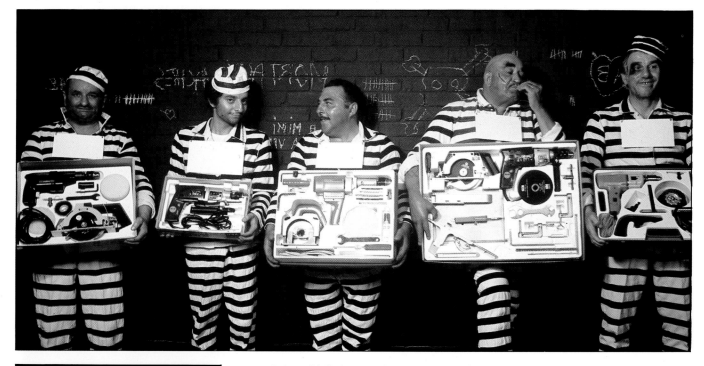

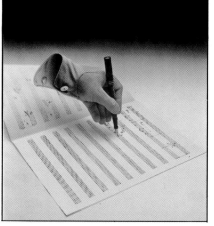

John Claridge's photographs of cars on location (page 128) do just that. This is accompanied by choosing wild, attractive settings, and then by waiting for interesting and exciting natural light conditions, which are helped along by colored and graduated filters. The results show the type of idealized conditions in which the experience of motoring would be heightened, even enjoyable.

Idealization at its most extreme can be seen in Michael Joseph's witty, glamorous reconstructions (*see* left and below). These complex tableaux rely on technical excellence, imagination and — importantly — the expectations of the audience. The rich detail demands to be closely studied, and entertains by confirming our preconceptions in a lively, tongue-in-cheek manner. We are not supposed to believe such scenes are real, but enjoy their jolly theatricality — and, of course, associate it with the product, port, for example.

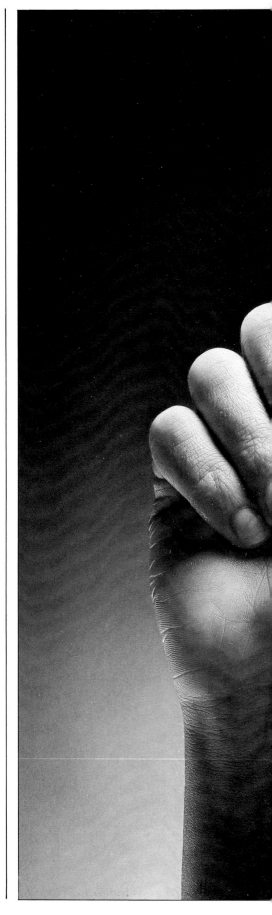

Given that advertising is in the business of creating images rather than reporting real life and events, technique has always been paramount. In particular, the techniques of fabrication have controlled the ambitions of art directors and photographers. Standards of image quality being high (large budgets ensure that), photographic re-creations are usually only attempted when they are thoroughly feasible. Major developments in this area have been happening over the last few years.

Special effects photography has come a long way from the colored gels and darkroom experiments of amateur photographic societies and magazines. There now exists an impressive battery of sophisticated techniques for combining and altering images. There is, in fact, an absolute and critical boundary in technique. This is the point at which *any* image can be fabricated with complete believability. It is not just a question of degree, with better and better results possible each year, but of a threshold which affects the style of advertising imagery.

As long as there are technical limitations to the image they want to create, the photographer and art director have two choices. They can rely on some suspension of disbelief by inviting the viewer to realize that the picture is a fabrication, as in the case of the surreal image of a gloved hand (page 135), or, they can choose another approach that does not rely on special effects. However, if the technology is available to cross this boundary, the viewer does *not* have to be privy to the fabrication. The photographer, with help from laboratories and retouchers if necessary, can go ahead and design any image, and present it as the real thing.

Few people are aware that this technical threshold was actually passed several years ago. Special effects photography can now accomplish its work without the viewer being aware, as the photographs of the jet fighters and hand demonstrate (*see* below and left). In the case of the jet fighters, no clues are given that the retoucher has been at work. In the photograph of the hand, however, it takes a little while to realize exactly what is wrong with the picture. It is, in fact, a clever piece of self-promotion for the retoucher, Michael Mann.

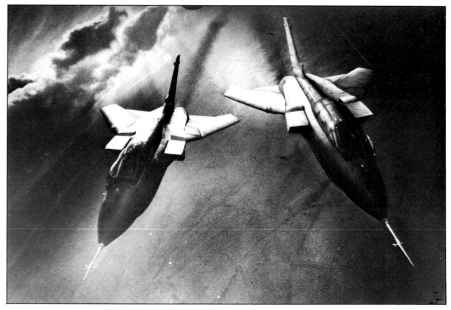

Above *The retoucher Michael Mann was called upon to create the near-miss shown in this photograph. Which jet is real? The one on the left; the other is completely painted in.*

Right *The extra middle finger in Michael Mann's amusing self-promotion is painted. To fit it in, the photograph of the hand was divided in two and duplicated with a gap, which was then retouched.*

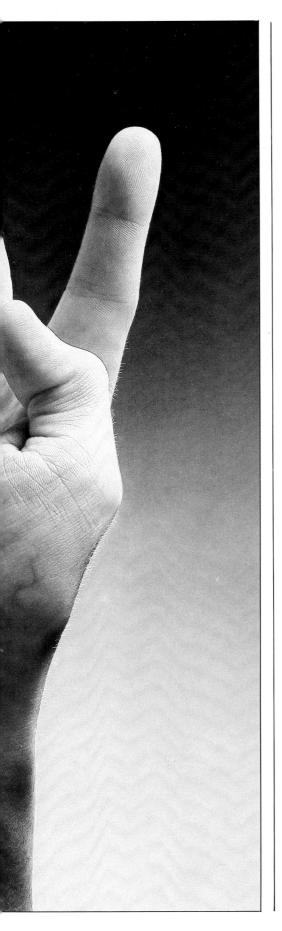

Much of the progress — in image combination, model-building, artwork backdrops, and so on — was actually made outside still photography, in the film world. Here, large budgets have funded the means for perfecting special effects, and the results can be of a very high order. But perhaps even more valuable than the development of particular techniques is that the major Hollywood special effects studios have shown that it is *possible* to fabricate images that seem completely authentic, given sufficient time and effort.

The elaborate twenty-first-century American megalopolis created for the film *Blade Runner* combined real location footage — shot in downtown Los Angeles with futuristic car and streetlighting props — with a matte painting of the upper levels of the city. The artist worked to a print and the filmed painting was combined optically with the live-action take. Sophisticated extra tricks, known as 'gags' in the business, boosted the glow from street lights and added rain effects, such as false reflections of the printed buildings, achieved by backlighting coloured gels that matched the neon lights, through scratches in a sheet of opaque glass.

The techniques involved in retouching and planning special effects photography are surprisingly complex and sophisticated, but the process is still determined, to a large degree, by the expectations of client and audience. This may weigh against originality, but in practice it is only one of several factors. Retouching can be used to enhance the image, to clean it up cosmetically or to make it more elegant. Another reason for improving on reality is that the situation may just be unavailable. A new car, for instance, may only be available for photography in the winter and, for reasons of security, it may not be possible to transport it to another, more attractive location. One answer is to employ expensive retouching to provide the desired background and sky. The retouched photograph of the two aircraft in flight (*see* left) is an example of a situation which would be dangerous to set up in real life.

For all these forms of 'improvement', the level of photographic technique must be high enough to make the project worth attempting. Where a special technique is actually the center of interest, not just playing a supporting or cosmetic role, this requirement is crucial. To help achieve this authenticity, the photographer needs a model (or several) as the basis for the design, not just a repertoire of techniques. In the case of the film *Blade Runner*, director Ridley Scott and industrial designer Syd Mead first worked out a full background scenario for the year in which the film would be set, including the social theory, so that all the imagery would be grounded in what Scott called 'a very solid, mechanical logic'.

Being convincing is not just a matter of being faultless, however. Lack of character in a designed photograph can announce its lack of authenticity as strongly as any technical error, and experienced photographers involved in this kind of work know the importance of leavening a perfect setting with a little unpredictability. This may seem to contradict the initial aim of idealizing a scene, but this principle of idiosyncrasy simply borrows authenticity by recognizing that real-life situations contain elements that have no good reason for being there, and which an average designer would not normally include.

Time and effort are the only two factors limiting the spread of prime quality special effects work. Up to now, advertising has been the main instigator and user, because of the money available. However, as such techniques as photo-composition to add backgrounds become standardized photographers are learning to use them outside advertising.

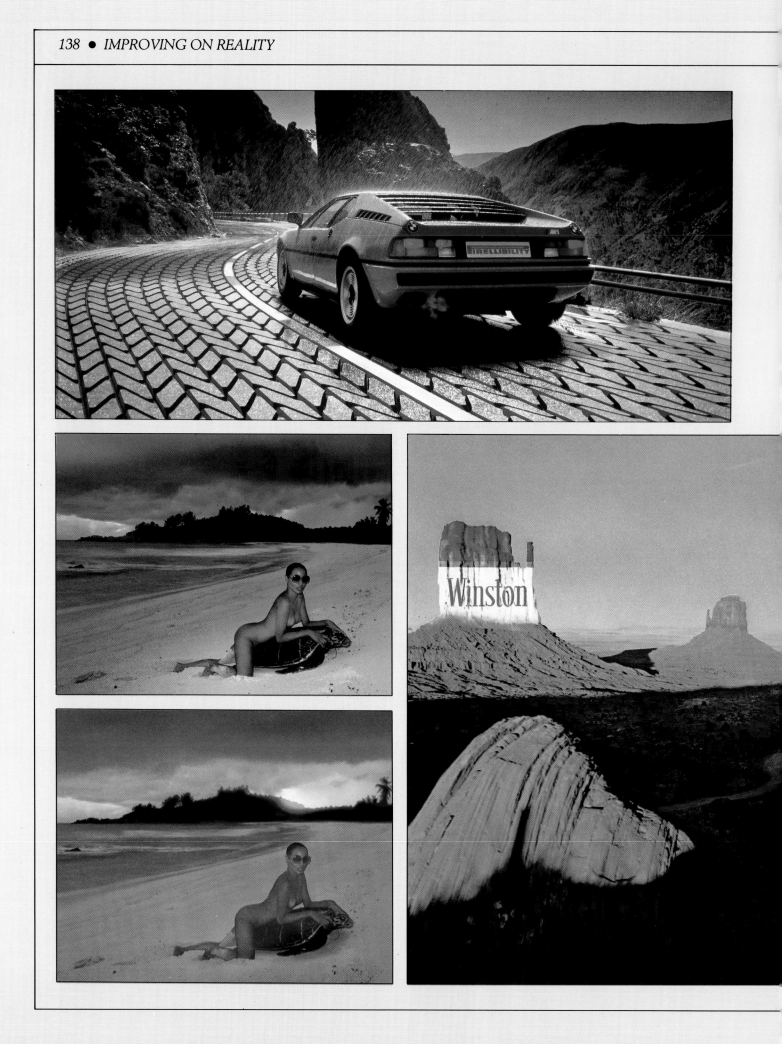

Left *As one of a series of advertisements for a tyre company, this complex example of photo-composition replaces a normal road surface with the tread of a tyre.*
Below left *Color changes are a reasonably straightforward part of the retoucher's repertoire. Here, selective dyeing has been used to change a blue-toned photograph by John Thornton into a more conventional orange sunset.*
Below *Monument Valley, already a favorite with landscape photographers, here finds its way into advertising. The campaign called for representations of the pack to be worked into American landscapes. Here, it appears on one of the Mittens, by means of careful application of bleach and dyes, performed by Tantrums, a printing and retouching studio.*
Right *In a complex assembly of 17 different images, a number of techniques have been used to illustrate a magazine story on particle physics. Each element was prepared specially, using streak photography for the round spheres and electrical discharges for the 'forces', and the whole assembly was made by photo-composition, duplicating each onto a single sheet of film.*

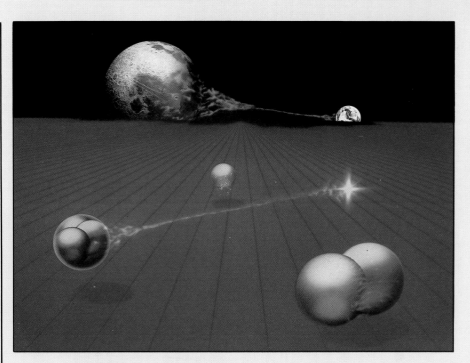

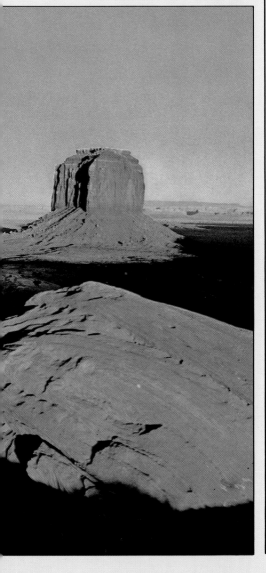

Record promotion has tended to cultivate bizarre visual tastes to suit the style of some rock music, and album covers feature quite spectacular special effects. These are most often used to create surrealism and fantasy, as the Hipgnosis examples (pages 201-3) show.

Editorial demand for constructed images is also high — in magazines and for book covers in particular. As techniques improve, producing special effects is becoming less expensive, with the result that their use is slowly permeating through the major fields of photography, photojournalism excepted, for obvious reasons (at least, officially).

Just the possibility of limitless fabrication and improvement is beginning to alter the rules of the game. In the past, special effects were so primitive that their role was as graphic tricks, occupying a fairly trivial or curious place in photography. When applied to making an altered picture look authentic, they were usually seen as attempted distortions of 'real' photographs. Now that their use is widespread and sophisticated, the division between 'real' and 'fake' no longer makes much sense. The Winston ad (*see* left) is obviously not trying to fool its audience. It is using special effects (in this case) re-touching on a transparency) as a means of producing the image. The next few years will see these and other effects become more commonplace in *different* areas of photography, not so much to perform the outright fakery (although this is inevitable where scruples are low), but as an illustrative style. Most of the pictures in this chapter are drawn from what is sometimes called illustrative photography, in which the picture's task is a visual exposition of an idea or concept — whether a text story, music or advertising message.

Some of these special effects techniques, although a part of photography, are a type of illustration in themselves, and so ideal for the purpose. They are, in fact, beginning to blur the distinction between pure illustration and photography. Pictures such as that above, in which photography is used to generate entirely designed images (an analogy of sub-atomic structure), clearly encroach on what was once the preserve of the illustrator. The development of photographic illustration promises to be one of the most interesting, and perhaps even controversial, features of photography in the coming years.

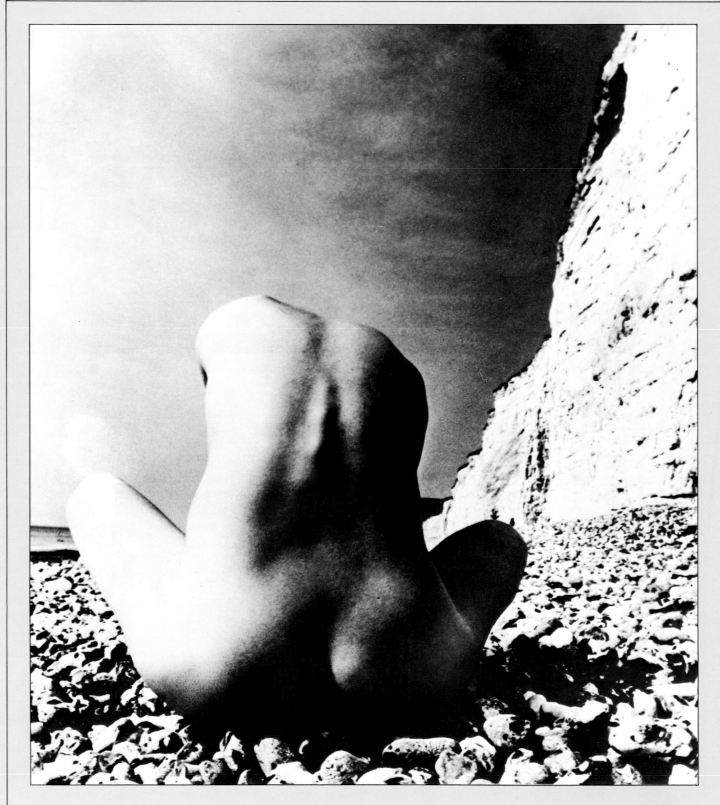

Above In 1945 Bill Brandt bought a second-hand wooden Kodak camera from a shop near Covent Garden, London. Its special feature was an extremely wide-angle lens with an aperture so tiny that it produced almost no image on the ground-glass screen. He said, 'The lens produced anatomical images and shapes which my eyes had never observed,' and became so fascinated with these distorting optical effects that he spent more than 15 years photographing nudes in this manner.

CHAPTER 6

Style and Conceit

'I am not interested in nature, I'm interested in my own *nature.'*
Aaron Siskind

'I want my sitters to be recognized, not my work.'
Snowdon

The major concern of this book, and the exclusive issue of this chapter, is a concept that is widely used but rarely defined. The concept is style, and it is a notion that is curiously imprecise. When a critic, Vicki Goldberg in this instance, writes: 'This is not to say that Snowdon doesn't have Style. He has vast resources of it, the same way that some men have sex appeal or inherited money', you know that she believes Snowdon to be a good photographer; but you also realize that she is not going to give chapter and verse about it. The very vagueness of its common usage makes the word 'style' one of the most valuable in the vocabulary of photographic art — at least, for those using it. It can identify photographers, demonstrate one's own taste, pass judgements, or just inspire aphorisms.

Aphorisms about style are popular partly because they can neatly sidestep the problems of analysis. 'Style is the bottle, not the wine', runs an article devoted to the subject in *American Photographers*'s five-year anniversary issue, which continues, 'It is the medium, not the message', and, 'Style is the signature and measure of talent.' Style is also apparently elusive (the same essay ends by acknowledging the author's failure 'to capture the chimera').

Confusion exists largely because there are two important ways in which 'style' can be used, and these are interconnected. In one sense style is simply the manner in which a particular photographer works, the fashion of picture-taking by which he or she can, with luck, be identified. In the other sense, more apparently the 'chimera', style is a quality of excellence — not just a manner of working, but a fine, perceptive manner.

In either use — and the two have a way of becoming mixed once the conversation begins — there is usually an unspoken acknowledgement

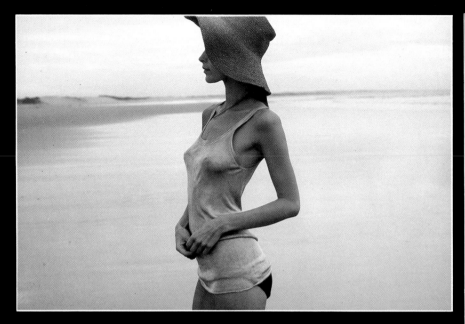

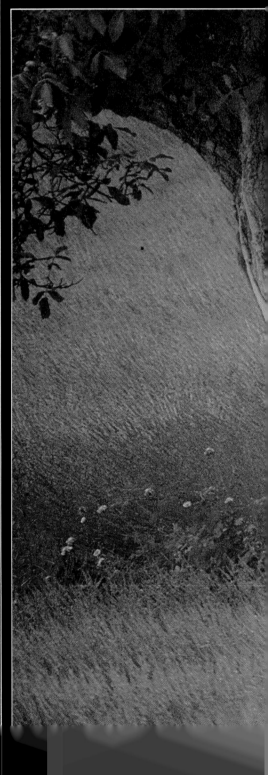

Left *and* **below left** *David Hamilton, who changed career from magazine art director to photographer in the late 1960s, has developed a particular technique (soft-focus diffusion and a leisurely pace of shooting in order to gain the confidence of his models) and a consistent theme (young girls). Together, these aspects have become an instantly recognizable trademark.*

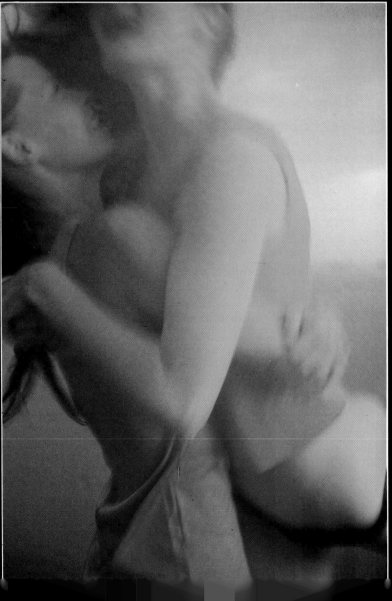

Below *André Martin's highly characteristic pastoral studies of France are made principally, as here, with a long-focus mirror lens. Used from a low viewpoint, so that there is a great visible depth in the subject, the extremely shallow depth-of-field of this lens throws much of the image into a soft, dappled focus. The particular way in which the image appears to be diffused is due to subtle interference from the small, centrally situated front mirror.*

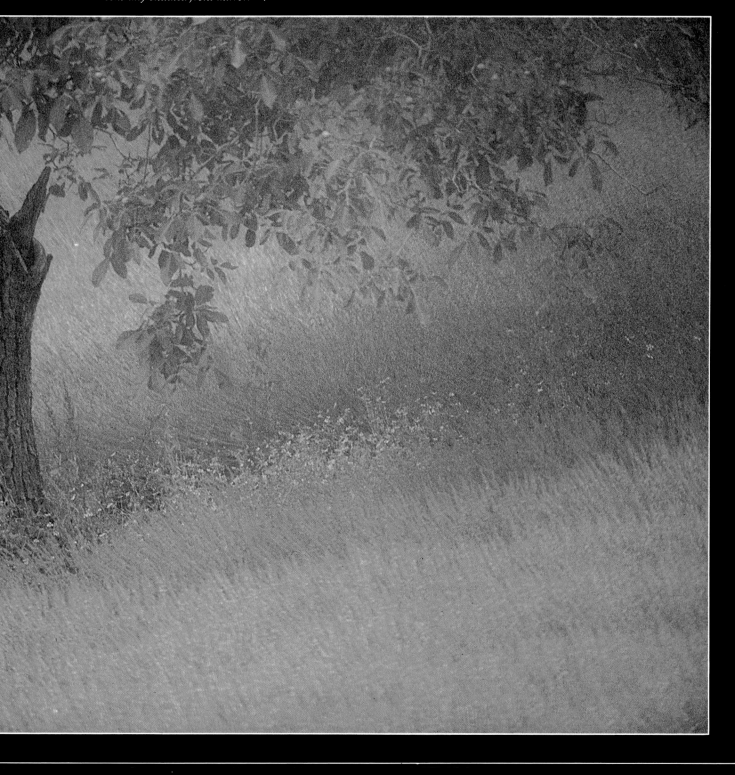

that style is a positive quality. Style in its general sense means a combination of imagination and visual fluency, and this is the meaning (to avoid confusion) that is intended as the title of both this book and this chapter. Style in its *specific* sense means an identifiable manner of taking photographs, but one that is, by implication, of merit. In other words, we might say, 'Expert photographers can always turn out a good picture', but, '*This* photographer always turns out *this* kind of good picture.'

Unfortunately, in the world of photography all is not quite so simple. In particular, when we look at the individual, identifiable kind of style, the facts do not always bear out the theory. It is widely assumed — or taken for granted — that great photographers can be identified by certain traits, and one of the consequences of this belief is that a particular style is a desirable thing to have. On closer examination, these issues are not so straightforward.

To begin with, the recognition of style is a basic tool in art criticism and art history. It makes it possible to clarify, draw relationships and show influences. Quite naturally, the critics and historians of photography have expected to find similar stylistic differences in their subject. Perhaps even more important is that both critics and the audience for photography feel more at ease when the work they are examining can be pigeon-holed. Goldberg says in one review, 'I think most of us are more comfortable when a photographer has a style than when he doesn't. It is so reassuring to recognize an image before you read the label.' Being able to do this provides a comforting frame of reference.

Photographers themselves can be expected to share these feelings; in addition, many have a vested interest in style either as a mark of quality or territorial signpost. To become known because the public recognizes certain characteristics is obviously satisfying. In addition, because photography is a major commercial medium, and many of the best photographers work professionally, this can also be financially rewarding. With large numbers of photographers competing for assignments, anyone with an identifiable (and useful) trademark has an advantage. For picture editors and the other people who commission photographs, the easiest method of finding the best people to do certain jobs is to have a ready system of classification. A photographer showing his portfolio to a potential client may not be given an assignment on the spot, but if there is something distinctive in his work, it will be noted for future reference.

As a result of this, the people involved — both photographers and critics — on the whole strive to reinforce the notion of identifiable styles. But while such motives are understandable, how does this work in practice? First, consider the work of one or two widely known photographers and examine what makes their work recognizable. David Hamilton is a well-known modern photographer, whose output has a strong commercial element. The photographs on page 142 are absolutely typical of nearly all his published work. What makes these pictures identifiable is that Hamilton usually photographs young girls, often partly clothed, and does so in a way that is partly lyrical and wistful — by means of soft focus and muted colors — and partly candid. There is usually a relaxed air of sexuality, achieved through pose, undress and close contact between the models. As Hamilton has specialized in this combination of subject and treatment, he is rightly identified with it. Any other photograph that appears to be similar could be said to be in his 'style'.

If this type of simple analysis were possible for each photographer's work, all would be perfectly straightforward. But few photographers use the same subject and treatment over and over again, as does Hamilton. And, if a photographer's style can be identified in such an easy way, is the concept so useful? To take another case, one of Bill Brandt's best-known series of pictures, an example of which is shown on page 140, is of nudes photographed with a special camera. The camera's lens had an extremely wide angle of view and this characteristic could produce extreme distortion. Brandt was clearly fascinated by this, and over a few years made a number of studies in which he explored the distortion effect. These pictures may not seem so unusual now that fish-eye lenses are commonplace, but many people found them so then.

When Beaumont Newhall, photography's chief historian, discussed these pictures, he said: 'Bill Brandt ... changed his style during the 1950s: with the use of an extremely wide-angle lens he created highly abstract studies of nudes.' Even if Newhall was trying to be succinct, this seems a disappointingly brief explanation for a style. Brandt, in this series of nude studies, is displaying the distorting properties of a special wide-angle lens that has a minute aperture and so great depth of field. It might be too harsh to say that he was just playing with a new lens, but its effect so dominates the image that there is little room for whatever other subtleties Brandt was capable of producing. Since few photographers would have turned out substantially different photographs under these conditions, the grounds for describing this approach as a trick of technique, rather than a style, are quite good.

Another example of a photographer whose work is recognizable is Ernst Haas. His swirling picture of a bullfight on page 18 was achieved by means of a long exposure and deliberate movement of the camera. This is quintessential Haas, rich in color and form; he admits to feeling at the time (the 1950s) 'a tremendous longing for color'. Once again, it is relatively easy to describe what makes these pictures recognizable.

From this limited examination of three photographers' work, the identifying features seem to consist of just two elements: subject matter and technique. Both, though useful for making classifications, are essentially easy to detect and describe; neither are elusive. As Susan Sontag says, 'It requires a formal conceit (like Todd Walker's solarized photographs or Duane Michal's narrative-sequence photographs) or a thematic obsession (like Eakins with the male nude or Laughlin with the Old South) to make work easily recognizable.' Sontag's 'formal conceit' is, by another name, technique, and this seems to have a peculiar prominence in photography.

One of the recurring themes in this book has been that photography is tied almost inextricably to the real world. The standard use of a camera is as a recording instrument, making images that are essentially straightforward in appearance — we could say realistic, to the extent that this is possible in a flat, two-dimensional medium. This simple fact has influenced the development of all photographic materials and processes. From the beginning, most of the technical side of making a picture was predetermined, with the photographer following certain operating instructions. Recently, nearly the whole of this process has been available fully automated and the average photographer effectively excluded from the technical aspects. Automation, and most of the progress in new materials, has been directed towards realistic recording. Automatic exposure is designed to produce images that cover a standard range of tones, whatever the conditions of the subject. New color films

Right *and* **far right** *The sequential picture stories of Duane Michals have become so identified with him that similar attempts by other modern photographers are invariably seen as an imitation by most audiences. This sequence, made in 1969 and entitled* Death Comes to the Old Lady, *is typical of much of Michals' work. The story is clear, if allegorical, and appears in a way similar to a clip of film — the raw material for a sequence of real movement.*

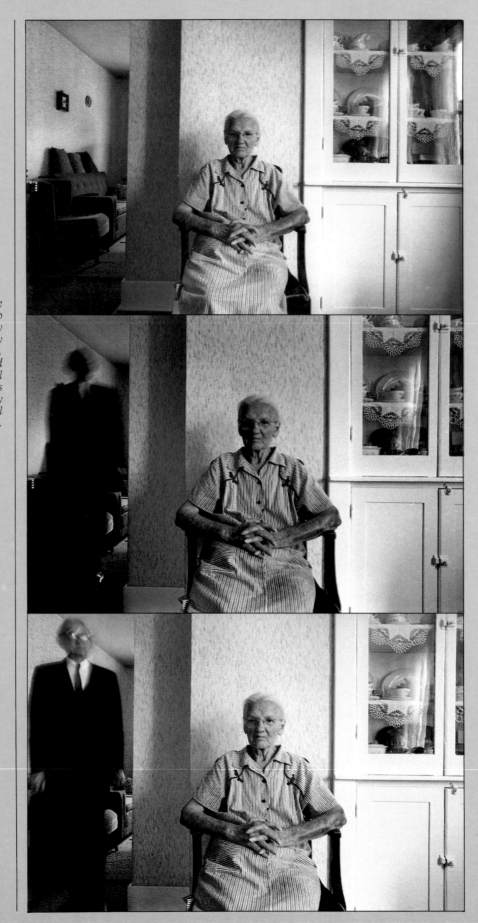

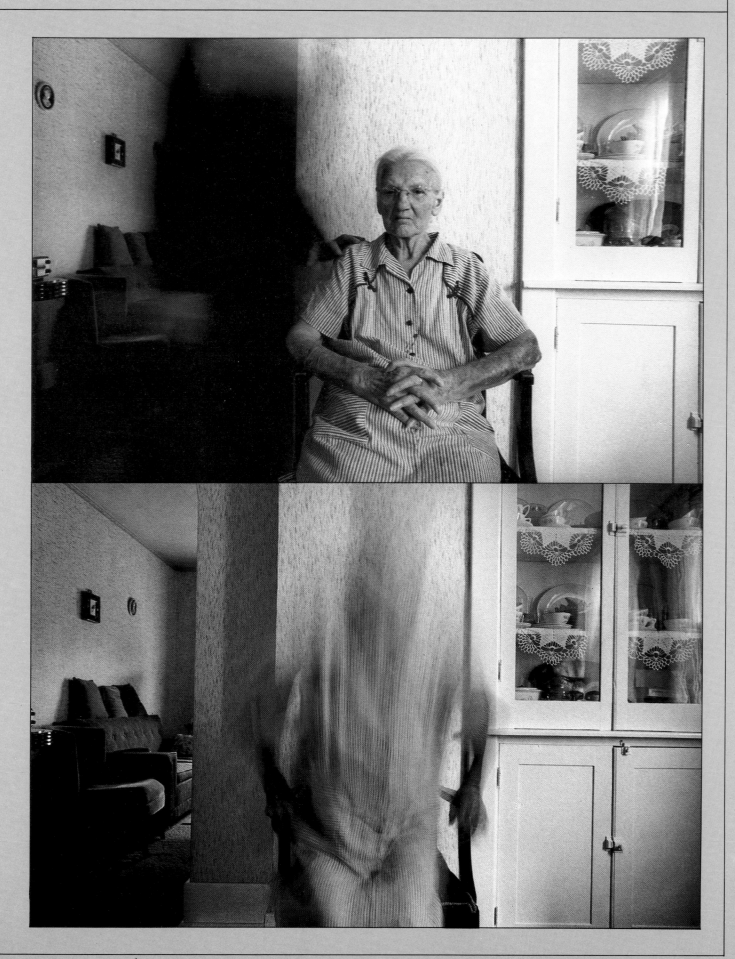

render hues more accurately — that is, more like the originals. Other hard-worn improvements in film technology are also designed for more realism and accuracy: finer grain, better resolution, more latitude to record a wide range of tones.

None of this constant technical progress gives the photographer more choice in the execution of a picture. At best, it could be said that it gives a photographer more freedom to concentrate on other aspects of picture-taking, but the *intention* of the manufacturers is to meet the wider public's demand for greater ease and simplicity. Indeed, many of the idiosyncracies of certain materials, which many photographers enjoyed, have been steadily ironed out. When Kodachrome II film was discontinued in the 1970s, a number of photographers bought up quantities of the remaining stock because of the special qualities of color they felt it had. When Polaroid's SX-70 film was improved, the same thing happened, because the slow hardening of chemicals in the old film made it possible to alter the image by pressing on the surface once it had been exposed — a vogue technique at the time.

While an artist must develop a particular way of working, a photographer is not compelled to; the camera and the process will take care of that, *unless* deliberately altered. But the opportunities for making such alterations are mainly limited to the obvious. Using a very slow shutter speed — of, say, one second — with a quickly moving subject is one example of a special technique; photographing through a set of prisms to break up the image is another. Yet a photographer who uses one of these deliberate techniques is inevitably drawing attention to the fact and is virtually *adding* to the image, as is the case in the photographs shown here by Hamilton, Haas and Brandt. The inescapable fact is that most technical departures tend to look like tricks rather than methods. There is remarkably little middle ground where the photographer can use technique subtly to display a personal style.

What opportunities exist are mainly in those areas of photography that involve a secondary process; principally, this means negative film that the photographer can print with some flexibility — and for many photographers this part of the activity becomes the most important. Most professional photographers, however, use color transparency film, since that is what publishers require for photo-mechanical reproduction. In theory, the separation processes used by printers give scope for adjusting the image; in practice, the photographer hardly ever has the chance to become involved. The fine control of image quality is, therefore, mainly restricted to photographers who exhibit their work, and produce a small number of prints as the end product. (This is not to say that photographers whose work is published do not care about the quality of reproduction, but that they have less opportunity for control.)

The second means of identifying the work of a photographer — and hence the other major component of style — is the subject matter, Sontag's 'thematic obsession'. The majority of photographers tend to specialize to some degree, sometimes because they are drawn to some place or situation, or because they have found that they are particularly able with a certain class of subject. Ansel Adams, for example, concentrated so heavily on the grand scenery of the American West that if we see a photograph of Yosemite or Big Sur, and it appears to be taken in a richly detailed, romantic manner, we think of Adams as a likely candidate. Similarly, Don McCullin has mainly photographed war and the bleaker human conditions; Lennart Nilsson has specialized in technically innovative medical pictures; William Garnett has chosen aerial views of America as his exclusive concern. Nevertheless, describing the theme of a photographer's work is a matter of no great complexity. As the basis for an exploration of photographic development and practice, it offers meagre material.

A further complication if personal style is seen as based on such simple matters is that the work of different photographers can look very similar. The photographs by the Formalists of Weston's generation often seem interchangeable — a close-up of weathered boards could be assigned to, say, Edward Weston, his son Brett, Ansel Adams, Minor White, or a number of others. Patterns of bent reeds could be Brett Weston or Harry Callahan. A certain type of cool, unfussy studio portrait could be by Snowdon or Penn. To Susan Sontag, 'Many of the published photographs by photography's greatest names seems like work that could have been done by another gifted professional of their period.'

One reason for this is that certain subjects encourage plain technique, so that some work appears similar because it shares a lack of contrivance (Snowdon's and Penn's portraiture are instances of this). Another reason is a convergence of talents and ideas, so that, without conscious imitation, some photographers arrive by similar routes at close results. Compare, for example, Brandt's distorted nudes with those by Kertész. The *technical* methods are different, but the idea and the effect have a great deal in common. Or compare Kertész' photograph of Mondrian's home (*Chez Mondrian*, 1926) with the portrait (*Piet Mondrian*, 1942) by Arnold Newman. Both photographers have taken the quite clever but predictable route of composing their pictures in the manner of Mondrian himself (pages 150-1). 'A skilful photographer', says John Szarkowski, 'can photograph anything well.' We might go further, and say that many of the skills acquired by photographers encourage similar solutions to photographic problems.

Yet, despite such evidence, the search goes on for stylistic differences. Most of the styles that tend to be cited are obvious techniques of the kind that have just been discussed. A portrait made up of several overlapping exposures by Alvin Langdon Coburn, for instance, is described in the *Life Library of Photography* as an example of 'multiple-image style', just as Newhall talks about Bill Brandt. One reason for this is simply that photography has had a relatively short history and for much of it was not widely considered worthy of critical examination. Another reason is that, in searching for stylistic difference on the lines of those visible in painting and other arts, critics have been dealing with a situation in which the equipment and manner of taking most photographs is basically similar, yet there are differences of technique. Because some photographs stand out for their use of specific techniques, as we have seen, the temptation to assign the status of style to these has been too great to resist. If it is felt that there ought to be stylistic differences, and there are some distinctions available, then they tend to be called 'styles'.

In this simplistic climate of assessment, photographers whose body of work displays consistency are easy to categorize and tend to feature widely as examples in histories of photography. By the same token, however, photographers who have less confined ambitions and more eclectic tastes, cause the compilers and classifiers more trouble. 'For photographers who don't so limit themselves,' says Sontag, 'their body of work does not have the same integrity as does comparably varied work in other art forms', thinking of artists such as Picasso. Yet some of the most influential and gifted photographers have done just this, pursuing their varied interests.

In an interesting example of the kind of convergence of ideas that complicates the whole issue of style, these examples show how two established photographers can take a basically similar approach to the same subject. That subject is the painter Piet Mondrian; the photographs are by André Kertész (Chez Mondrian, 1926) (below) and Arnold Newman (Piet Mondrian, 1942) (right). Both photographers have taken the sensible, if unremarkable, route of composing their photographs in Mondrian's own unmistakable style.

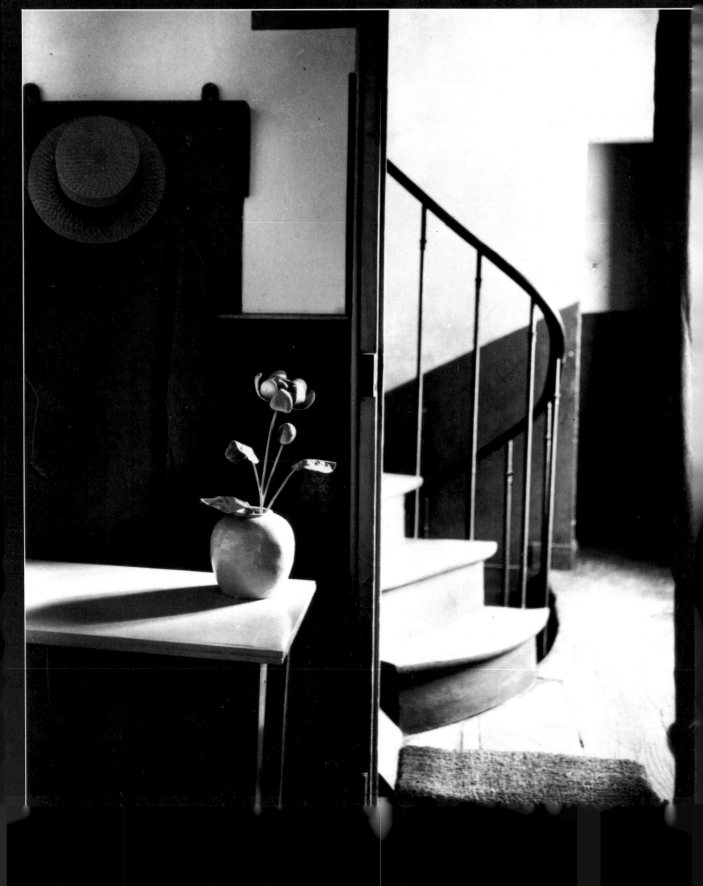

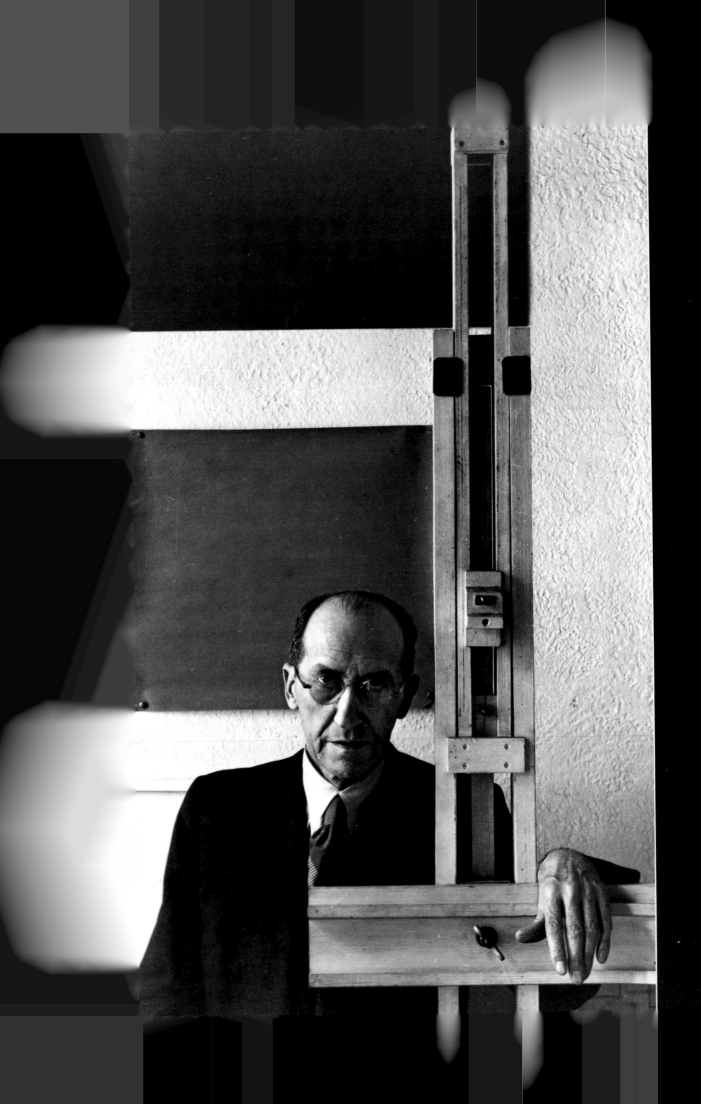

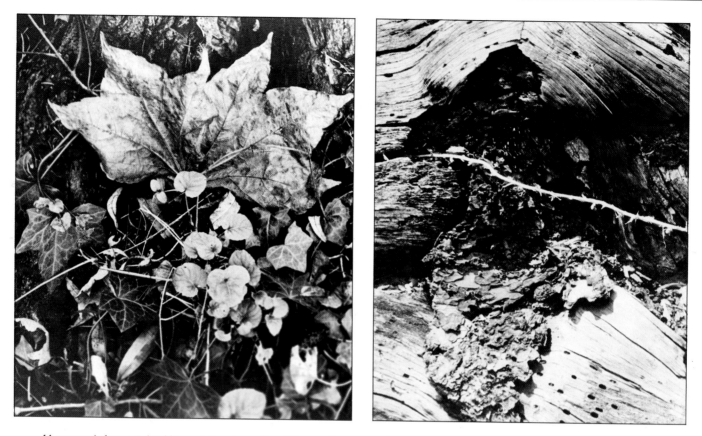

Above and **above right** *Although the different periods of Paul Strand's long photographic career may seem to be distinct, he did move back and forth between his thematic interests, as these two examples show.* Légion d'Honneur, Orgeval *was made in 1974* (above), *nearly 40 years after* Tree Stump and Vine, Colorado (1926) (above right). *A thread of interest throughout his life was to portray things as they are. In 1923 he said to Stieglitz: 'Notice how every object, every blade of grass is felt and accounted for...'*

Paul Strand's career began when he was 17 and, like other productive photographers of stature, he developed and experimented, making use of different types of subject and treating them in different ways. Most commonly, Strand is thought of as having two important styles; as a *Time-Life* obituary put it: '... the conscious artist whose youthful curiosity and consummate craftsmanship revolutionized the art of photography ... and the political partisan who saw in his art a means of changing the world.' The first direction is probably epitomized by a crisp, high-contrast abstraction of a white fence in New York, taken in 1916, the second by a portrait of sombre, impoverished Mexican peasants against an adobe wall.

In fact, there are more than two 'styles' identifiable in Strand's work. There is his earliest work, fuzzy under the influence of the salon photography of the time. There are unpretty candid shots of down-and-outs taken at the same period as the abstractions of man-made objects. Another area of his work explored nature in a similar Formalist manner to Weston. Moreover, these different sides to Strand are not neatly divided by time. There are 'social comment' pictures from almost the beginning of his career, and formal compositions from almost the end.

Whereas the reaction of many photographers is to move on and change once they feel they have exhausted the possibilities of one way of working, occasionally one will just stop. The work of Robert Frank had a seminal influence on street photography with the publication in 1959 of his book *The Americans*. In it, he outraged the conservatives in photography by making two radical departures from what was accepted: he paid attention to the ordinariness in American life rather than the special and spectacular, and he chose to treat it in a random, seemingly casual way, abandoning the regular standards of design and precision. In its time, *The Americans* was largely ignored, but its influence has since grown steadily as a number of photographers came to realize that

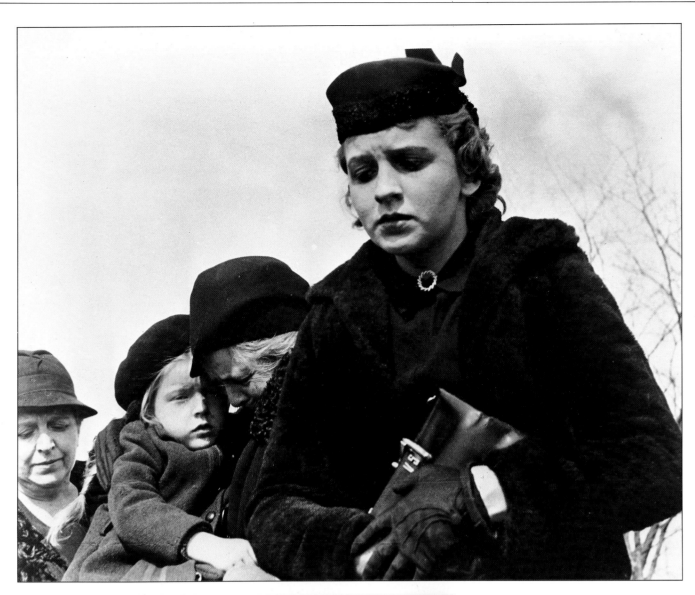

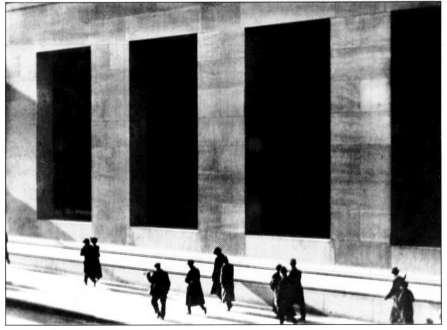

Left and **above** While many of Strand's early pictures were of urban subjects, such as Wall Street (**left**), taken in 1915, in some of his later work he also returned to the theme of the machine age and industrial society. These citizens, dwarfed by skyscrapers, are nevertheless individuals; individuality is also evident in Strands portrait of a grieving widow, Virginia Stevens (**above**). Any attempt to categorize such a varied body of work would inevitably lead to banalities.

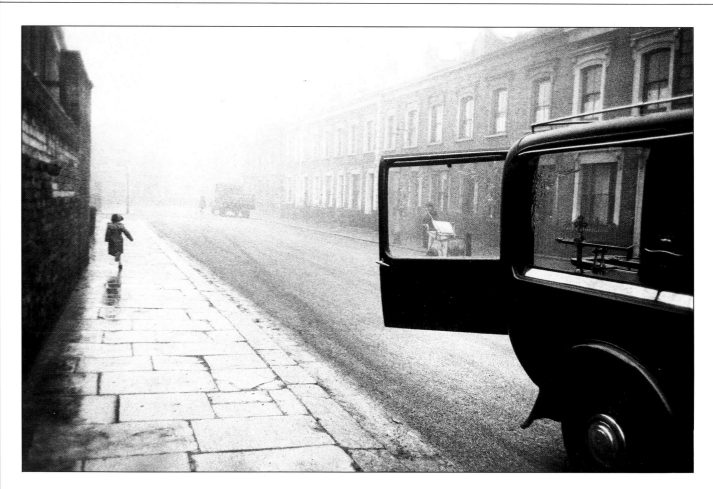

Above and **right** *Robert Frank's position in the history of modern photography as the social iconoclast of American life has resulted in his American pictures being the only ones of his that most people know. As the smoggy scene in London of 1951 shows (above), Frank did, in fact, take other photographs. This photograph also shows what an important influence the tone of the object matter can have on what is assumed to be a photographer's style. A first-time viewer could be forgiven for not first thinking of Robert Frank as the author of this gloomy Brandt-like scene, with its densely printed blacks. More 'characteristic' in its subject matter and informal composition is the photograph of a liquor store in Arizona (right). When this picture was taken, 1956, such a casual approach to theme and technique was rare, and not widely appreciated.*

Frank's style offered a new direction that had plenty of scope for development. Frank's randomness in particular was a kind of escape from what some photographers saw as the tyranny of Cartier-Bresson's 'decisive moment'. As Garry Winogrand, a successor to Frank's way of working, put it, 'No one moment is most important. Any moment can be something.' Frank, however, had completed what he set out to do, and after *The Americans*, moved on to film making, never to return seriously to still photography. He said, 'I had done it. I had made a book without interference. At best, to go on would have been a repetition.'

Another photographer whose attitude towards personal style has also been refreshing, although in a different way, is Lord Snowdon. While other portraitists, such as Avedon and Newman, work to place their own stamp on the picture, Snowdon prefers an unassuming approach, saying 'I want my sitters to be recognized, not my work.' And the result is just that — his portraits are individually excellent, carefully lit and sensitively timed, but there are no special trademarks.

How this contrasts with the work of another portrait photographer of note — Karsh, whose 50-year career has been directed towards highly distinctive photography of the famous, in the grand manner. The style of a Karsh portrait is deliberate, and comes from a theatricality of both pose and lighting. His subjects, who are usually people of public stature, are directed into poses that fulfil the viewers' ideas of greatness. They are not bathed in a simple, diffuse light, but spotlit from several directions — outlines and highlights often pop out from dark backgrounds creating high contrast. The Karsh signature is clear in all his work, but it is also, as with other photographic styles that are based heavily on technique, very obvious.

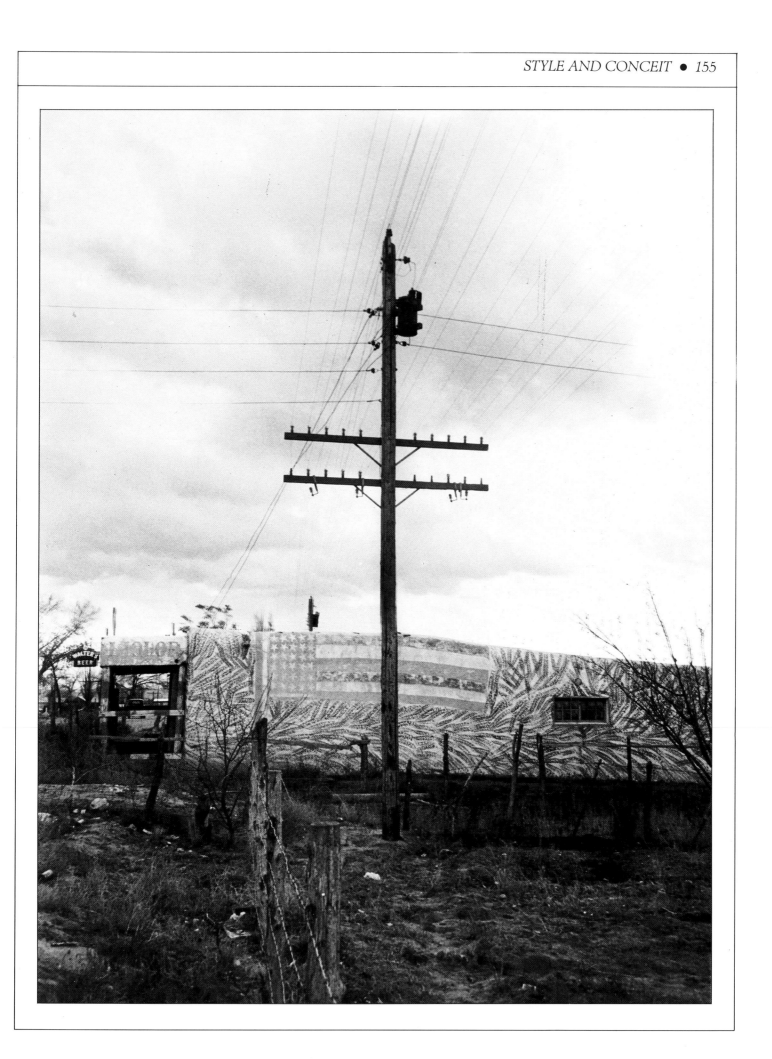

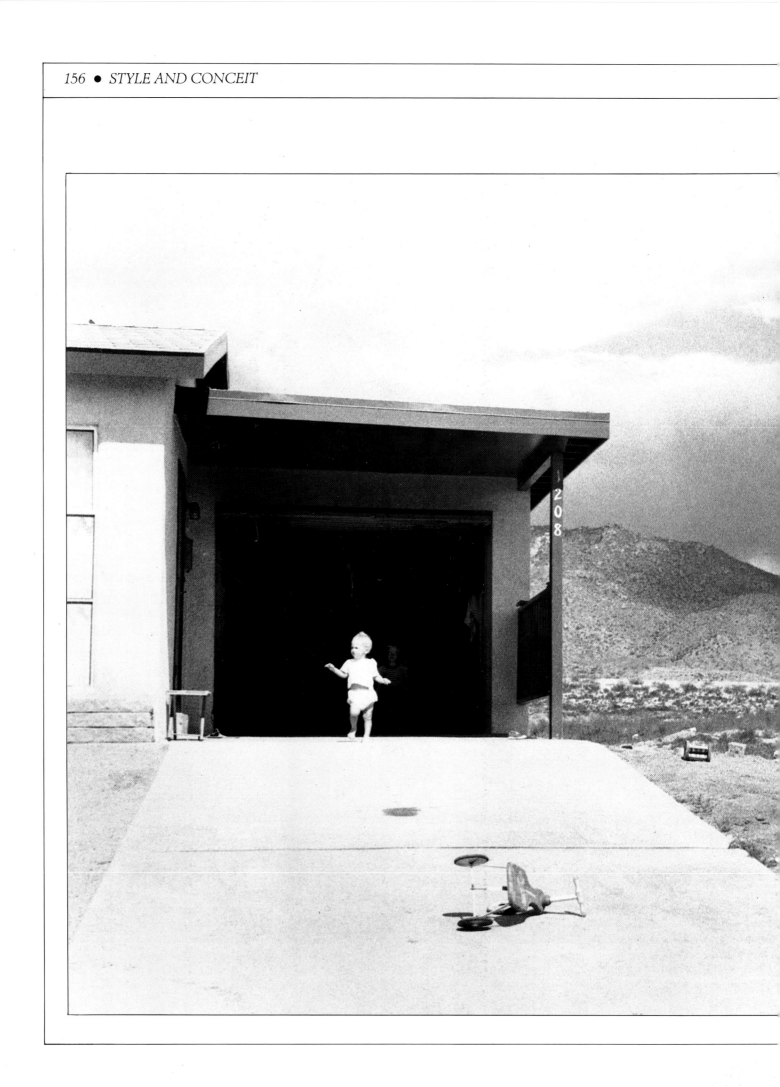

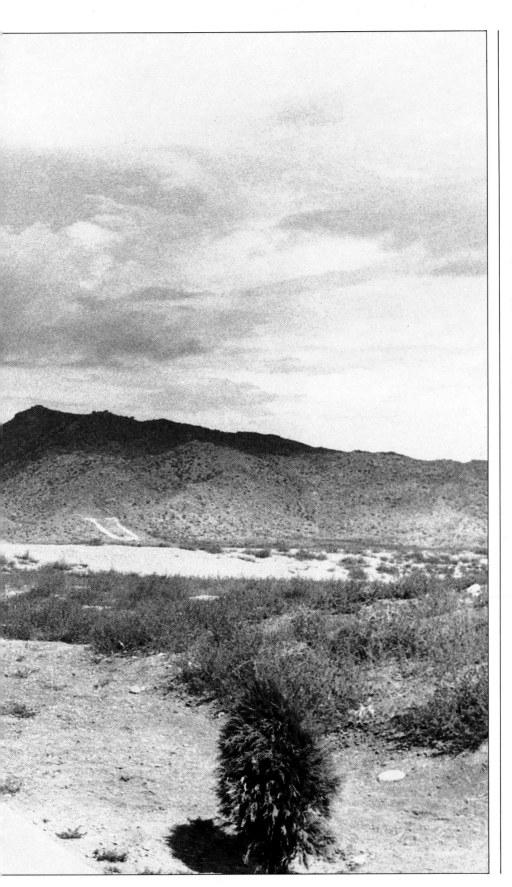

Left *In his interest in the ordinariness of life in contemporary America, Garry Winogrand acknowledged the influence of Walter Evans and, more intermediately, Robert Frank. Never very interested in articulating or explaining his approach (this photograph is captioned simply* Untitled, Albuquerque, 1958), *Winogrand said, 'Most photographs are of life, what goes on in the world. And that's boring, generally. Life is banal, you know. Let's say that an artist deals with banality.'*

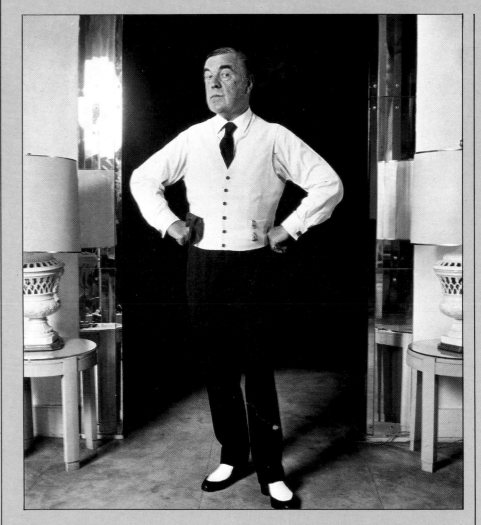

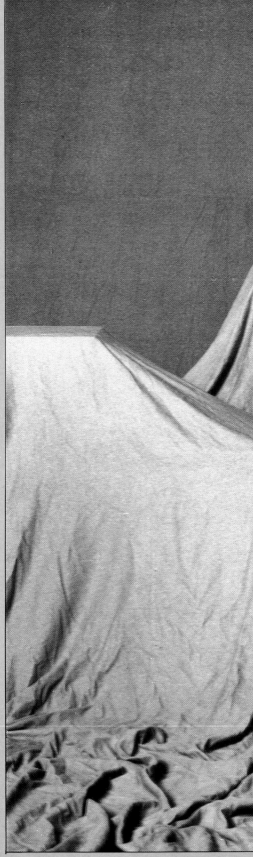

Above *and* **right** *Two portraits by Lord Snowdon, one somewhat mannered and formal in design, to bring out the personality of its subject, royal couturier Norman Hartnell* (**above**), *the other a surprisingly bleak photograph of Sir John Betjeman, Poet Laureate* (**right**), *just before his death in 1984. Both illustrate the intention of one notable photographer not to be constricted by a recognizable style. If any of Snowdon's pictures share a common feature, it may be the particular degree to which the light is diffused (he has a small daylight studio), but the effect can be seen in pictures by other photographers.*

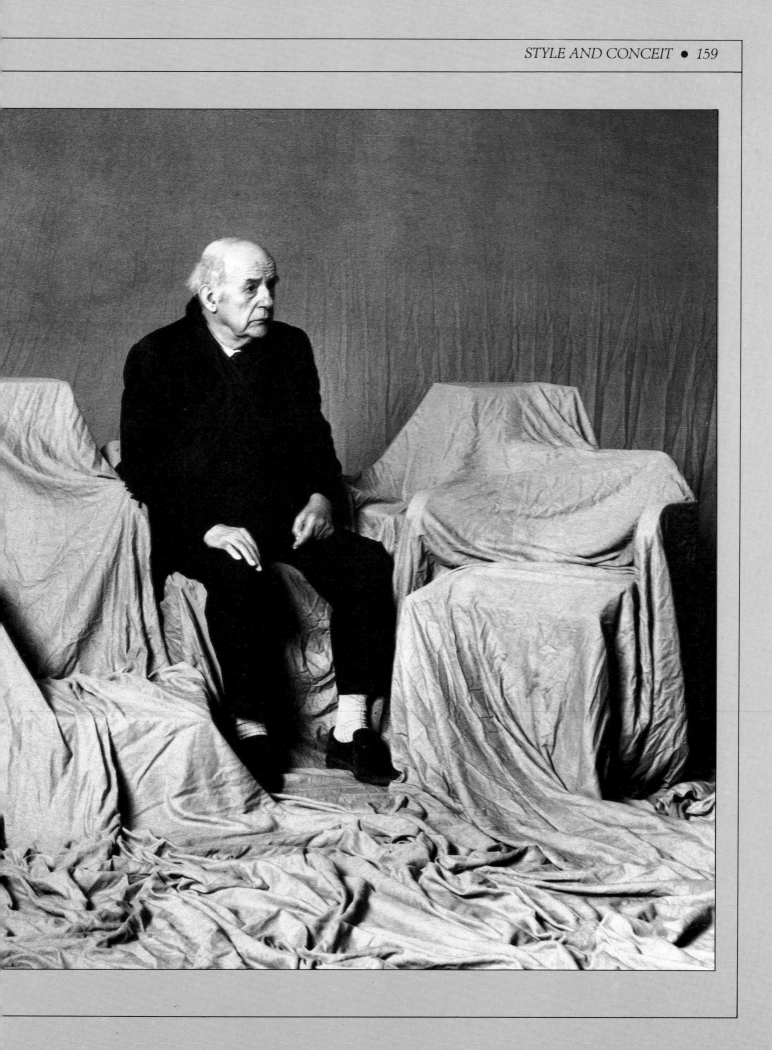

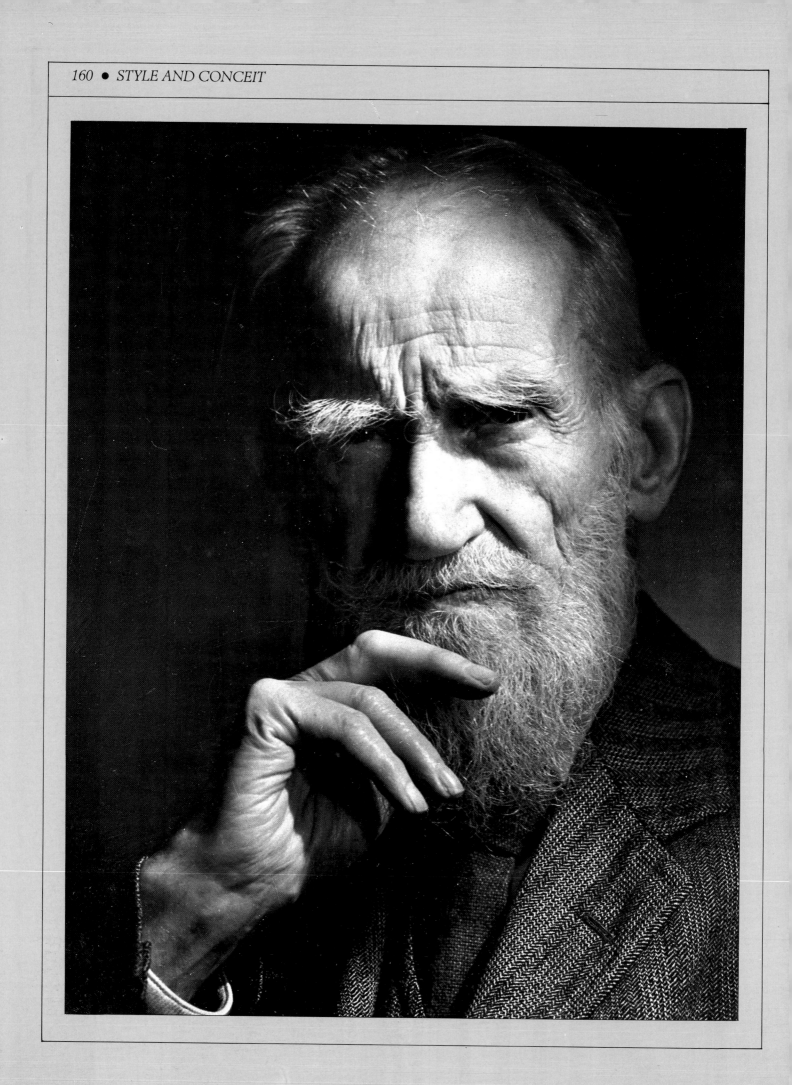

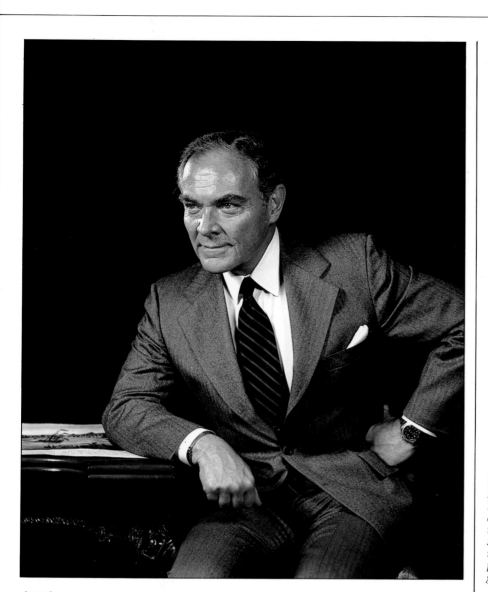

Far left *and* left *Two photographs by Karsh, one of George Bernard Shaw (*far left*), the other of Alexander Haig (*left*), demonstrate his consistently grand, mannered style, imposing his technique of strong lighting on all his subjects. The result is generally an heroic kind of portraiture — great men presented as great men.*

The attitude of needing a style is pervasive, even among professional photographers who are content simply with producing a good job that satisfies the needs of the client. As style really means, in most cases, a trademark, it is not surprising that speciality of technique is rampant. Moreover, for all the reasons mentioned, many photographers have been tempted into thinking that a recognizable technique is the same as artistic quality.

There is nothing wrong with using a set of techniques as a trademark, but this has little positive value in encouraging the development of a photographer's work. Indeed, once a photographer becomes aware of what other people begin to call his style, he may even begin to allow it to lead his work, risking freshness and originality. In its much more important sense, style is clearly not a store-bought quality, and cannot be cobbled together from one or two techniques and a distinct theme. It is a visual sensitivity to the subject — whatever subject — that is in front of the camera. Sensitivity in its turn involves both the willingness and application to examine, explore and consider. When the techniques have been learned and added to the files, the essence of photography is being able to show a subject in a manner that adds to our knowledge of it. This is style, and it is developed by the processes of looking and evaluation. Its role as a means of identifying an author is entirely secondary.

CHAPTER 7

The Element of Craft

'There is no substitute for fine craft; we can have craft without art, but not art without craft.'
Ansel Adams

'I don't care if you make a print on a bathmat — just as long as it is a good print.'
Edward Weston

As the quotations at the beginning of each chapter help to show, differences of opinion both keep photography vital and contribute to defining areas of interest. In fact, many of the most interesting developments in photography have been inspired by such disputes. Here, the issue is the role of craft in a medium that can, and often does, manage entirely without it: even a gorilla once made the front cover of *National Geographic* with a self-portrait.

In photography craft comes into play at two important stages. Once the photographer has established a general direction or approach, craft involves the application of certain skills or techniques to ensure that the image is produced without blemishes or faults. Once the photography is completed, craft again has a bearing on how the image is developed or presented. Although both roles seem fairly straighforward, many photographers express an ambivalent attitude towards craft.

For anyone familiar with the work of Ansel Adams and Edward Weston, the two quotations at the beginning of this chapter may not sound completely representative of their opinions and work. Adams was too perceptive a photographer to idealize craft, despite his own mastery of it, and was at pains to stress that the strength of a good photograph does not merely rely on the way in which it is presented. Weston, for his part, went to considerable effort in printing his negatives. Both photographers, although founders of f64, a group that exalted craftsmanship, expressed mixed feelings about it.

Such attitudes seem to be fairly common. Eugene Smith said 'I absolutely despise printing', yet once spent five days and five nights

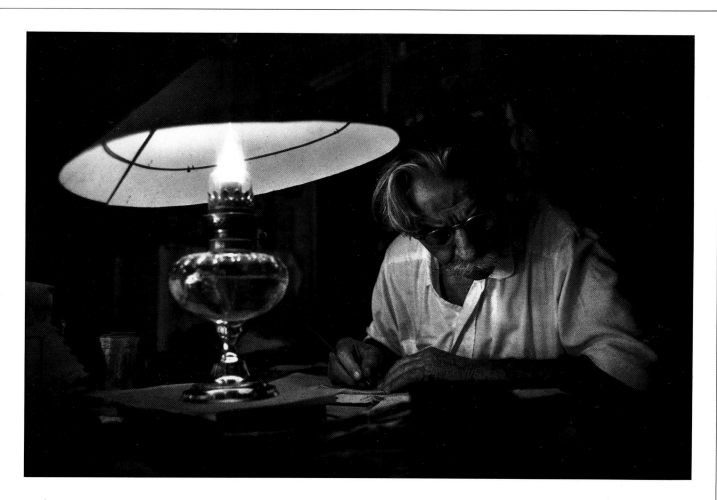

making the print that would be the lead picture for a *Life* story on Albert Schweitzer. In saying, 'I only use the camera like I use a toothbrush. It does the job', Don McCullin sounds less than fascinated with technical matters, yet he prints his own negatives (itself rare for a photojournalist) with great care and delicacy. These inconsistencies, though minor, are evidence of a perpetual tug-of-war between, on the one hand, an appreciation of craftsmanship — the intrinsic value of a thing well done — and a mistrust of skills that might interfere with the captured image.

For many photographers, the moment of *taking* the picture is the real focus of their ability. This is easy to appreciate in those situations, so common in photography, in which extremely fast reactions are the only way of making the image; an event unfolds, rapidly, in front of the camera, and it is only by being able to compress skills learned over a long period into a very short instant that the photographer can hope to succeed. Here, the taking of the picture is the single important element in the process; and a subsequent avoidance of craftsmanship, or at least of contrivance, can even serve to display the talent of the photographer. The ability of someone like Henri Cartier-Bresson is underlined by his refusal to alter his photographs — what the audience sees is what he took, warts (rarely any) and all.

Even in less urgent conditions, many photographers, certainly photo-journalists, have a strong feeling that the unpredictable process of looking at and working with a subject — up to the point of firing the shutter — is where the heart of photography lies. Studio still-life photography, for example, may seem to be highly formal and disciplined, but the best images from this field are rarely produced perfectly to plan. In the course of positioning camera, subject and lights,

Above *Despite his deep dislike of what he called 'the discipline of the darkroom', W. Eugene Smith regularly went to immense efforts because he needed technique to help him convey his strongly felt emotions about his subjects. Usually working quickly and discreetly, as his journalistic assignments usually demanded, Smith often found himself faced with hard work in the darkroom to overcome lighting problems during the shooting. For this photograph of Albert Schweitzer at his desk (1954), Smith had used a slow shutter speed (1/5 or ½ second), a fast lens, and a flashgun covered with a handkerchief and bounced off the floor (to give detail to the background). The main light, however, was the oil lamp, and although by Smith's judgement the negative 'wasn't a bad one', it took him three hours to make the first good print. He burned in the papers and envelopes intruding at the left, burned the entire lamp shade strongly, and then applied ferricyanide reducer to the flame, which understandably appeared as an extremely dense patch of silver on the negative.*

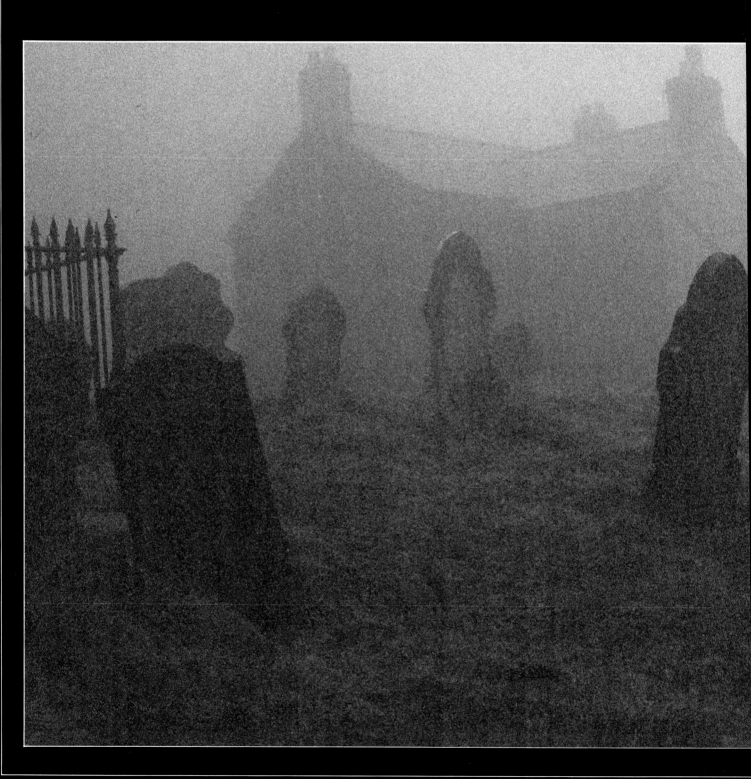

Below *Returning from an assignment in Port Talbot, Wales, Jim Arnould lost his direction in heavy mist, but found this intriguing small chapel. Wanting to enhance the sense of atmosphere with a strong texture of grain, Arnould loaded his camera with a high-speed transparency film, Ektachrome 400, and deliberately underexposed by two or three stops, later pushing the development of the film by the same amount. Push-processing exaggerates the appearance of the grain structure that is already pronounced in a high-speed emulsion.*

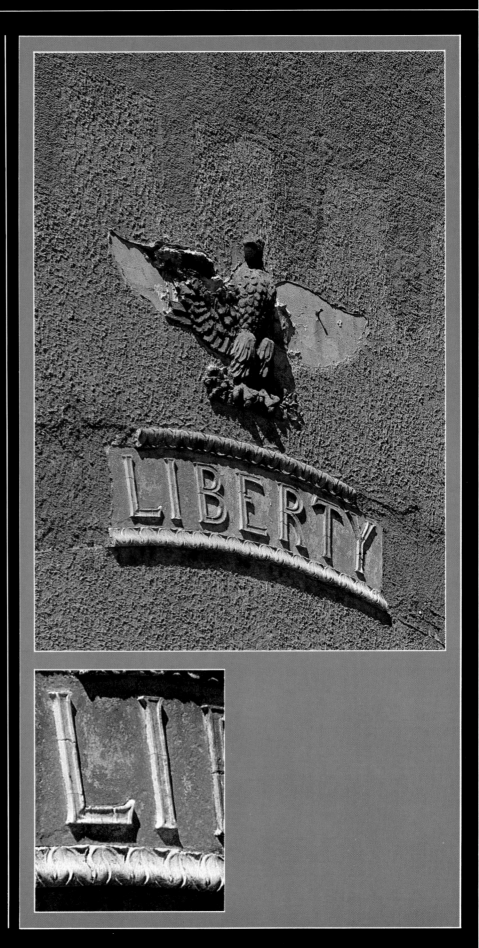

chance and suggestion often play an important part, and inspirations are not generally inhibited by the stark, workmanlike surroundings of a typical studio. These inspirations may be small ones — a coincidence of lines here, the play of light there — but they are an important part of what many photographers actually value most in their work: the unique and hard-to-define idiosyncrasies lying behind the execution of every single picture.

Craftsmanship is frequently mistrusted because it is a form of deliberate interference. Indeed, craftsmanship in any medium, implies a disciplined and careful approach, while the taking of a photograph can be fascinatingly and delightfully imprecise. The part of each photographer's personality that enjoys the surprises in taking pictures is usually suspicious of the perfecting influence of craft.

These suspicions are deepened by the knowledge of how a photograph can be manipulated. The hidden technologies in photography — retouching among them — can actually replace certain skills of picture-taking, such as the quick-wittedness to capture fleeting moments. Photographers whose work depends more on the physical world around them rather than their imaginations, can view the calculated manner of planning and producing pictures as running directly against what they see as the essential spontaneity in photography. Craft is closely linked to this idea of improvement and manipulation and so shares some of the disapproval. There is an underlying opposition between the crafted image and the picture that is more obviously 'realistic', capturing the moment with all its irregularities and peculiarities.

Despite this attitude, at a basic level craft is essential just for the sake of efficiency — producing pictures without blemishes and to a level of quality that enables whatever the photographer found important at the time to be fully expressed. A stage further on, craftsmanship can be used to *develop* some of the image qualities, for instance by heightening contrast in a picture that relies on a certain starkness for some of its effect, or by increasing the visual weight of a stormy sky in a landscape for greater impact.

Beyond this, the actual crafting of the image — the balancing of tones and colors, the selection of paper, and so on — can itself be perceived as a quality of its own, and one that may even be admired as much as or more than the picture's content. Further, while the finish of a photograph is unimportant for some images, it is vital for others. It is hard to imagine the effect of a Weston or Adams print if it were produced indifferently, with an inadequate range of tones, blocked-up highlights and blemishes.

Careful workmanship and production skills appeal to the personality of some photographers, who find them a down-to-earth and satisfying means of expressing themselves. In many areas of picture-taking there is a constant uncertainty about ultimate success; street photography is a prime example of this, where a day's hunting may produce several exciting, unrepeatable pictures — or nothing at all. For some people, this very uncertainty dims some of the pleasure; printing a negative, however, while it can demand great skill, is a more predictable activity — from the moment of entering the darkroom, the photographer can be fairly certain of being able to improve the print, given sufficient time and effort. From the point of view of personal gratification, there may be more excitement in capturing a picture, but it is not something that can be planned. Craft in photography, however, ensures a degree of satisfaction.

There is some justification for dividing craft into two: that involved in taking a picture and that involved in presenting it. The craft in picture-taking lies in basic precision — in focus, exposure, the selection of the appropriate camera controls, the movements of a view camera, and so on — and in choosing the materials and equipment that seem to suit the subject and the style of the photograph. A 35mm camera may be eminently suitable for candid photography, for example, or a view camera may make it possible to treat some subjects in searching detail.

At this stage, the variables that determine the quality of the picture are these: the pattern, size and texture of grain, the sharpness, the amount of detail, the contrast and separation of tones; in color photography the richness, purity, delicacy and saturation of the colors add an extra, complex and largely subjective dimension. These parameters can be controlled to a large measure — perhaps more than most people would imagine — by means of the film and equipment used to take the picture.

Most of the variables at the point of taking the picture depend on the film. There are relatively few manufacturers of film, Kodak being by far the largest, and the production quality is uniformly high. There are some very small differences between makes of the same type of film, unimportant in black-and-white and only marginally significant in color . Regular film is available in three forms — black-and-white negative, color negative and colour reversal (for transparencies) — and the color films are available balanced either for daylight and flash or for tungsten lamps. Selecting from these is fairly straightforward, depending on how the pictures are to be used and, in the case of color film, on the general color of the lighting. More creative choice is offered by the size of the film and its sensitivity, for, while these are practical matters, determined by the camera format and the amount of light available for photography, they also affect the appearance of the picture. The larger the film, the more detail and the smaller the grain, relative to the film, while the faster the film speed, the more the graininess and the less the contrast (in color film this is an apparent difference only).

A landscape, for example, that contains a large amount of fine detail, such as grasses and intricately textured rock, and includes delicate transitions of tone, such as a clear evening sky, may suggest a precise, grainless treatment — best handled by a large-format view camera and a fairly slow, fine-grained film. Alternatively, another photographer may decide to enhance the wildness of a stormy landscape by using graininess to break up the image; this can be done by using a fast, grainy film in a small size, such as 35mm, or even an enlargement from a small section of a 35mm frame.

Two specific films work in such distinctive ways that they have an important effect on image quality. One is Kodachrome, the other is the relatively new dye-image black-and-white negative emulsion. Kodachrome differs from all other regular color reversal films in that the color dyes are added by the manufacturer, Kodak, during the processing; as used, it is actually a black-and-white film. For various reasons, this special processing makes it possible for Kodachrome to be the least grainy of color reversal films, and its sharpness and delicacy can be exceptional. Although sold principally for amateur use, it has a professional following among magazine and advertising photographers that sometimes amounts almost to bigotry. Dye-image black-and-white film has a similar technical edge over regular silver emulsions; because it replaces silver grains with small clouds of dye, it can resolve very great detail and has no real graininess.

Even though modern camera equipment is all made to high standards, choice can still influence the quality of the picture in many situations, particularly those which are out of the ordinary, such as extreme close-ups and extreme magnification of distant views. For specialized uses, certain lenses in particular are more accurate than others. Lenses can be judged on their ability to resolve detail, their contrast, freedom from flare, accuracy of color, and relative freedom from the standard ailments that plague all optical systems. Complete freedom from aberrations is not possible, so that if a lens has to perform one particular task as well as possible — such as reproducing the dimensions of a flat copy — the manufacturer concentrates on correcting just the important aberrations, sometimes at the expense of others.

Closely tied to the performance of different films and lenses is the use of appropriate filters — not the bizarre pieces of colored glass and prisms that produce garish and banal trick photographs, but the ranges of filters that adjust color imbalances and alter tonal rendering. Filtration, at least as far as it is discussed here, is a production aid rather than as a special effect, can be applied with considerable sensitivity. For example, the relative tones of colors as they appear in a black-and-white photograph can be altered by using a colored filter over the lens. Whatever the color of the filter, it will lighten the tone of any subject that has the same color. Red lips photographed through a red filter will appear pale; through a

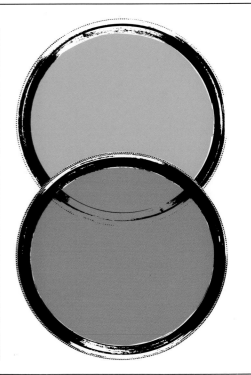

Right *Precisely because color is absent in black-and-white photography; its tonal rendering can be manipulated by using colored filters over the lens. A filter of a certain color lightens the appearance of that color in a print, and darkens its opposites. In practice, the colors of landscapes tend to be muted, so that the effects are generally subtle rather than obvious. In the photograph of El Morro National Monument in New Mexico, the desired effect was a distinct but gentle tone to the sky, both to reveal the delicate clouds and to enhance the lightness of the snow. The filter chosen was a Wratten 15 (deep-yellow) which needed an extra exposure of about one stop.*

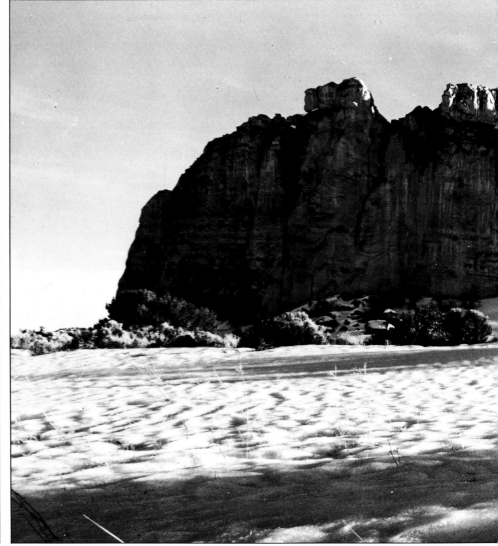

Below *In the more dramatic composition of the Saint Francis of Assisi Mission in the settlement of Ranchos de Taos, also in New Mexico, a Wratten 25 (red) filter was used in order to heighten the tonal contrast much more, to assist the slightly abstract composition. A red filter darkens a blue sky substantially, and deepens the shadows, which are also bluish.*

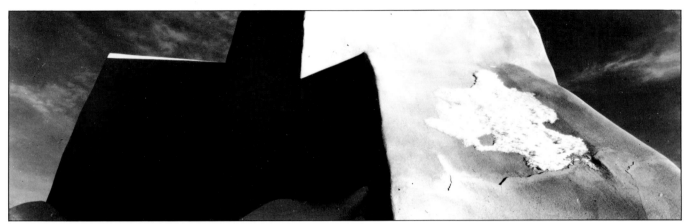

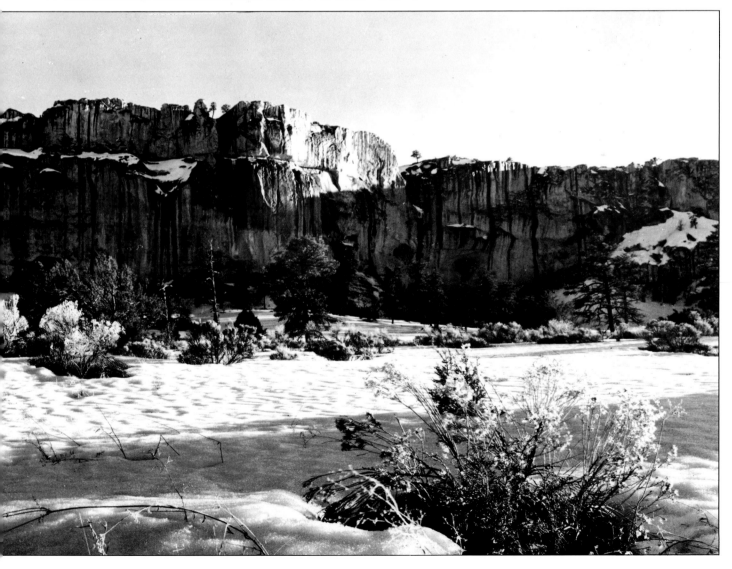

Right and **below** *Early film was sensitive to blue light — it was orthochromatic as opposed to the panchromatic black-and-white films in general use today. One of the effects of this, of some importance to landscape photographers, such as Carleton Watkins, whose best work is from the 1860s and 1870s, was to render all but the darkest skies a uniform white. The wet plates that he used reacted so much more strongly to the blueness of the sky than to the terrestrial features that they were recorded as dense areas on the negative. Many photographers of the day, in order to 'normalize' their images, resorted to printing in clouds shot (with a much shorter exposure) from another negative. More often, however, photographers adjusted to this discrepancy by composing their images so that the sky area would be of little consequence. In the photograph of Cathedral Spires, Yosemite, taken in 1865 (**right**), the white sky plays little dynamic part in the image. Indeed, the shaping of the top of the frame seems a recognition of this. Interestingly, however, the blue sensitivity of the film had, on occasions such as this, one benefit: it emphasized the depth and distance by enhancing the haze. Ansel Adams, who later made Yosemite his special photographic province, saw the value of increased blue sensitivity through the use of a blue filter. He said, 'In his desire for photometric accuracy in color rendition, the modern photographer, even though he has such greatly improved materials, has sometimes lost a feeling for light and atmospheric depth.' Nevertheless, what the improved sensitivity of modern materials has done for landscape photography is to encourage compositions that rely more heavily on the sky for balance. The photograph (**below**) of the Storr on the island of Skye in Scotland uses the rhythm of the broken clouds at the top of the picture to balance the unusual rock shapes below.*

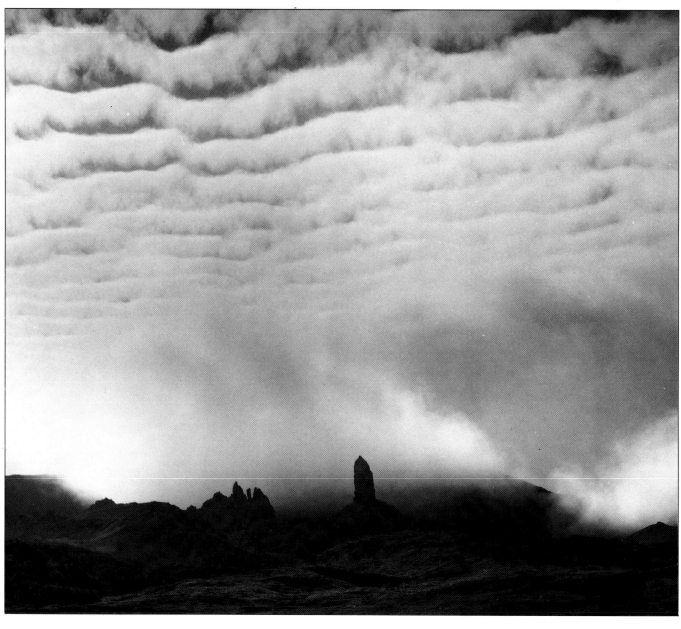

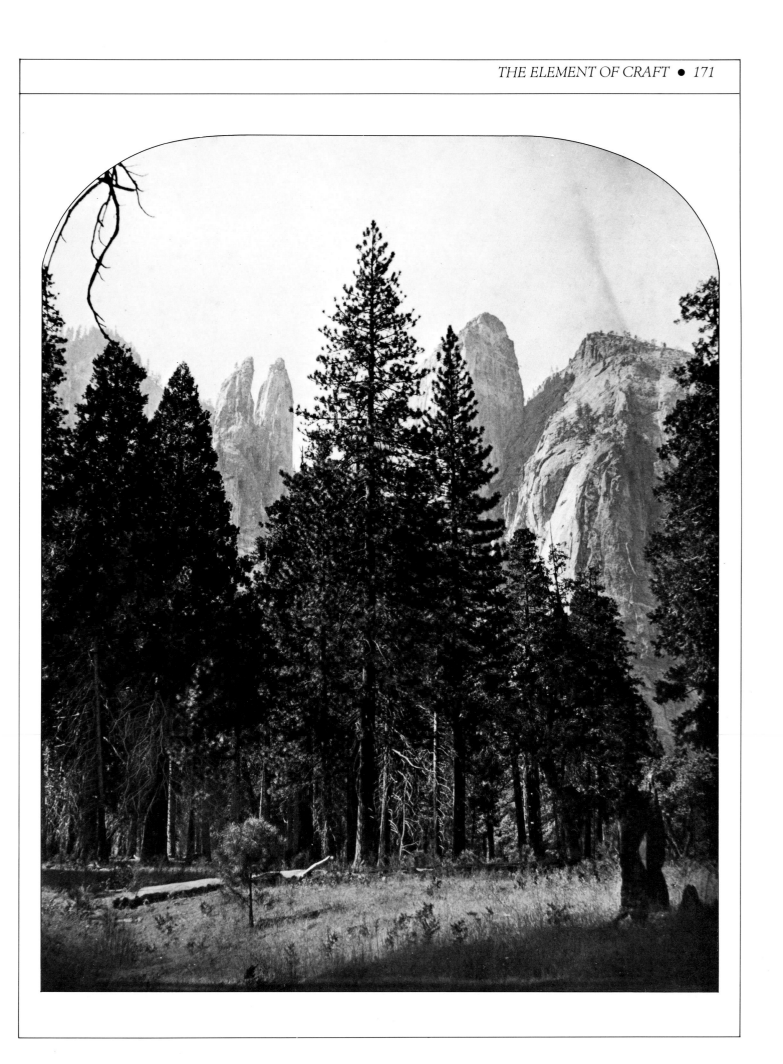

green filter, however, they will appear almost black. Since the colors of landscapes are generally more earthy and less pure than those of artificial and painted objects, filtration usually has a more gentle effect on the photograph.

Blue skies are a special case, however, for not only can the hue be intense, but even modern black-and-white film records blues deficiently. Simply to restore the expected, natural appearance, a yellow filter is needed. Early emulsions hardly recorded blue at all, and skies of whatever composition appear white in early plates. One incidental effect of the improvement of black-and-white emulsion and the additional use of darkening filters (yellow, orange and red) is that skies could be made a strong, even dominant, part of the composition.

Colour film offers fewer possibilities for control at the picture-taking stage, as there is no opportunity to be selective in the ways just described. One filter has virtually the same effect on all the colors; a pale blue filter will make the whole picture bluish, and, while it may have slightly less effect on anything blue in the scene, this is swamped by the overall cast. Color film does, however, impose its own quite rigorous standards of accuracy, as color, although usually judged subjectively by eye, is judged very precisely. A five-percent difference in overall hue can be noticed by most people, and is generally perceived in terms of rightness and wrongness. Audience reactions to the appearance of a black-and-white picture are much more tolerant of image qualities than they are to a color photograph. As a result, filters in color photography are mainly used in a corrective way, to counter the small differences between batches of film, the effects of ageing on emulsion, and the color differences between varieties of light.

Where craftsmanship really has the opportunity to dominate is in the way that the photograph is prepared and presented – 'post-production' in commercial technology. From the point at which the image has been recorded on film, there are boundless possibilites for changing it; these can vary from simply ensuring basic standards of image quality, to salvaging a disaster, or showing off a special technique.

Such forms of craftsmanship are most effective where the final product is a print and it is significant that many — perhaps even most — of the photographers who see themselves as craftsmen prefer to work with negative film rather than reversal and with black-and-white rather than color. Of the several means of producing a print, the regular negative process offers the greatest range of control at a reasonable cost (highly sophisticated processes such as platinum printing and dye-transfer printing can offer extraordinary control, but are difficult).

If the choice of film, equipment and filters at the *time* of shooting seems extensive, the permutations of materials and processes *after* the exposure has been made are even more so. If desired, these fine controls can be used to such a great extent that most of the final effect of the photograph is the result of work in the darkroom and workroom. The laws of optics and the relative standardization of film emulsions limit the expressive opportunities for craftsmanship behind the camera. From the darkroom onwards, however, a great deal can be done, so much so that the techniques used by certain photographers can be very distinctive.

To detail all the means of control would require a large technical manual, but they lie in these areas: the processing of the film, treatment of the developed film, choice of printing paper, and subsequent treatment of the print.

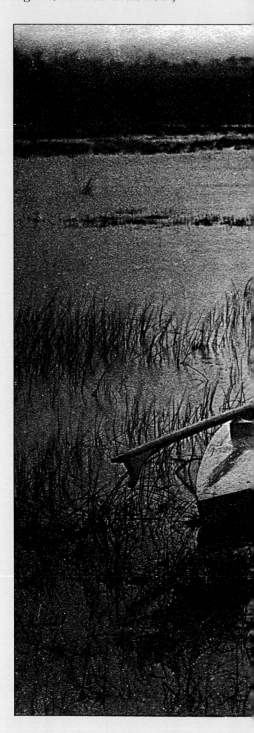

Below *Platinum printing was invented in 1879 by an Englishman, William Willis, and remained popular until the price of platinum itself rose too high. Apart from much greater permanence than even silver, the advantages are in what George Tice, who has revived the process, calls 'the unique beauty of a soft, full-scale platinum print'. The extremely fine particles of platinum are spread throughout the paper, so that there is no emulsion as such, and the surface is quite matte. Because it is produced by a partial 'printing-out' process, exposed in contrast with the negative, the shadow areas are self-*

masking. This means that, as the long exposure (half an hour is not uncommon) continues, the darkening shadow areas hold back more and more light. The result is a very long tonal scale, revealing great detail. Peter Henry Emerson was one of the platinotype's most ardent users, producing, principally in the 1880s, a series of naturalistic photographs of life in rural East Anglia. The print quality of photographs such as this platinotype, Gunner working up to fowl, *taken in 1886, was an important part of Emerson's work.*

There is sufficient variety in the choice of black-and-white developers and techniques that the film and its processing need really to be considered as one. At the point at which the exposure has been made, the film carries what is known as a latent image — undetectable but capable of being brought out by further treatment — and the film, with its layers of (usually) silver halide crystals, has *potential* characteristics. The processing stage plays a large part in determining how dark or light the image will be, how much contrast the pattern of graininess will display, and how sharp the image appears. Some kinds of developing solutions, for example, are particularly energetic, and so have some of the effect of using a faster, more sensitive film. Others develop a more abrupt edge

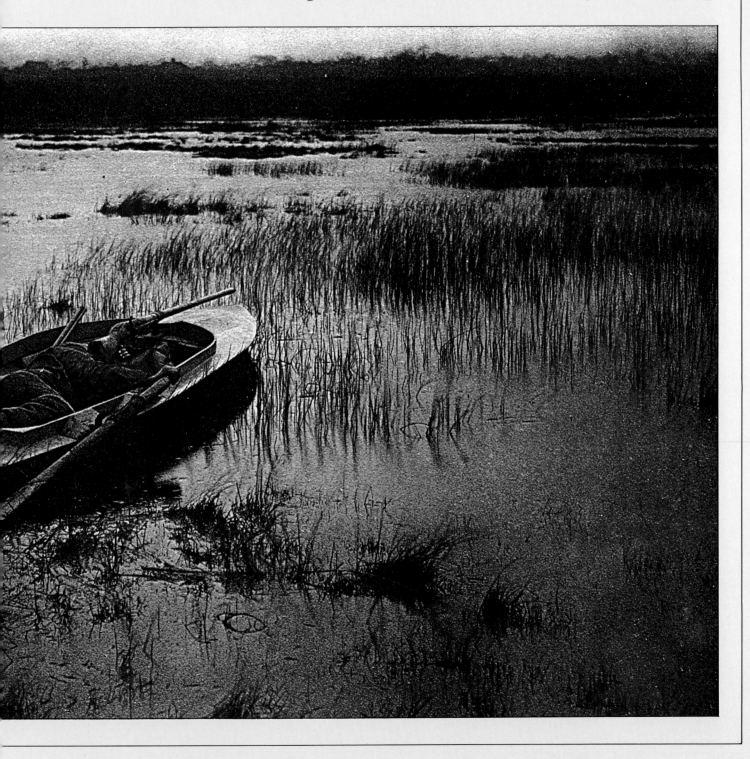

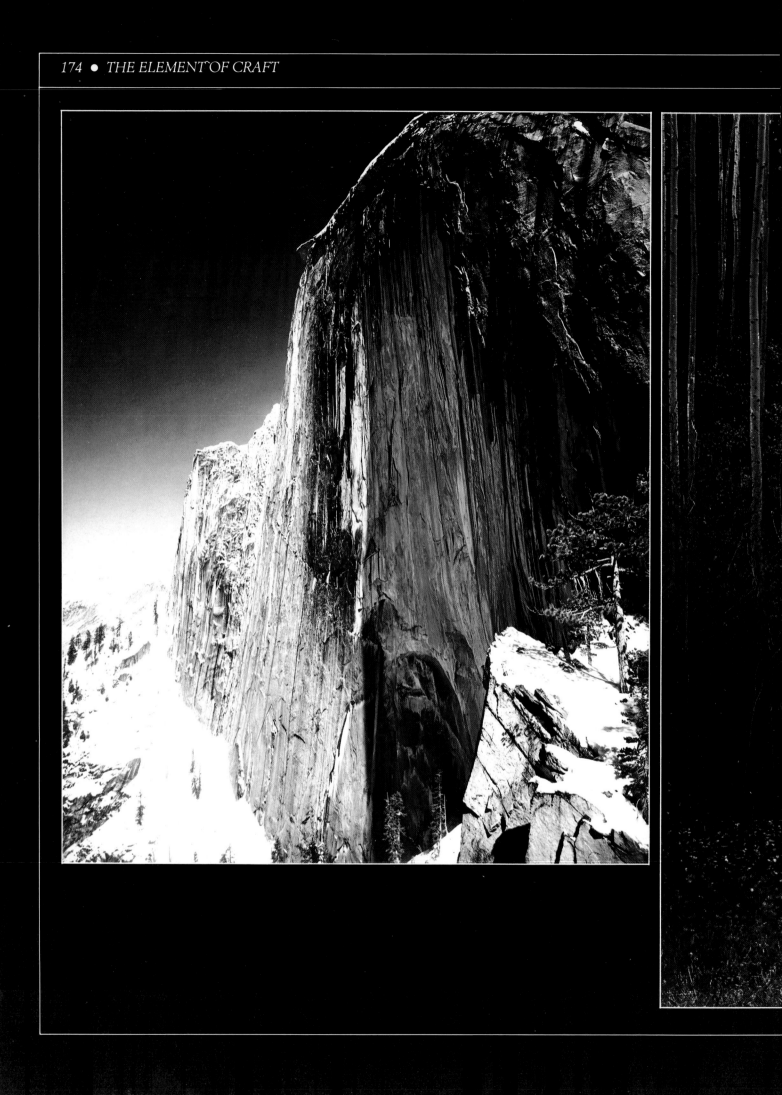

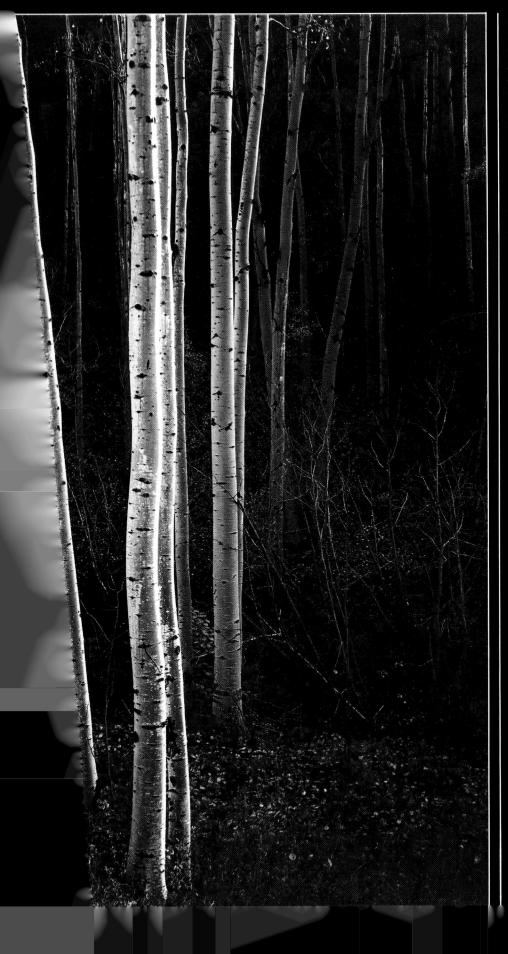

Far left *Photographed in the spring of 1927 in Yosemite, this rich, well-proportioned view, entitled* Monolith, The Face of Half Dome, *was made by Ansel Adams near the beginning of his career. Although by this time he had not yet conceived his Zone System method of assessing exposure and contrast, the hallmarks of quality and craftsmanship are abundantly evident. One of the factors influencing Adams' careful, deliberate way of working, not necessarily obvious to modern photographers, was the physical bulk and weight of the glass plates and view camera that he used. On that day's photography, Adams climbed 4,000 feet carrying a '6½ x 8½ Korona View camera, with two lenses, two filters, a rather heavy wooden tripod, and 12 Wratten Pan-chromatic glass plates'. In other words, in terms of picture-taking capacity, the equivalent of one-third of one roll of modern 35mm film. This completely prevented casual shooting, yet after a morning of photograhy, Adams had only two remaining plates for this view. As soon as he had exposed the first, he realized that the yellow filter that he had used would not deepen the sky and shadows sufficiently to do full justice to the sculptural shape of the Dome. 'I had only one plate left,' he wrote, 'and was aware of my poverty. I saw the photograph as a brooding form, with deep shadows and a distant white peak against a dark sky.' To accomplish this, he used his other filter, a deep red. Already having spoiled two negatives when wind moved the camera, and another when he forgot to stop down the lens, he was understandably anxious about making his last exposure. The cropping of the frame at the top right into the dome seems a little brave, given that Adams had only one negative to expose. In fact, it was slightly damaged in a fire in 1937, a compositional loss, Adams felt, that he 'could do without'.*

Left *The tonal range in this photograph by Ansel Adams of Aspens in northern New Mexico is its most interesting quality from the point of view of darkroom craft. 'In black-and-white photography,' Adams wrote, 'normal exposure and development would have produced a rather flat and gray image. I visualized the images as stronger, in accord with the mood of the hour and place.' He achieved this by two means: using a yellow filter to deepen the shadows slightly (the fill light was from a blue sky), and extending the development time (which increases contrast). Another technique that Adams used here was to select a high acutance developer so that the intricate details of autumn leaves and bark would be preserved.*

The Zones

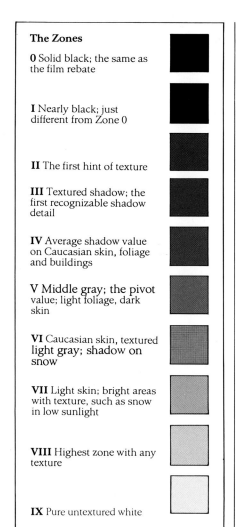

0 Solid black; the same as the film rebate

I Nearly black; just different from Zone 0

II The first hint of texture

III Textured shadow; the first recognizable shadow detail

IV Average shadow value on Caucasian skin, foliage and buildings

V Middle gray; the pivot value; light foliage, dark skin

VI Caucasian skin, textured light gray; shadow on snow

VII Light skin; bright areas with texture, such as snow in low sunlight

VIII Highest zone with any texture

IX Pure untextured white

The Zone System

Devised by Ansel Adams and later developed by Minor White and others, the Zone System is essentially an aid to deciding the level of exposure and degree of contrast in a photograph, and relies on what Adams called 'pre-visualization' — the opportunity and ability to decide before *taking a photograph exactly how it should appear when finally printed. At every stage of the process, from measuring the brightness in the original scene to making final adjustments to the enlargement, all the tones are assigned to zones. There are, arbitrarily, 10 of these, from solid black (0) to pure white (X), as shown in the strip* (**left**). *The range of the subject, the film and printing paper can be worked out in terms of these zones, and potential problems realized at the start. For instance, if the brightness range of a scene covers eight zones, but the film can only record seven zones, one solution might be to reduce the development (while increasing the exposure proportionately). The photographs* (**right** *and* **below**) *illustrate the Zone System as applied to a typical situation. Probably the most important step in this method is to choose the most important tone, and assign this to a particular zone. Such calculation is clearly only practical for certain kinds of photography, where there is time to think and plan. Nevertheless, with experience this can all be done surprisingly quickly. Ansel Adams, discussing the application of the Zone System to one print, wrote, 'People have said to me, "Why don't you just* make *the picture and forget all that technical gobbledygook?" … Because of ample practice in the field, the technical considerations were decided in about three seconds.'*

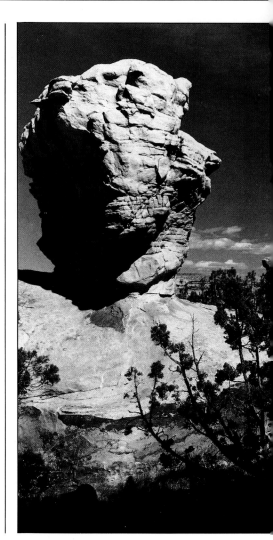

Measurements given in candles/ft² and f-stops

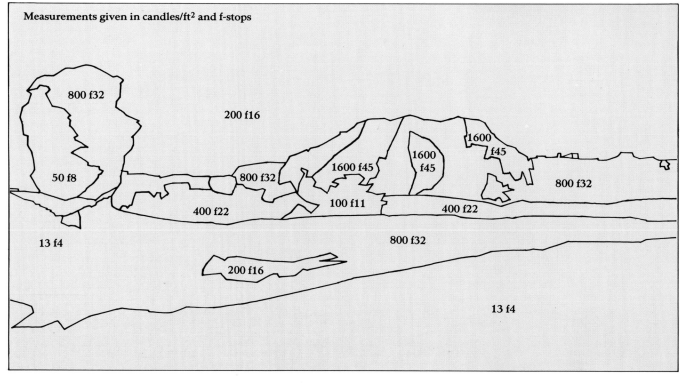

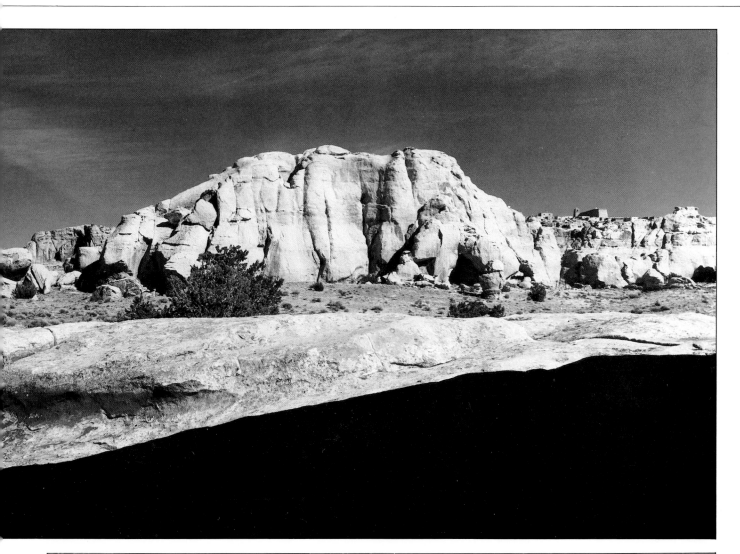

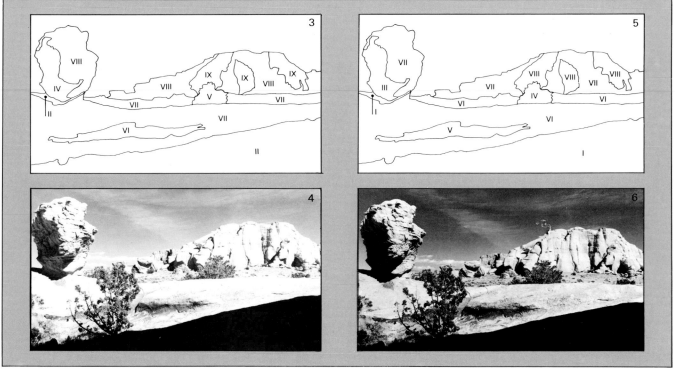

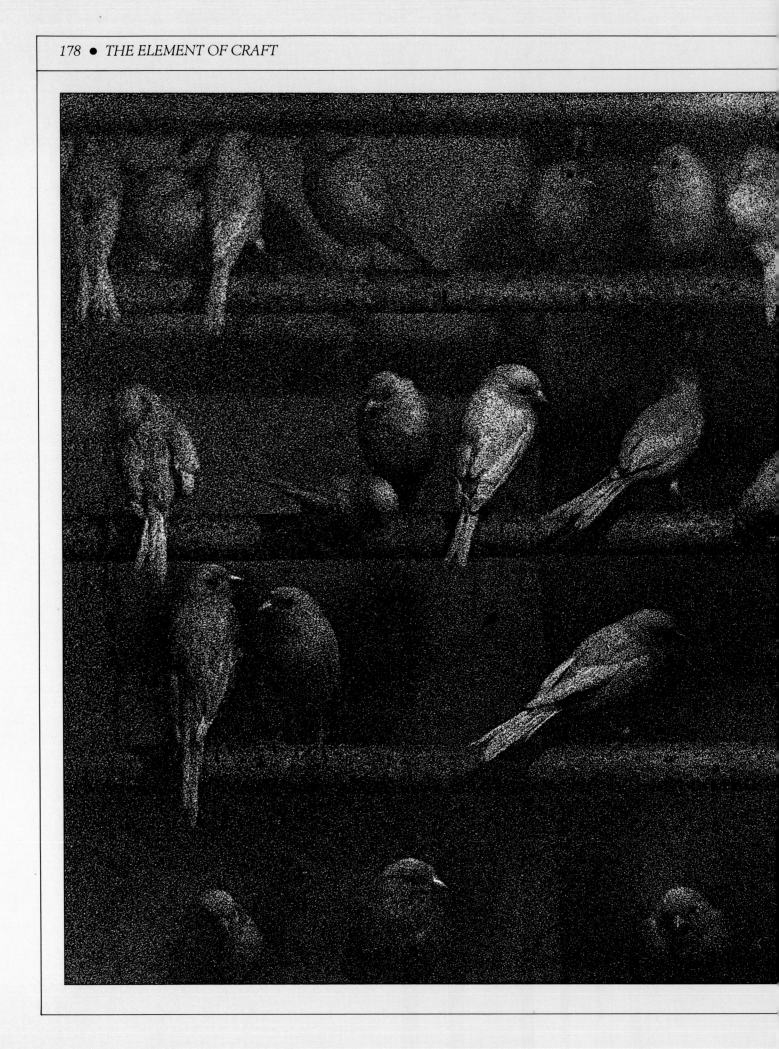

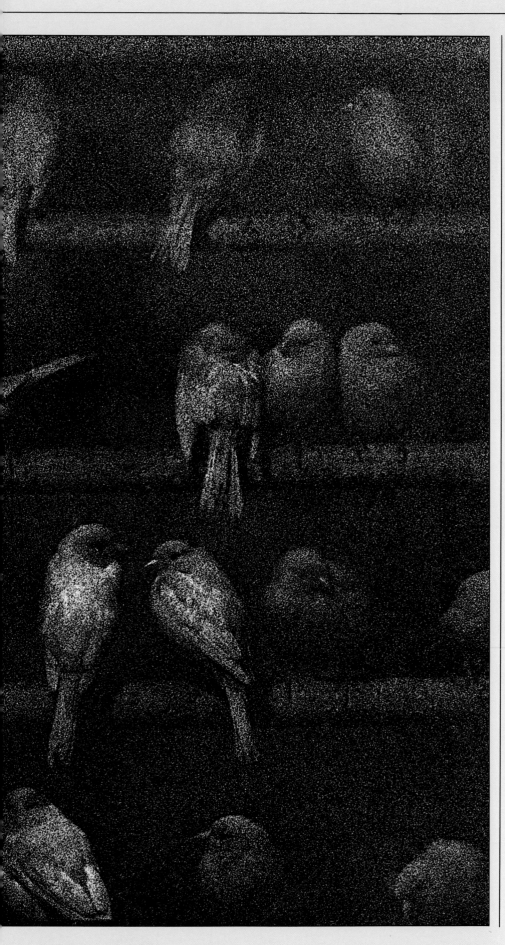

Left *The special grain texture of this photograph, The Birds, by George Krause, was achieved by high intensification of a Tri-X negative. Krause has experimented with the graphic possibilities of different chemical intensifiers, because of their effect on the graininess. In this example, he used a proprietary brand, Victor's Mercury Intensifier. Mercury intensifiers work principally on the thin areas of a negative, helping to separate tones and increase contrast.*

between the lighter and darker parts of the picture, and this tends to make the whole image look sharper. By altering the dilution of the developer, its temperature, or the time it is applied to the film, the density and contrast of the picture can be altered even more.

As the examples show, none of these possibilites has a gross effect — at least, not without ruining the image — and the way in which they are normally used by those photographers who take trouble over them, is to perfect the negative. For this reason, they are not for everyone; many photographers are dismissive of such techniques on the grounds that small technical improvements are unimportant compared with the content and structure of the image.

Others, such as Ansel Adams, have seen such techniques as an integral part of making photographs, one step in a continuous process in which the photographer decides how the final image should look and then sets out to achieve this by all available methods. Adams himself used the term 'pre-visualization' to signify the start of this process, implying a methodology that is, at heart, the approach of a craftsman.

Even when the processing is completed, not all of the possibilities for treating the negative have been exhausted. By bathing it in certain chemicals, the density of the image can be either weakened or strengthened. This is performed by solutions known as reducers (which remove some of the silver) and intensifiers (which add deposits of another metal to the silver). Moreover, depending on the formula of the solution, the contrast of the image can either be altered or not. Practically, intensifiers and reducers tend to be used for salvage operations on negatives that did not turn out as expected, but they can have more positive uses. George Krause, whose print *The Birds* appears on page 78, has a particular affection for a mercury intensifier (incidentally, highly toxic). He uses the solution, not so much to correct exposure mistakes as to restructure the pattern of the grain and to increase the separation of tones. The print shown here is an enlargement from a section of a Tri-X

Right and **far right** *In both of these surrealistic photographs, Jerry Uelsmann has put most of his attention and effort into the darkroom stage of the process, printing several negatives in combination. Although he will sometimes take photographs deliberately to fit a preconceived idea, more often he relies on a large stock pile of negatives. The juxtapositions tend to occur after the event rather than before.*

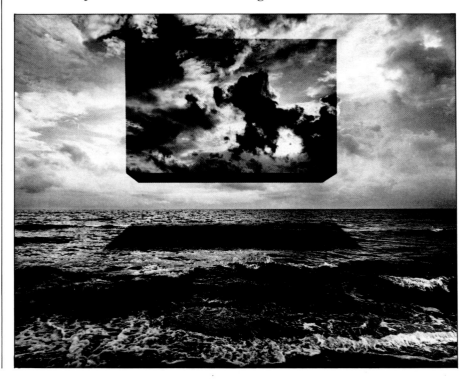

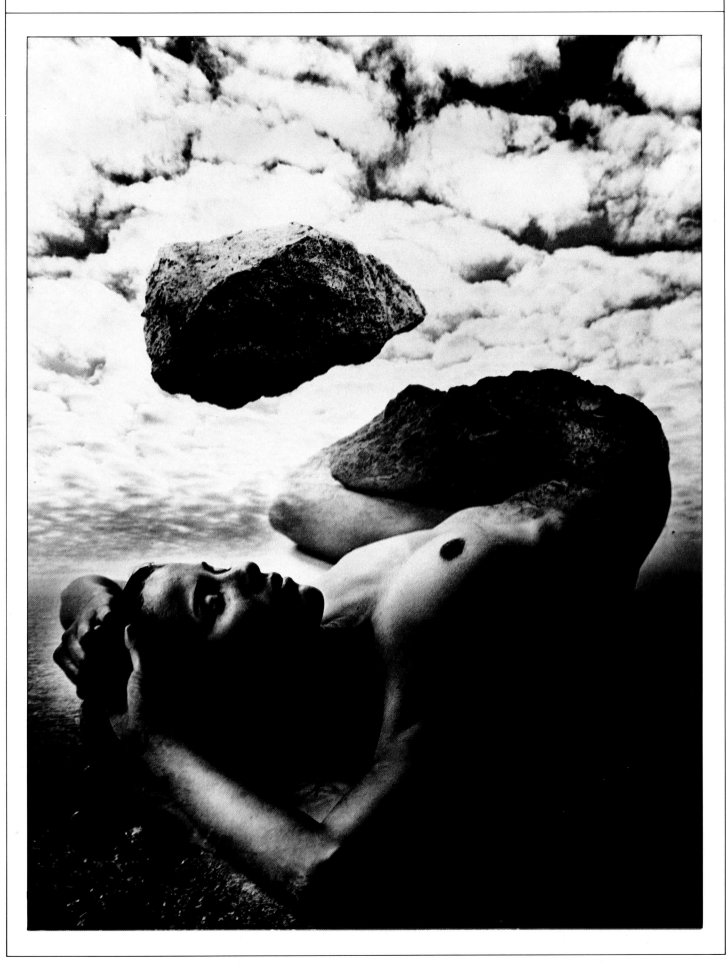

negative that has been strongly intensified, and achieves much of its effect from the detailed graininess. To Krause, this pattern 'resembles aquatint or fine mezzotint', a preference which is a legacy from his early days when he was working as an intaglio print-maker.

The major set of quality controls, however, apply to printing. In black-and-white printing, a wide variety of papers is still available, even though mass production is steadily moving towards standardization. There is variety in several qualities: in contrast, the maximum density of black, the maximum brilliance of highlights, finish and glossiness, texture of the coating, tint, response to toners, the chemical process itself, and the thickness, absorbency and texture of the paper base.

As the examples on page 184 show, even despite the inadequacies of photo-mechanical printing, the black-and-white photographer has a broad palette from which to choose. There are even fashions in the choice of paper. The degree of smoothness of finish tends to arouse definite feelings among photographers, with a basic polarity between those who prefer the softer tones of matt paper and those who prefer the depth and crispness of a glossy print. The greatest brilliance is possible on a paper that has a smooth, glossy surface, as this gives the least scattering of light. The reflectance range (black to white) on the best of such papers can be more than 1:100. Matt papers, on the other hand, have a reflectance range of about 1:25, which in practice means that the deepest blacks and most reflective whites are not possible. Ferrotyping, now rarely practised, was a means of adding an even higher gloss to glossy paper, by drying it in contact with a polished metal sheet; its extreme reflectance, however, makes the print difficult to view.

Color printing has a much smaller range of possibilities, and the controls that do exist are more in the printing stage than in the choice of paper. Moreover, the very existence of color in the image tends to push the style of reproduction towards realism — there is less acceptable scope for interpreting the colors of a recognizable scene than there is for manipulating its monochrome appearance.

Printing skills are largely concerned with controlling the lightness and darkness of local areas of the picture, and the effect is, naturally, influenced very strongly by the contrast of the paper being used. It is also determined by the light source used in the enlarger — a single lamp, focused through condenser lenses, gives more contrast than a diffused light (and also, incidentally, shows up any imperfections in the emulsion more clearly). In addition, the choice of developing solution can affect the contrast and the tint, while the method of processing also offers control.

It is interesting to compare the way in which Ansel Adams works, with the procedures of another photographic craftsman of great skill, Jerry Uelsmann. Adams' pictures are, to use Weston's expression, essentially 'straight', while Uelsmann works very much from his imagination, using, in a Magritte-like fashion, unexpected juxtapositions. Here the approach is what demands craftsmanship; Uelsmann's printing skills are necessary in order to make the images work at all.

Uelsmann's techniques in combining images are relatively straightforward, but the high degree of craftsmanship is necessary to make the components blend successfully. The blending applies not simply to the 'joining' of the different negatives, but to the tone, contrast and perspective as well. In the photograph on page 181, the negative of the torso and the joining rock have been printed separately onto the same sheet of paper, each shaded with card so that alone they grade to white, in the manner of an old-fashioned portrait vignette. Through experience,

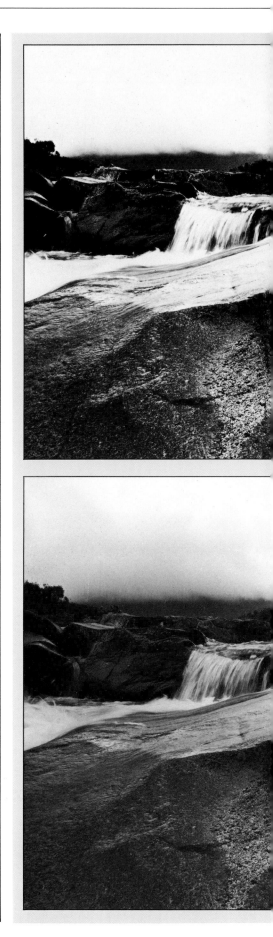

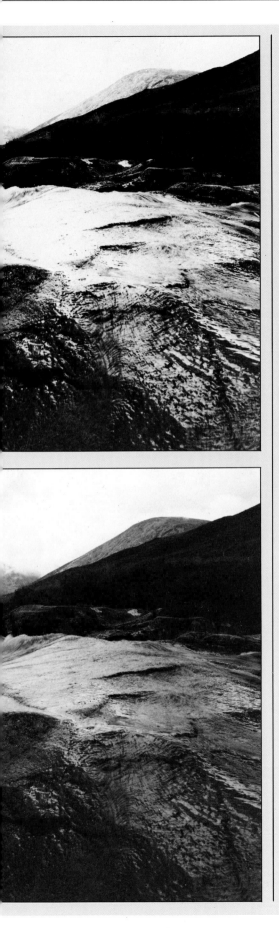

1

2

3

4

5

Below *Printing papers are available in a range of grades from 0 to 5 — soft to hard — to accommodate differences in contrast between negatives. These five strips illustrate how the same negative will print on papers graded from 1 to 5.*

Above left *Printing on the hardest grade of paper. grade 5, makes full use of the paper's tonal range but gives a harsh image that has no detail at either end of the scale.*
Below left *Paper graded 1 is fairly flat and is intended for negatives with high contrast. It will reveal the greatest amount of detail but a negative with a normal range of contrast will result in a print that extends neither to black nor white. Grade 2 is considered 'normal'.*

Printing controls *To Ansel Adams, who was a master craftsman of black-and-white photography, 'the negative is similar to a musician's score, and the print to the performance of that score. The negative comes to life only when "performed" as a print.'*

Aside from the use of different grades of printing paper, printing controls — varying the amount of light that reaches the paper by shading or printing-in — are an important means of interpreting a negative.

The same negative has been printed three *times (***below***), to accentuate different aspects of the same scene. All were printed on a medium-grade paper at f11; the diagrams (***right***) show the exposure time in seconds for the different areas of the prints. While such controls can be used merely to extract the maximum amount of information from a negative, they can also be used more creatively — to build an image in the darkroom whose tonal range may bear little resemblance to the original negative.*

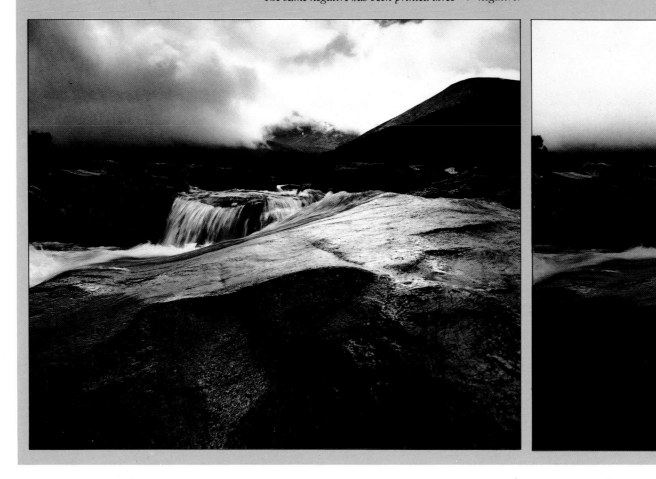

Uelsmann controls this shading in opposite directions so that the transition is smooth.

The contrast of different negatives used in this kind of combination is likely to vary and, as an aid to matching the contrasts, Uelsmann uses variable-contrast printing paper. Unlike the fixed range of grades in regular paper, this will give high or low contrast depending on the color of the filter used over the enlarging lens. Hence, negatives of different contrast can be compensated for individually on the same sheet.

After the print is made, the workroom offers still more possibilities for manipulation, including toning, which can be performed solely to keep the print from deteriorating or, as has already been seen on page 178, to add color , together with all the techniques of the retoucher. At its least controversial level, retouching is a matter of removing or obscuring small blemishes, but, used more heroically, it can substantially alter the whole nature of the picture.

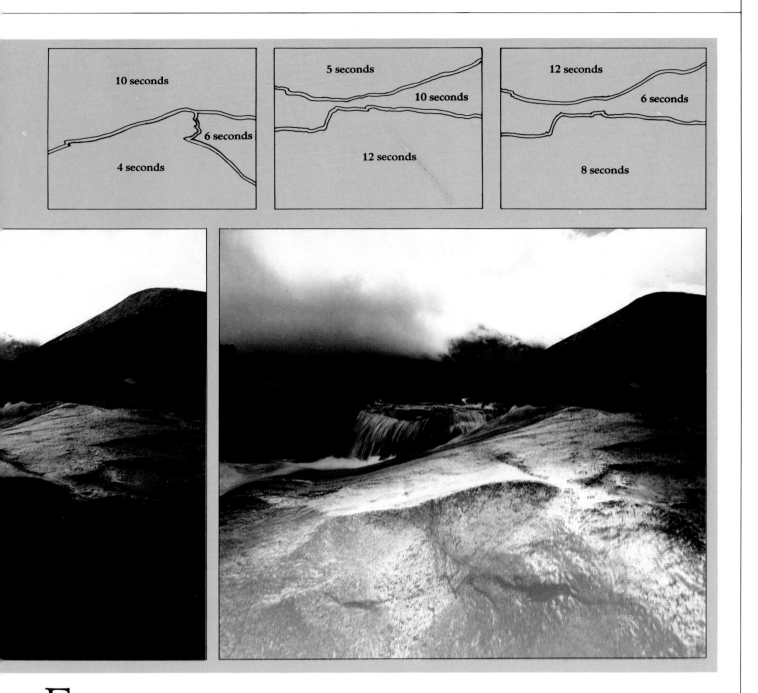

From this survey of craftsmanship in photography, it is evident that enormous effort can be put into the production of a single photograph. While this type of approach is critically important to only a section of practising photographers, and matters most when the final product is an original print, it has a broader appeal to the viewing public, for reasons that can perhaps only be fully appreciated by examining real prints rather than reproductions. Although the techniques may sound dry and technical, the final effect is very much a sensual one.

There is another reason for the appeal of the crafted print. Craftsmanship is tangible evidence of skill, apprenticeship and effort — old fashioned values in many ways. Where photographs are displayed — in galleries and magazines — the way they have been executed can account for a substantial part of the pleasure of looking at them. Finely crafted prints reassure audiences that what is on display is worthy of appreciation, and carry their own guarantee of excellence.

CHAPTER 8

Playing to the Gallery

'If the viewer doesn't get it, you've failed to communicate.'

Elliott Erwitt

'There's no audience as far as I'm concerned. I'm the audience.'

Joel Meyerowitz

Taking pictures can be, and often is, a private matter, destined for no wider publicity than a family snapshot album. The same cannot be said of the photographs in this book, which are public in the sense that they have been put on display, where they can be judged by an audience. But just as the types of role played by photography vary from the highly personal to the frankly commercial, its audiences range from a relatively small, dedicated group of gallery visitors to the public at large, for whom photographs in magazines and newspapers and on hoardings are part of daily life. The issue is further complicated by the fact that many people take pictures themselves, or at least have a basic familiarity with the technology — a degree of participation which influences their expectations of what the 'experts' should achieve.

How these different audiences modify or influence photography is the subject of this chapter; but this relationship is by no means as straightforward as it might first appear. The complexities can be highlighted by examining two extremes: 'private' or personal photography, and commercial photography, as typified by advertising work.

Personal photography, in which the photographer follows his or her own inclinations, may be seen as having a strictly limited context. On the level of the family snapshot — as long as the snapshot stays in the photographer's wallet — this holds true. Once photography that was conceived privately begins to be displayed publicly, however, other issues come into play.

A good example of photography of a very personal nature being offered for public scrutiny lies in the 'equivalence' photographs of Alfred

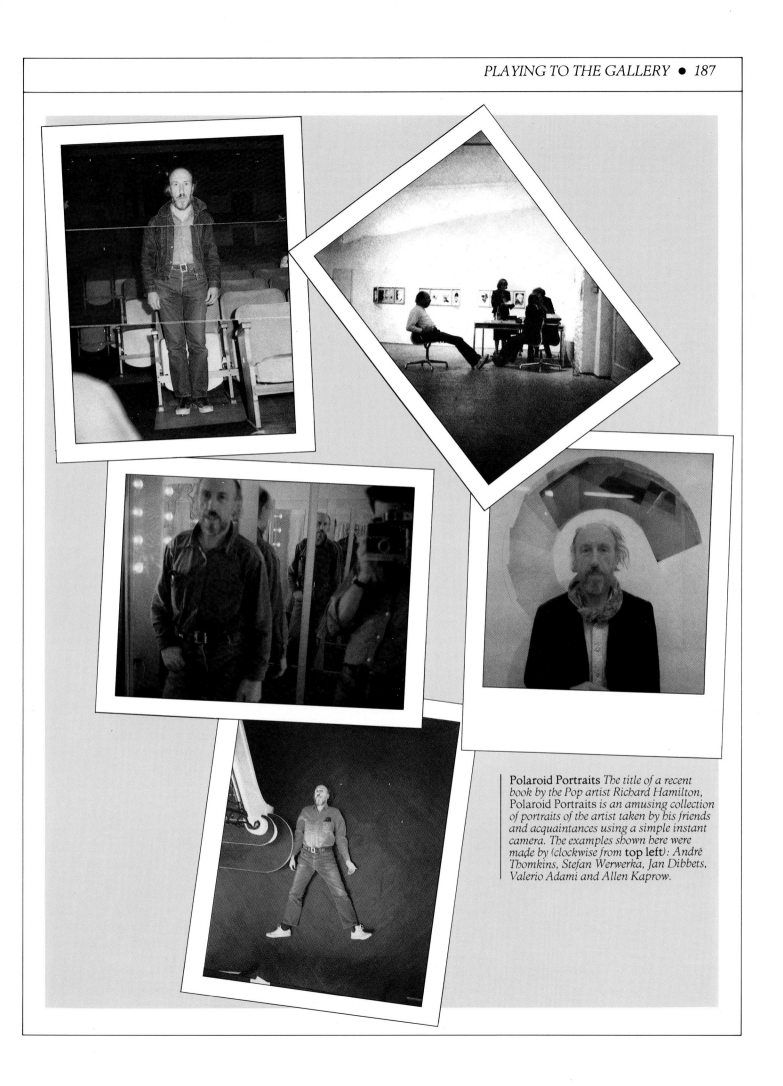

Polaroid Portraits *The title of a recent book by the Pop artist Richard Hamilton, Polaroid Portraits is an amusing collection of portraits of the artist taken by his friends and acquaintances using a simple instant camera. The examples shown here were made by (clockwise from* **top left**)*: André Thomkins, Stefan Werwerka, Jan Dibbets, Valerio Adami and Allen Kaprow.*

Stieglitz and Minor White. Their work represents a personal exploration of private feelings — but it had declared a public function. Minor White stated that he wanted to challenge 'the tyranny of visual facts' and expressed his intentions in the well-known phrase: 'To photograph some things for what they are, and others for what else they are.' While these are ambitious aims — the very naturalism of most photographic images, and many of White's in particular, can inspire different interpretations — such work is no more 'private' than other art forms. In other words, interpretation and involvement on the part of the audience is welcomed and invited. White is also on record as saying that 'the meaning appears in the space between the images, in the mood they raise in the beholder'.

In a different way, more recent experiments in private-made-public photography have explored the value of the personal snapshot. Some of the more interesting results have come from artists established in other fields. David Hockney, for example, has constructed giant collages of instant prints, assembled in sequences that challenge the single-instant, single-viewpoint image. The Pop artist Richard Hamilton recently undertook a project in which friends and acquaintances photographed him with a standard instant camera. The results, published in a new book, make no attempt to elevate the snapshot to the status of art, but light-heartedly present the variety of interpretations that emerged despite the limitations of subject matter and means of expression. Participants included Paul and Linda McCartney, and artists such as Rauschenberg and Anthony Caro.

At the other extreme from such private work is photography that is aimed wholeheartedly at an audience. Advertising photography is the least complicated example of this — it exists to help present a case for buying a product or service. Even here, however, the best work in the field is not obvious in its pursuit of its audience. Most advertising is concerned with persuasion (and reassurance) and photographers must generally work quite hard for the viewers' attention. This in turn means using imagination and being in some way different — different, that is, not only from other advertisements but from what the viewer expects. One practical dilemma is that it is not as simple as might be imagined to find out from an audience what type of advertising it will respond to best. Various kinds of consumer research are used, but what people say they like is not always what they will go for on the day. Further, by following the *stated* tastes of a large number of people, advertising, including its imagery, can sometimes drift down towards the lowest common denominator of interest. For this reason, advertising photography at its most competitive level often has to rely on unusual ideas — ones that are products of the imagination of the art director or the photographer rather than feedback from a prospective audience.

What these two cases illustrate is that private photography can venture into the public sphere, while the most public of photography can be fundamentally affected by personal tastes. It is reasonable to expect other types of photography to exhibit a similar mixture of responses. Even individual photographers hold different attitudes towards their viewing public, as the quotations from Elliott Erwitt and Joel Meyerowitz point out. Erwitt's photography provides good examples of what could be called a positive attitude towards the audience. While he has two distinct areas of work, commercial and personal, all his pictures are directed squarely at the viewer. His non-commercial photography, though personal in the sense that it is not assigned work, nevertheless has a sizeable public following. Most of these pictures make a humorous point, and humor absolutely requires that the audience sees things in the same

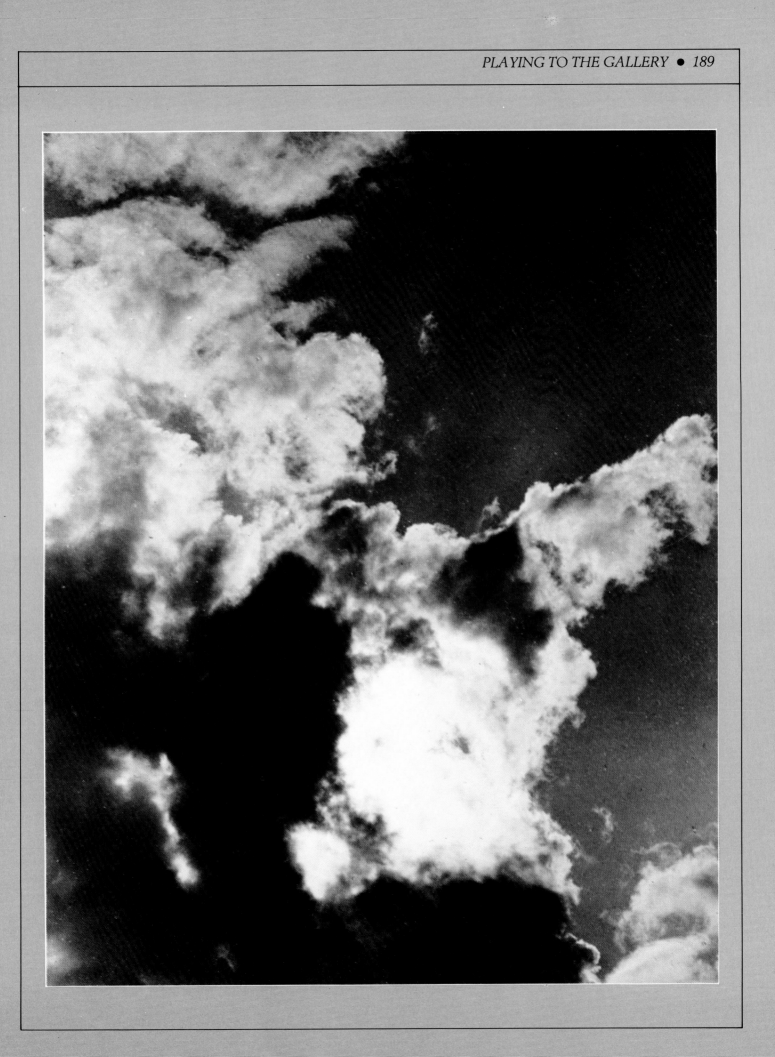

Below Luncheon at the British Embassy, Tokyo, February 14, 1983, *David Hockney. In a recent series of photographic collages, Hockney has been challenging the single-instant, single view-* point image. *This collage, arranged to put the viewer in Hockney's place, contains small sequences intended to convey an impression of the whole event, rather than just one moment.*

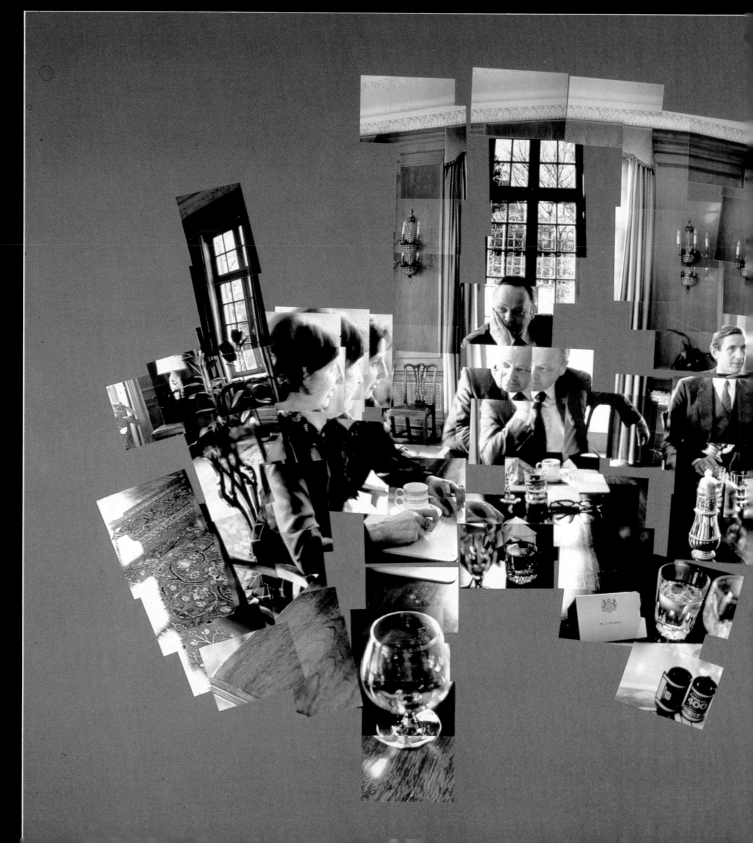

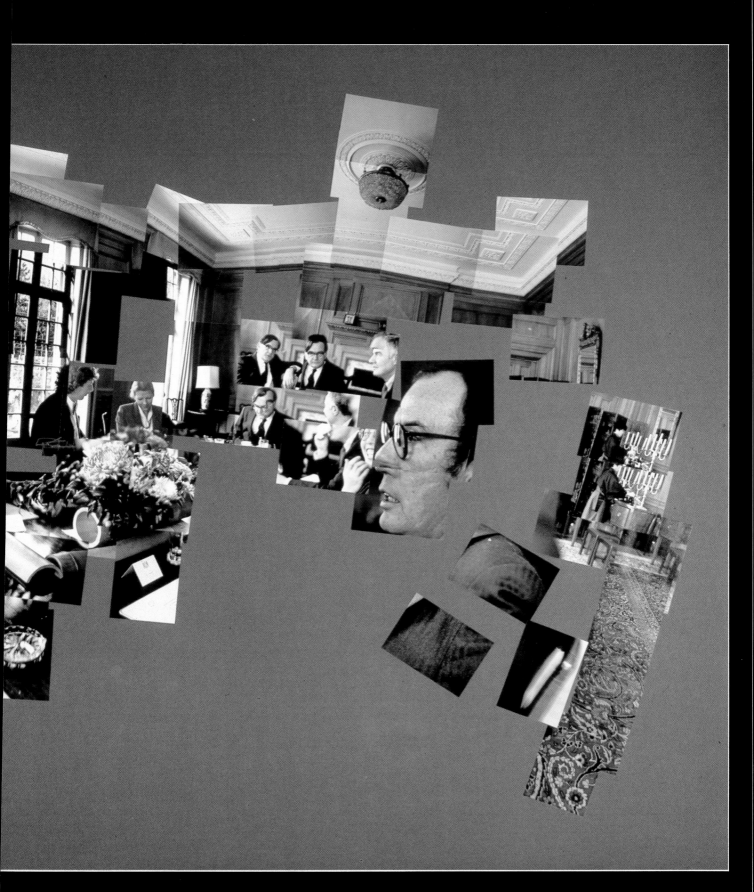

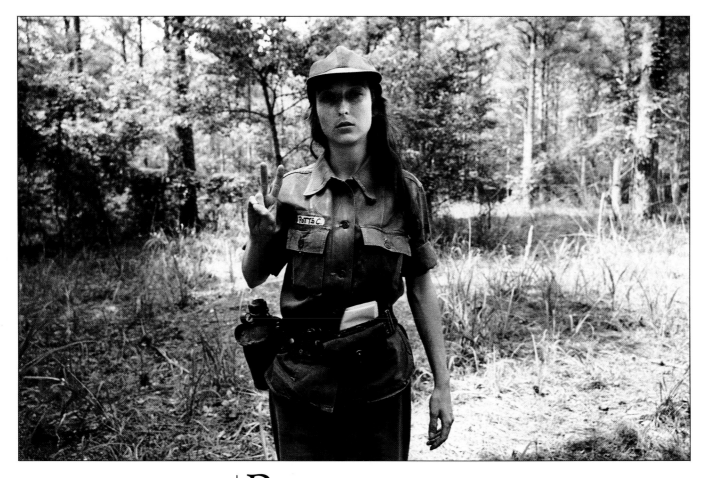

Reportage photography has, in theory at least, no crowd-pleasing role to fulfil. It is certainly aimed at an audience but, unlike advertising, its role is to present information. Nevertheless, as it is the response of an audience that determines the success of a shot (or at least the professional appraisal of that response), working photojournalists are obviously aware of who will be looking at their work, and how. In the context of rapidly unfolding events, time and circumstances may not allow the photographer the opportunity to shape the material, but in calmer moments it *is* clearly possible to play to the viewer's likely responses. In Mary Ellen Mark's picture of a WAC in battledress, there is gentle humor at work, of a kind that anticipates the reaction of the audience.

There is no point in disguising the fact that photojournalists are consciously working to the requirements of drama, actuality and human interest which editors believe will sell newspapers or magazines to the widest possible readership. To experienced photojournalists some images, as they take shape in the viewfinder, clearly announce themselves as potential lead pictures or double-page spreads. In this sense, every professional news photographer is his or her own picture editor.

At a deeper level, too, editorial and commercial photography tends to reflect the underlying values of its audiences, but not always deliberately. Aesthetically, photography is still dominated by Western tastes, due partly to tradition and partly to economics. The *market* for most photography is in the West — that is, the money spent by the public on the media that use photographs is mainly in the United States and Europe. Even the one large non-Western market for published photog-

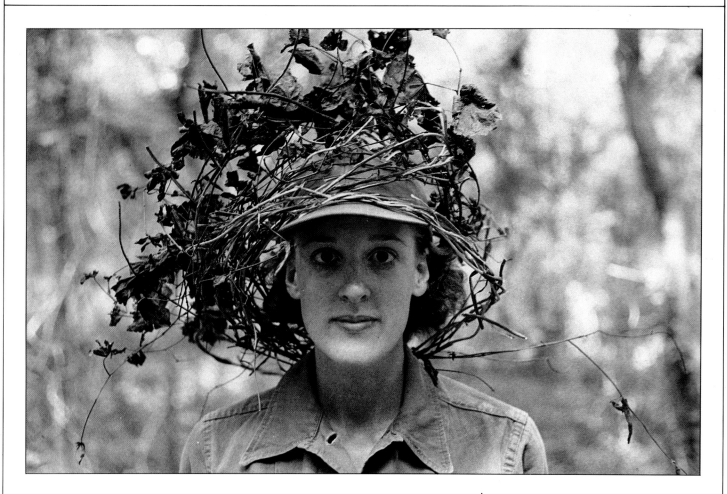

raphy, Japan, is not distinctively different in its reportage and advertising imagery, and generally seems to reflect Western standards. Traditional Japanese design in certain areas, such as food and household objects, is renowned for its simplicity and elegance, but any expectations that this might be reflected in the general run of commercial photography are likely to be dashed. It is significant, for example, that in Japanese advertising and fashion photography, even a large proportion of the models are from the West: the suggestion of Western origins may enhance certain products in the public's mind.

The result of the West's domination of the market is a bias in the kinds of photography, particularly advertising and reportage, that are internationally directed towards a mass audience. This manifests itself in various ways, two of the most obvious being on the one hand a kind of parochialism and, on the other, an interest in certain travelogue subjects specifically for their exotic nature. The parochialism is a natural editorial matter, reflecting local interests; it is not surprising, for instance, that most American general-interest magazines mainly run photographs of American topics that are not always easily appreciated by people in other countries. Naturally enough, since most high-circulation photo-publications are located in the West, it is the values of a Western readership which largely determine the ground-rules. Furthermore, in dealing with stories from 'abroad', there is often an assumption that anything very different from average Western values is simply unusual. It is these tastes that define the 'exotic' in photography.

Quite why the West has such an appetite for a dynamic image-making industry is a large question. Traditions of individual enterprise, of shaping the world through technology, and an accompanying ideology of

Above and left As part of an essay on the Women's Army Corps, in the photo-journalistic tradition, Mary Ellen Mark here catches the humor of a slightly ridiculous camouflage 'bonnet' on a wide-eyed trainee and the wistful expression of another recruit giving the victory sign in a peaceful glade (left). '...We didn't want to put them down,' Mark writes. 'We tried to see the funny side of it and sometimes the lonely side, to break through to the people and see what their life was really like.' The immediate journalistic concern here, where humor is the intention, was to recruit the appreciation of the audience. Mark has done this through knowing what most people (not necessarily the WACs) will find amusing. In the camouflage picture, she stressed the humor by closing in and using shallow depth-of-field to separate the camouflage from the background (with which, of course, it is supposed to blend). To achieve this shallow focus, Mark used a high shutter speed (1/1000 second) and a neutral density filter to allow a wide aperture of f2.

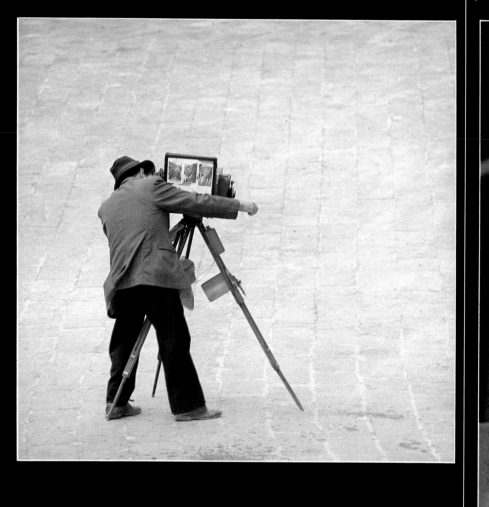

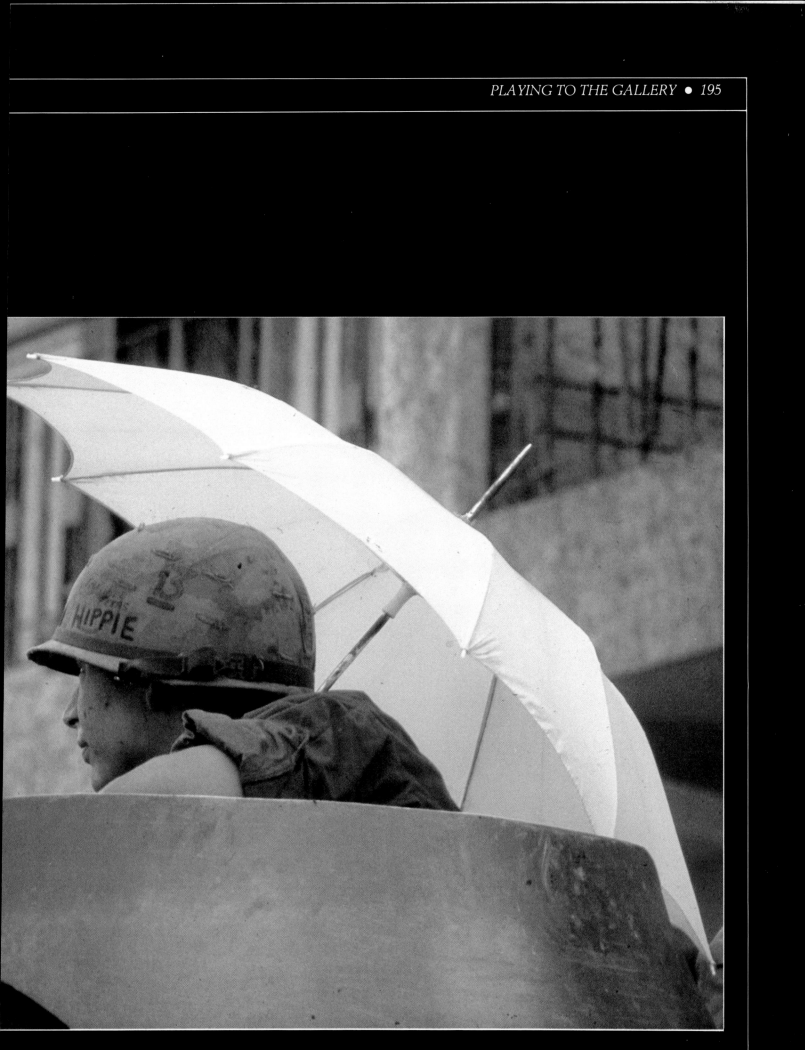

Right *Elliott Erwitt is possibly better-known for his 'anti-photographs' of the funnier side of canine life than for his more serious photojournalism. The idea for his aptly named book* Son of Bitch, *in which the dog pictures first appeared, came by chance: 'Every once in a while I take time out and look at contact sheets of pictures that I've taken during the year, or during the past years. I noticed without any special purpose I had a great number of dogs in the photographs. And so I said, "Gee, maybe I can do a dog book or something." There seems to be a lot of dogs.'*

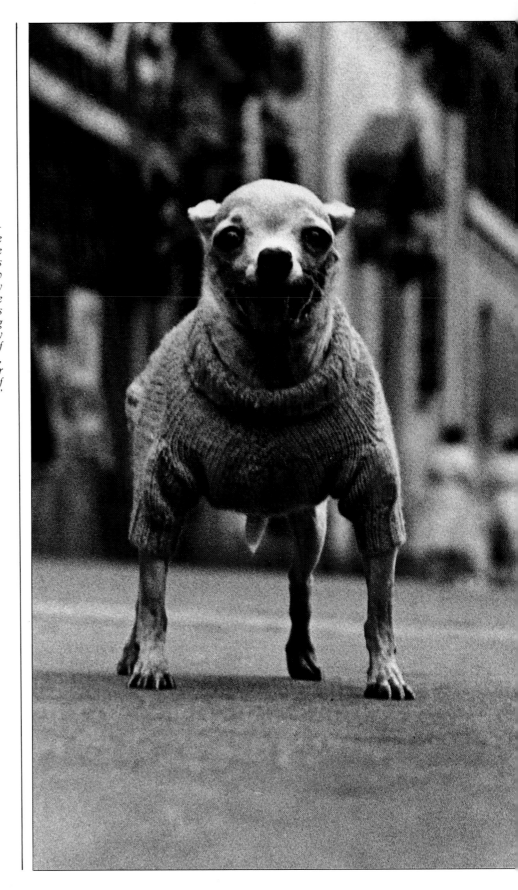

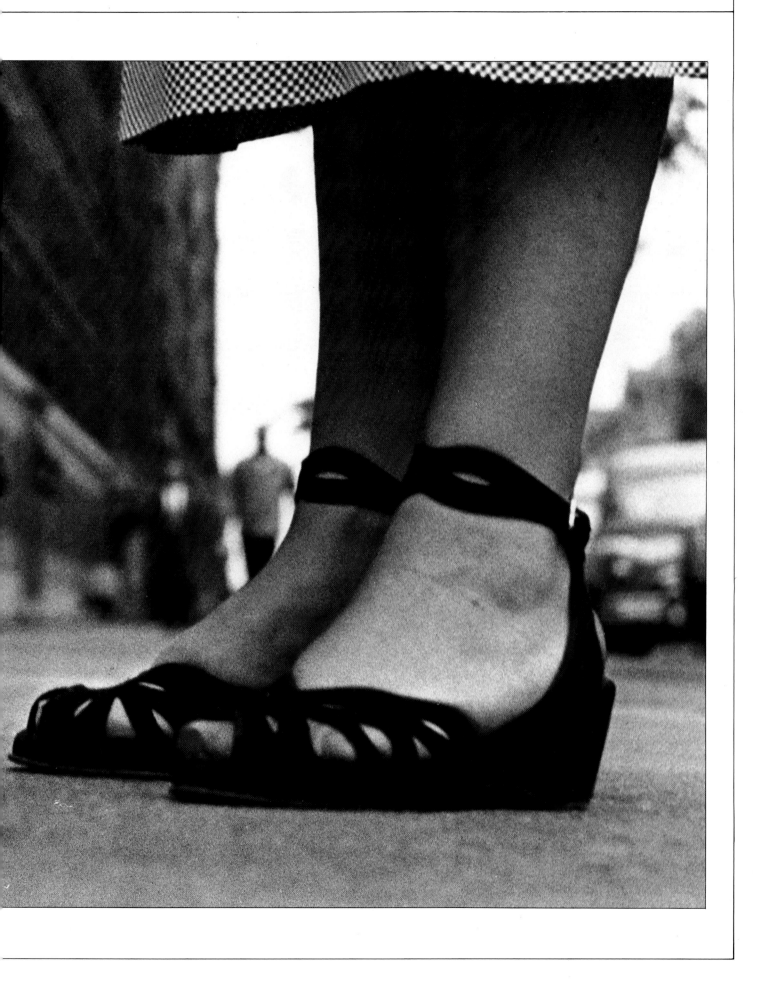

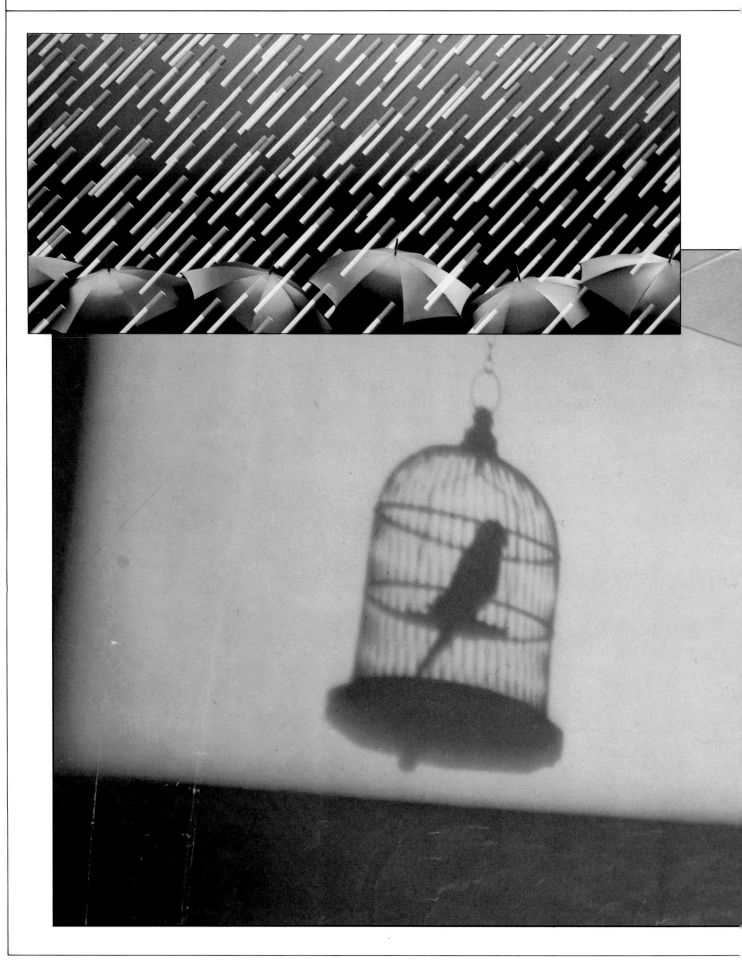

Left *and* **below** *Consistent winners of British advertising awards, the Benson and Hedges cigarette advertisements make use of enigmatic and oblique humor coupled with a distinctive visual style, a strategy that has been developed and controlled by the advertising agency, Collett Dickenson Pearce. Humor and indentifiable visual characteristics are important to an industry that is restricted in what it can show, say or imply about its product. Current regulations state that the cigarette pack itself may be shown, but no gratification implied. Hence, Benson and Hedges rely on intriguing and entertaining their audiences.*

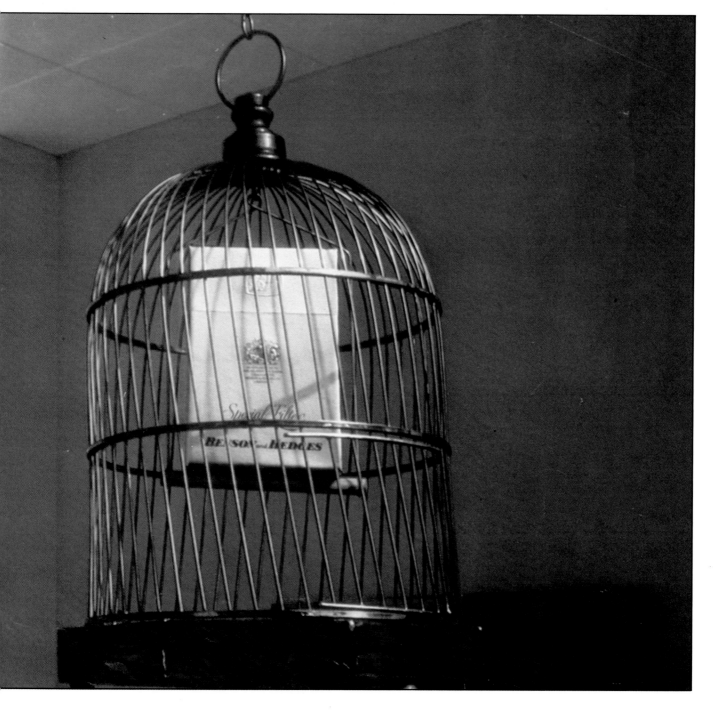

Below *Another example of the series of Benson and Hedges advertisements. Fashion has a major influence on the creative treatment an agency decides upon. This 'surrealist' campaign, begun in the 1970s, produced many imitators.*

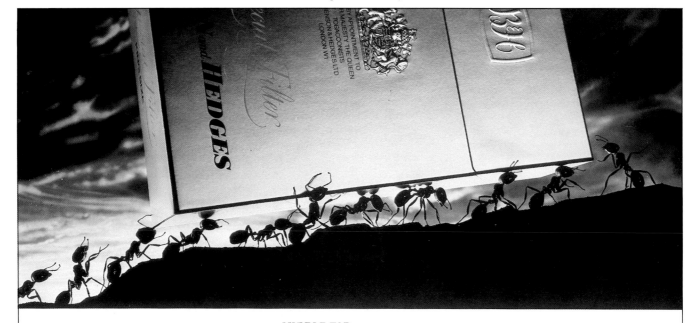

MIDDLE TAR As defined by H.M. Government
DANGER: H. M. Government Health Departments' WARNING: THINK ABOUT THE HEALTH RISKS BEFORE SMOKING

optimism and renewal, quite different to the contemplative philosophies of the East, are distinct cultural elements that have encouraged the rise of the image. Expressed as a desire for new experiences and new information and a quest for self-definition, these needs can be uniquely fulfilled by photography. Reportage and travel photography offer the power of appropriation on a global scale — of remote places and dramatic events. Portraiture and fashion photography provide a set of strategies for personal knowledge and development.

Specific examples provide an insight into the way these needs are met. One of the most distinctive audiences is the record-buying public, which contains some sharp divisions that are reflected stylistically in the design of record covers. Although record covers may superficially seem a limited, not to say trivial, medium for pictures, certain factors — particularly the emergence of a high-spending, style-conscious youth market — in the last quarter-century have given them disproportionate importance. The impetus came from the growth of rock music, not so much because of the volume of sales, but because of the cultural differences that the music reflected and helped to create.

At a certain point in the mid-1960s, record-cover illustration turned from what had been essentially straightforward designs towards those that were frequently enigmatic and highly imaginative. An important function of those new designs, such as the examples shown on pages 202-3 by Hipgnosis, has been to help maintain a cultural distance between the values of rock music and the conservatism of Western society. The rock music audience demands, in other words, a distinctive visual style that deliberately stands apart from conventional imagery.

There is an accidental element to the development of record-cover design: the size of an LP and the need to give it a protective cover has meant that there is, simply, space to be filled. This alone would not have been sufficient to ensure interesting work, but because many of the young illustrators, photographers and designers of the time themselves identified with the growing rock culture, record-covers received a high level of well-directed talent, and continue to do so.

Photography has been used in record-cover design in two principal ways: to promote an 'image' by means of idealized portraiture, and as an illustrative technique, often used in combination with artwork. In both areas, experimental use has been particularly important: the surrealist, the cryptic and the deliberately unconventional have been the important methods of appealing to an audience that can at times be hypercritical. In the case of a major recording artiste or group, the actual effect on sales of the cover design is probably insignificant, and this in a sense has freed the designer to be eclectic. Within non-conservative rock music, the worst that seems to happen is trouble with the distributors over covers in dubious taste, as has happened a number of times to such design groups as Hipgnosis that specialize in this work. The audience for rock music, however, seems to reserve its criticism for the unadventurous.

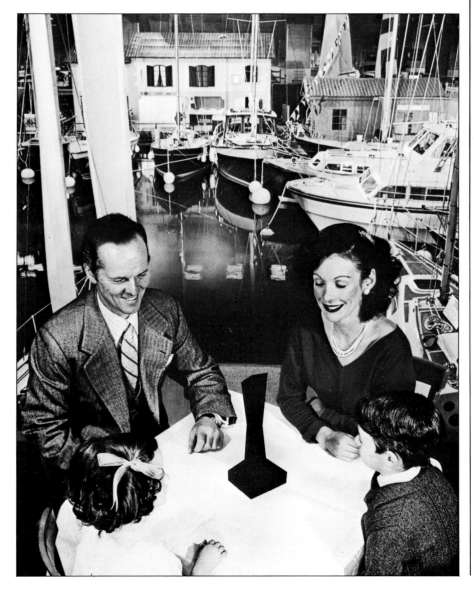

Left *This record cover for the 1976 Led Zeppelin album* Presence *was designed and produce by Hipgnosis, who specialize in this type of work. The basic idea was 'anachronism and obsession'; to achieve this, old photographs from the 1940s and 1950s were used for their nostalgic qualities and a mysterious, black object added to provide the disturbing 'presence'. This front cover was actually photographed by Hipgnosis themselves but was based on a real picture. The object was painted in, with no depth clues so that it looked like a 'hole'.*

Below *This front cover design by Hipgnosis for the 1971 Nice album* Elegy *was photographed on location in the Sahara desert. One of the problems involved in creating the shot was placing 60 inflatable red balls on the dunes without leaving footprints — an exercise that was completed successfully only minutes before the sun went down.*

Right *Another Hipgnosis design, this front cover for the 1975 Pink Floyd album* Wish You Were Here *was photographed in Los Angeles at the Burbank Studios lot. It took a week to find the right location and to arrange the stuntman. Associative, unusual imagery is what both the clients — the rock groups — and the audience have come to expect from album cover design.*

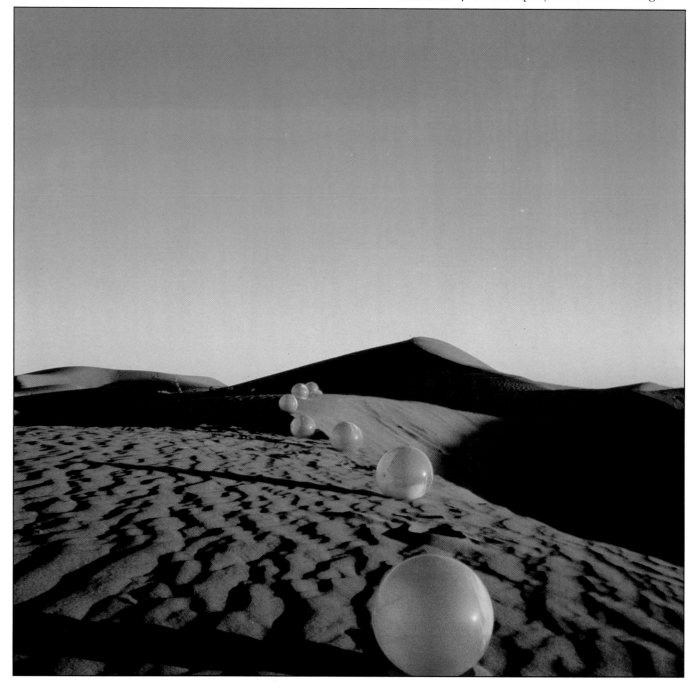

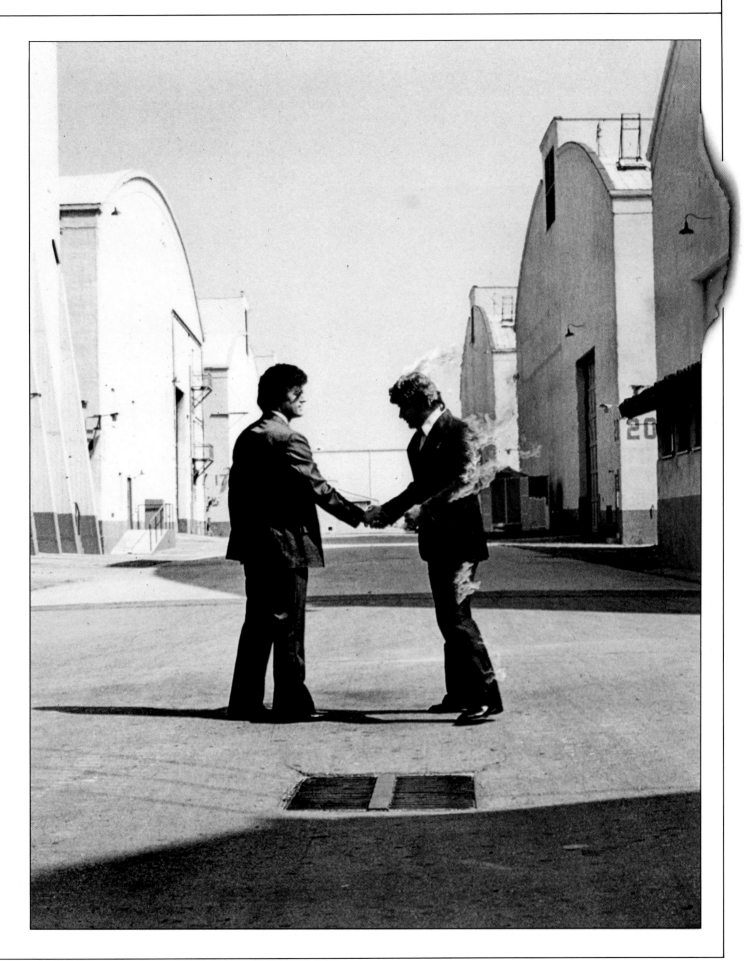

Below Hat check girl *(1946), Cecil Beaton. This ironically artificial and highly stylized fashion photograph is one from a series called 'The New Reality', made for* Vogue *and which showed chic models in mundane settings. Although the series proved very popular for a while, within a few years, it was decidedly out of date.*

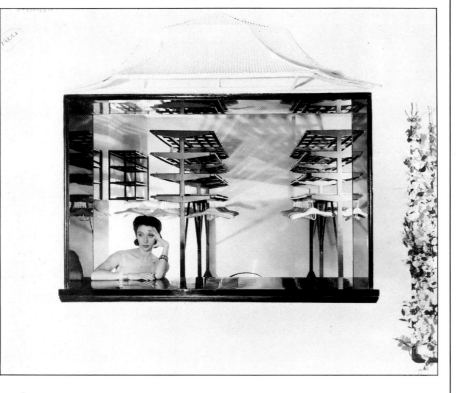

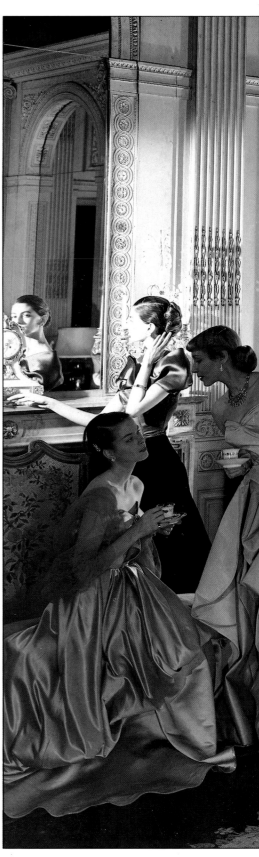

A larger specialized audience exists for fashion photography. It is a measure of the size of the market and its commercial importance that this field has attracted some extremely talented people, several of whom, including Penn, Avedon and Bailey, have built considerable reputations on this relatively narrow foundation. A clue as to why the standards of fashion photography are so high is furnished by the demands of the audience. The photographs, most of which are published in a few major magazines such as *Vogue* and *Harper's*, perform a triple role: partly advertisement for dress, jewelry and cosmetic manufacturers, partly news of changing fashion, and partly entertainment. To achieve the necessary results involves more than simply photographing pieces of material — it demands a sensitivity to an ephemeral field and a high order of visual imagination and style to be able to display a constant procession of clothes with enthusiasm and variety.

The key to all this is that fashion is very much a matter of the moment, and depends heavily on the creation of an aura that is necessarily imprecise and frequently elitist. Photography, as we have seen in other fields, can be used very successfully to idealize its subjects without being very obvious, and so is well suited to the fashion business. Photographs such as the examples on pages 206-7 have a flair that rubs off on the product, even if the dress appears at first glance to be a minor element in the picture.

One of the most interesting aspects of fashion photography is the speed of stylistic change. Fashion production has to anticipate the willingness of the public to shift its taste in a certain direction, and then to lead it; following demand is not enough. Fashion photography must match these changes, and the result is that it has become, for one sector of society, a very sensitive barometer.

Below *This carefully arranged tableau by Beaton is just as evocative of its period as the dresses it is designed to display. The rich interior, artificial poses and theatrical lighting combine to suggest an atmosphere of social superiority — an idealization to whet the appetite of the customers.*

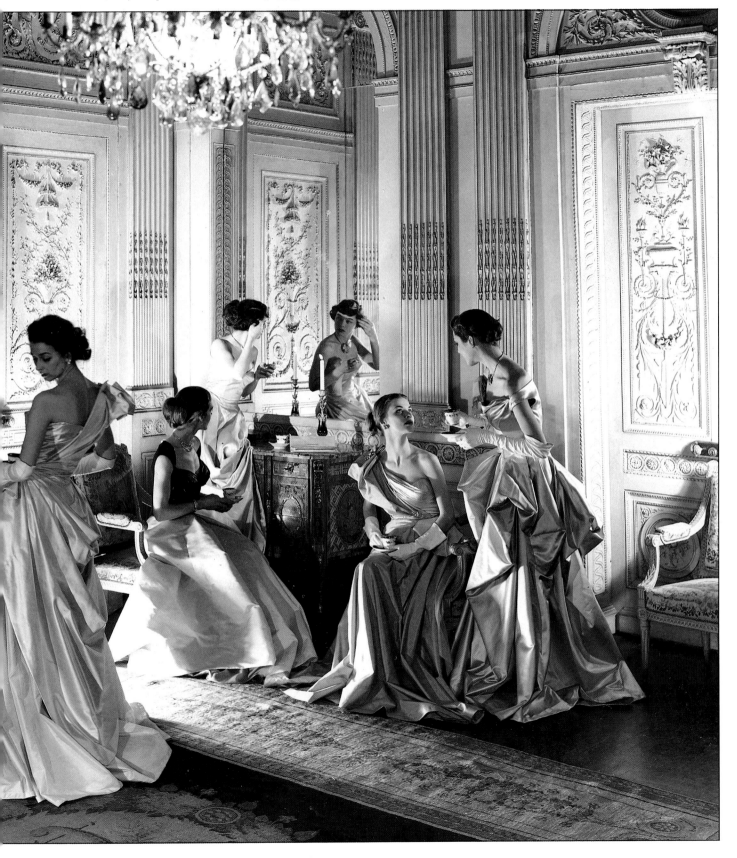

Fashion photography *Contrasted with Beaton's sophisticated chic on the preceding pages, these recent examples of fashion photography by Sanders illustrate just how much the manner of presentation can change. It is, in fact, in the very nature of this field of photography to look for change and to react, often in an extreme way, to what has gone before. These strong images may appear to display little of the products they are attempting to sell, but mood and emphasis — here a 1980s eclectic tribalism — is all-important in creating desirability.*

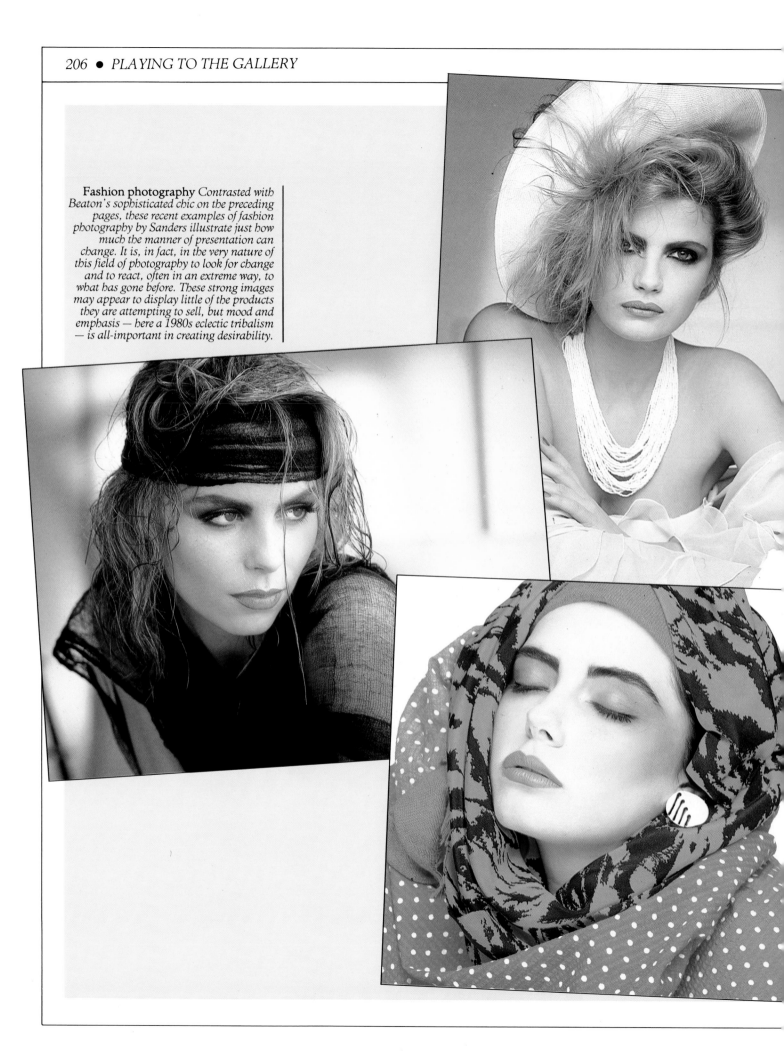

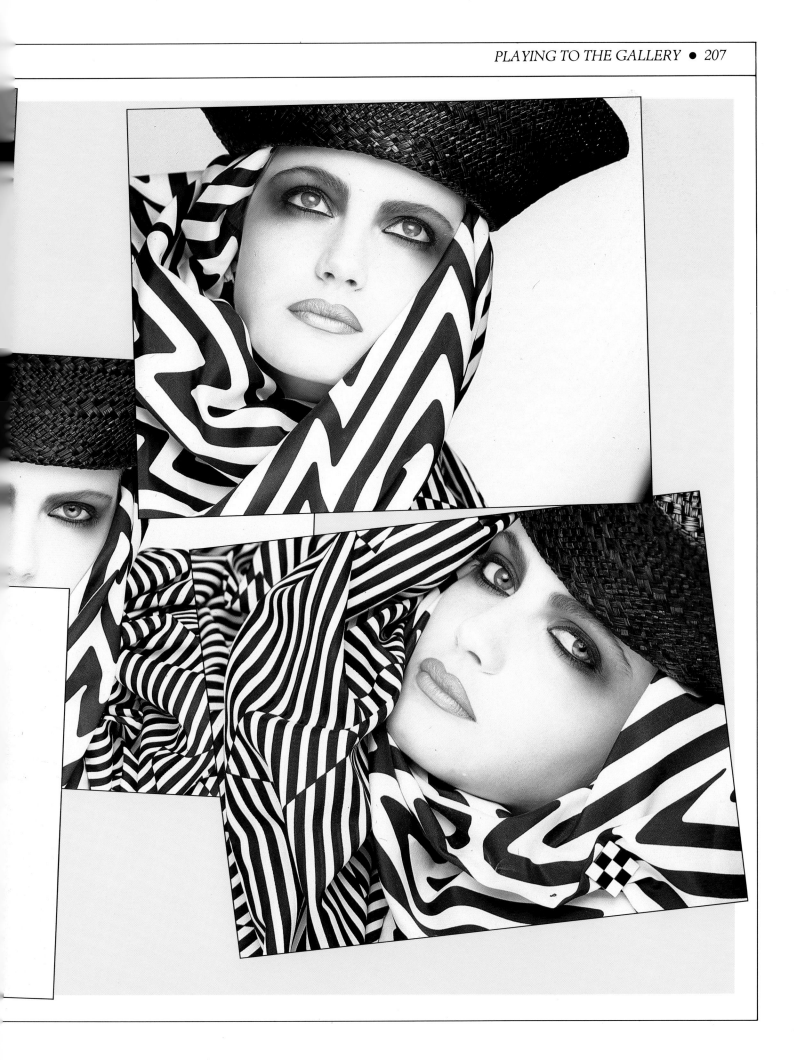

The purpose of this book has been to demonstrate ways of looking at photography in all its different contexts. Central to this task of appraisal is the need to understand the structure of the whole institution. Since its invention, photography has proved so useful that it has won itself a diversity of roles. It is an important tool for recording and discovering information about the physical world; it is 'worth a thousand words' of editorial copy; it can tell a story, amuse or idealize; it can sell a product, act as a cultural barometer or a personal exploration; it can be art, an icon or a snapshot. These different aspects reveal no common intentions. In a magazine such as Time, for example, a hard news photograph may well face a picture that is designed to sell a luxury product. That two such dissimilar images share the same process is merely a coincidence of technology; one is in no sense 'better' than the other; both must be judged on their own terms.

What further complicates the issue is that the different audiences at which this everyday tide of imagery is aimed are, in practice, often composed of the same people. Moreover, this mass audience is influenced by its own involvement as picture-takers. The technical process of taking pictures is so familiar and accessible, for the most part, that there is a natural tendency to ascribe more mysterious and arcane faculties to those 'experts' whose work we are invited to inspect and judge.

Photography is arguably the one true mass art. Familiarity with and participation in the medium puts most people in a far better position than they realize to assess and appraise its successes and failures.

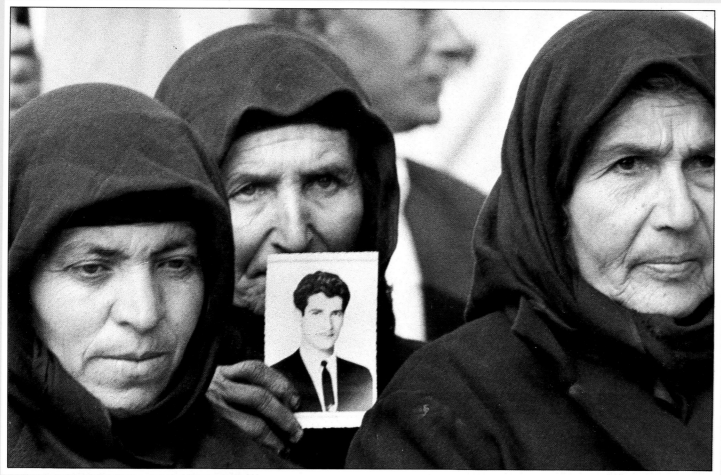

Cyprus, René Burri

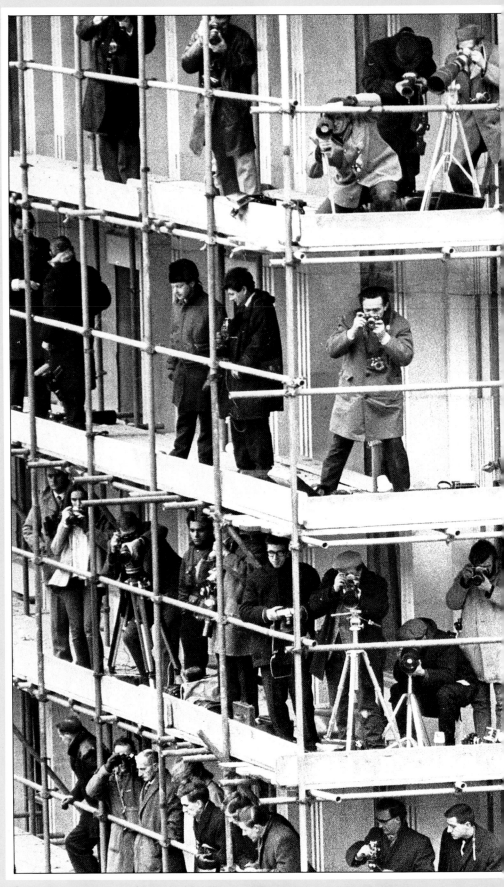

Photographers at the funeral of Sir Winston Churchill, 1963, Alan Ballard

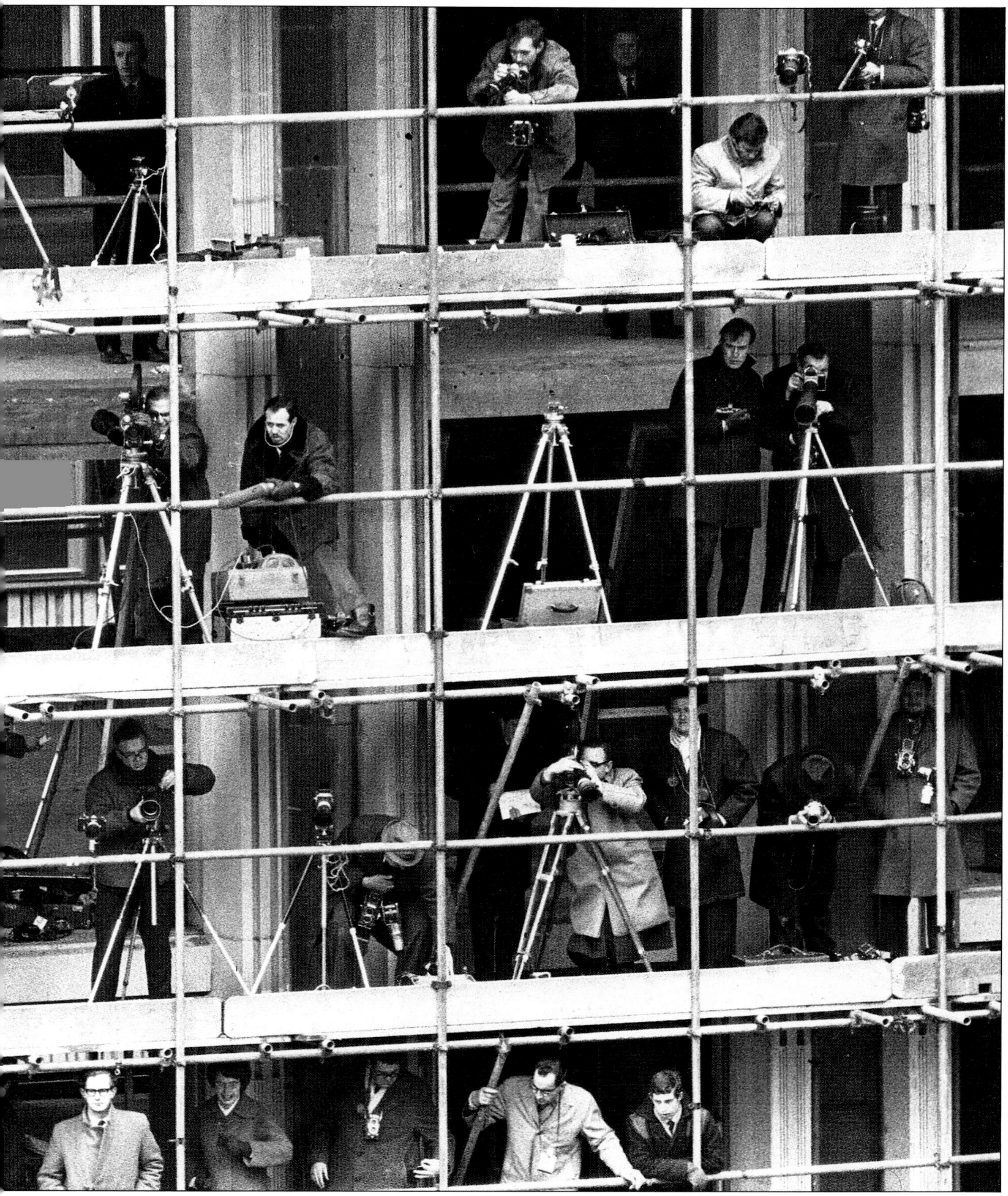

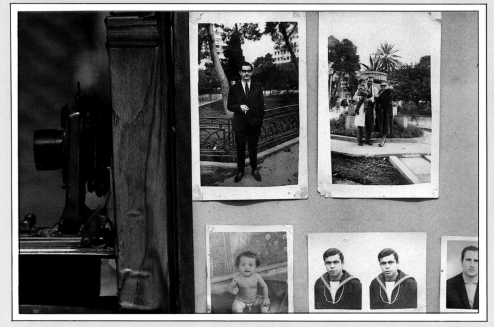

● *Portrait camera*

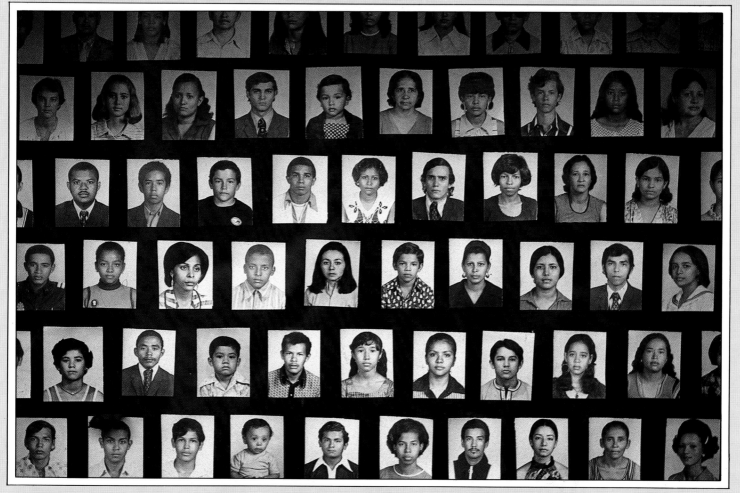

Columbian studio photographer's display

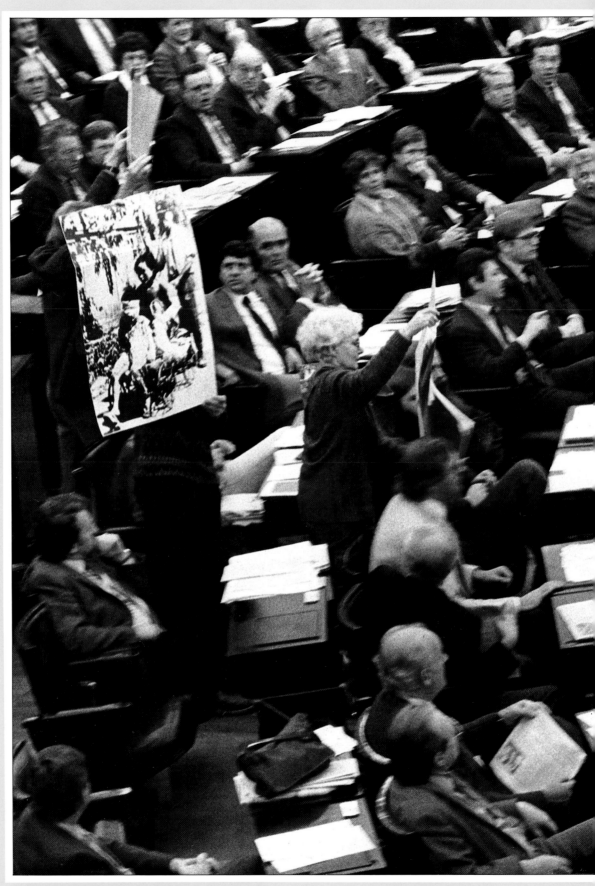

● *Greens Deputies display photographs during a Bundestag debate*

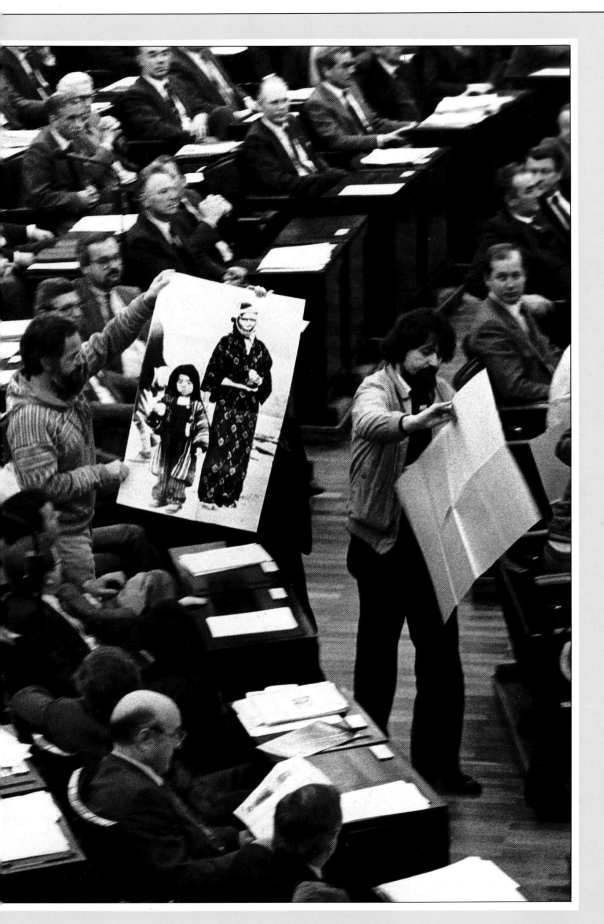

List of Photographers

*Principal photographers whose work is mentioned
or illustrated in the book.*

Ansel Adams, American 1902-1984
Robert Adams, American 1937
Duiane Arbus, American 1925-1971
Jim Arnould, British 1942
Eugène Atget, French 1857-1927
Richard Avedon, American 1923
José Azel, American
Sir Cecil Beaton, British 1904-1979
Werner Bischof, Swiss 1916-1954
Lester Bookbinder, American 1929
Bill Brandt, British 1904-1984
David Burnett, American
René Burri, Swiss 1933
Romano Cagnoni, Italian
Harry Callahan, American 1912
Julia Margaret Cameron, British 1815-1879
Robert Capa, Hungarian 1913-1954
Henri Cartier-Bresson, French 1908
John Claridge, British 1944
Brigitte Dahm, German
Franccoise de Mulder, French
William Eggleston, American 1941
Peter Henry Emerson, British 1856-1936
Elliott Erwitt, American 1928
Frederick Evans, British 1853-1943
Walker Evans, American 1903-1975
Horst Faas, German born
Robert Frank, American 1924
Jill Freedman, American
Michael Freeman, British 1945
Ralph Gibson, American 1939
Robert Golden, American, 1945
Ernst Haas, Austrian/American 1932
David Hamilton, British
Richard Hamilton, British 1922
David Hockney, British 1937
Philip Jones-Griffiths, British 1936
Michael Joseph, British 1941
Yousuf Karsh, Armenian/Canadian 1908
André Kertész, Hungarian 1894
Joseph Koudelka, Czechoslovakian 1938

George Krause, American 1937
Dorothea Lange, American 1895-1965
Jacques-Henri Lartigue, French 1896
Axel Lenoir, Swiss 1937
Mary Ellen Mark, American 1940
André Martin, French 1928
Don McCullin, British 1935
Joel Meyerowitz, American 1938
Duane Michals, American 1932
James Nachtwey, American
Arnold Newman, American 1918
Charles Nye, American
Tim Page, British
Irving Penn, American 1917
Timm Rautert, German 1944
Oscar Rejlander, Swedish/British 1813-1875
Marc Riboud, French 1923
George Rodger, British 1908
August Sander, German 1876-1964
Sanders, Scottish 1944
Yoshikazu Shirakawa, Japanese 1935
Stephen Shore, American 1947
Aaron Siskind, American 1903
W. Eugene Smith, American 1918-1979
Lord Snowdon, British 1930
Joel Sternfeld, American 1944
Alfred Stieglitz, American 1864-1946
Paul Strand, American 1890-1976
William Henry Fox Talbot, British 1800-1877
John Thomson, British 1837-1921
Pete Turner, British
Jerry Uelsmann, American 1934
Nick Ut, Vietnamese
Carleton Watkins, American 1829-1916
Dan Weiner, American 1919
Mike Wells, British 1951
Brett Weston, American 1911
Edward Weston, American 1896-1958
Minor White, American 1908-1976
Garry Winogrand, American 1928-1984

Selected Bibliography

About Looking, John Berger (Writers & Readers, 1980)

American Landscapes, John Szarkowski (MOMA, 1981)

The Americans, Robert Frank (Aperture, 1958)

Aperture Fall, 1969. Vol 14 No.2

Assignments, Snowdon

Basic design: The dynamics of visual form Maurice de Sausmafez (Studio Vista, 1964)

The Camera at War, Jorge Lewinski (Simon & Schuster, 1978)

Camera and Lens, Ansel Adams (Morgan & Morgan, 1970)

Cape Light, Joel Meyerowitz (NYGS, 1978)

The Complete Guide to Photography, Techniques and Materials, Michael Freeman (Phaidon, 1982)

A Concise History of Photography, Helmut and Alison Gernsheim (Thames & Hudson, 1965)

The Concerned Photographer, ed. Cornell Capa (Grossman, 1968)

The Creation, Ernst Haas

D&AD Annuals (series) ed. Edward Booth-Clibborn

D&AD/European Illustration

Darkroom, ed. Eleanor Lewis (Lustrum, 1977)

The Daybooks of Edward Weston

Edward Weston: The Frame of Recognition, ed. Nancy Newhall (Aperture, 1965)

European Photography, Edward Booth-Clibborn (D&AD/European Illustration) (annual series) 1981 edt.

Examples: The Making of 40 Photographs, Ansel Adams (Little, Brown, 1983)

The Extraordinary Landscape, William Garnett (NYGS, 1982)

Fashion: theory, ed. Carol di Grappa (Lustrum, 1980)

The Golden Age of British Photography 1839-1900, Mark Haworth Booth (Aperture, 1984) ed.

Images of the World (National Geographic Society, 1981)

Images d'une France, André Martin (Kodak Pathe, 1972)

In America, Ernst Haas

Intimate Landscapes, Eliot Porter (MMA/E.P. Dutton, 1979)

Jerry N. Uelsmann (Aperture monograph, 1971)

Life Library of Photography (Time-Life Books, 1970-3)

Lifework, Norman Parkinson (Weidenfeld & Nicholson, 1983)

Looking at Photographs, John Szarkowski (MOMA, 1973)

Mirrors and Windows, John Szarkowski (MOMA, 1978)

The Negative, Ansel Adams (NYGS)

The New Color Photography, Sally Eauclaire (Abberville Press, 1981)

The New Zone System Manual, Minor White, Richard Zakia, Peter Lorenz (Morgan & Morgan, 1976)

On Photography, Susan Sontag (1973)

Pencil of Nature, W.H. Fox Talbot (Plenum, 1968)

Photodiscovery, Bruce Bernard (Thames & Hudson, 1980)

The Photographer's Eye, John Szarkowski (MOMA, 1966)

Photography Year (annual series) (Time-Life Books, 1973)

Pictures on a Page, Harold Evans (Heinemann, 1978)

Polaroid Portraits, Richard Hamilton

The Print, Ansel Adams (NYGS, 1983)

Private Pictures, introduced by Anthony Burgess (Jonathan Cape, 1980)

Techniques of the World's Great Photographers (Phaidon, 1982)

Tim Page's Nam, Tim Page (Thames & Hudson, 1983)

Vietnam, Inc, Philip Jones-Griffiths

Visions and Images: American Photographers on Photography, Barbaralee Diamonstein (Rizzoli International Publications, 1981)

Voyage of the Eye, Brett Weston (Aperture, 1975)

Ways of Seing, John Berger

White Women, Helmut Newton (Quartet, 1976)

Worlds in a Small Room, Irving Penn (Secker & Warburg, 1974)

The World of Camera, C.J. Bucher (1964)

Yosemite and the Range of Light, Ansel Adams (NYGS, 1979)

Index

Page numbers in *italics*
refer to illustrations

Acknowledgments

KEY: (a) above; (b) below; (l) left; (r) right

The photographs on the following pages were reproduced by kind permission of the following:
11 Robert Capa/Magnum/John Hillelson Agency; **13** (a) Victoria and Albert Museum, (b) Royal Photographic Society; **15** José Azel; **17** Romano Cagnoni; **18** Ernst Haas/Magnum/ John Hillelson Agency; **20-1** Brigitte Dahm/Action Press; **27** Michael Gray; **28** by kind permission of Mrs Brandt; **31** (br) Jet Propulsion Laboratory; **33** (a,b) Henri Cartier-Bresson/ Magnum/John Hillelson Agency; **36** Ralph Gibson; **44** Pete Turner/Image Bank; **45** Joel Meyerowitz; **46** Brett Weston; **47** William Eggleston; **54-5** Romano Cagnoni; **56** James Nachtwey/Black Star/ Colorific; **61** Joel Sternfeld/ Daniel Wolf Inc; **63** (a) Old Dartmouth Historical Society Whaling Museum, Massachusetts, (b) Museum of Natural History, Los Angeles County; **70**, **71** Jacques-Henri Lartigue/John Hillelson Agency; **73** E.T. Archive; **78** (b) Royal Photographic Society; **79** Victoria and Albert Museum; **80**, **81** Library of Congress, Washington DC; **82** E.T. Archive; **83** BBC Hulton Picture Library; **85** Nick Ut/Associated Press; **87** Alpha; **88-9** Jill Freedman/ Archive Pictures Inc; **90-1** The Scotsman Publications Ltd; **92** UPI; **93** The Scotsman Publications Ltd; **95** © Arnold Newman; **97** (a) Romano Cagnoni, (b) Timm Rautert/Bruce Coleman Ltd; **98** Joel Sternfeld/Daniel Wolf Inc; **99** Charlie Nye; **100-1** Francoise de Mulder/TIME Magazine; **102** Imperial War Museum; **104** Horst Faas/Associated Press; **106** Werner Bischof/Magnum/ John Hillelson Agency; **107** W. Eugene Smith/Black Star; **109** (a) Philip Jones Griffiths/Magnum/ John Hillelson Agency, (b) Tim Page/Anna Obolensky; **110** (a) David Burnett/Contact/Colorific, (b) Mike Wells/Aspect Picture Library Ltd; **111** Joseph Koudelka/Magnum/John Hillelson Agency; **113** Associated Press; **114** (a,b) The Kobal Collection; **116** Robert Adams/MOMA; **119** Axel Lenoir; **124** Yoshikaza Shirakawa/Image Bank; **126** (br) Foote Cone and Belding; **127** (l,r) John Claridge; **130** (a), **131** Robert Golden; **134**, **135** (a) Michael Joseph; **136**, **137**, **138** (al) Michael Mann; **138** (b) Tantrums, (bl) John Thornton/Tantrums; **140** by kind permission of Mrs Brandt; **142** (a,b) David Hamilton/Image Bank; **143** Andre Martin; **146-7** Duane Michals/Sidney Janis Gallery, New York; **150** André Kertész; **151** © Arnold Newman; **152-3** The Paul Strand Foundation, as published in Paul Strand: *Sixty Years of Photographs*, Aperture, Millerton, NY, 1976, (l) copyright © 1976, 1977, (r) copyright © 1971, 1976, (a) copyright © 1976, (b) copyright © 1971, 1976, 1983; **154,155** Robert Frank; **156-7** Garry Winogrand/Fraenkel Gallery; **158**, **159** Lord Snowdon; **160**, **161** Karsh/Camera Press; **163** W. Eugene Smith/Black Star; **164** Jim Arnould; **171** Eston Gallery, Carmel, California; **173** Robert Hershkowitz; **174**, **175** Ansel Adams; **178-9** Geroge Krause; **180**, **181** Jerry Uelsmann; **187** Richard Hamilton/Edition Hansjörg Mayer; **189** Metropolitan Museum of Art, New York; **190-1** David Hockney, Tradhart; **192**, **193** Mary Ellen Mark/Archive Pictures Inc; **198-9**, **200** Collett Dickenson Pearce; **201**, **202**, **203** Hipgnosis; **204**, **205** Sotheby's; **206-7** Sanders; **209** René Burri/Magnum/John Hillelson Agency; **210-11** Alan Ballard/ Sunday Times; **214-5** Poly Press.

All other photographs by Michael Freeman.

While every effort has been made to acknowledge all copyright holders, we apologize if any omissions have been made.